Wisconsin
Our State, Our Story

Wisconsin
Our State, Our Story

Bobbie Malone
Kori Oberle

Published by the Wisconsin Historical Society Press
Publishers since 1855

© 2008 by The State Historical Society of Wisconsin

For permission to reuse material from *Wisconsin: Our State, Our Story*, ISBN 978-0-87020-378-7, please access www.copyright.com or contact the Copyright Clearance Center, Inc. (CCC), 222 Rosewood Drive, Danvers, MA 01923, 978-750-8400. CCC is a not-for-profit organization that provides licenses and registration for a variety of users.

www.wisconsinhistory.org

Photographs identified with WHi are from the Society's collections; address inquiries about such photos to the Visual Materials Archivist at Wisconsin Historical Society, 816 State Street, Madison, WI 53706. A list of image credits can be found starting on page 245.

Printed in the United States of America
Designed by Zucker Design
Cartography by Earth Illustrated, Inc.

15 14 13 12 11 10   2 3 4 5 6 7 8 9 10

Malone, Bobbie, 1944-
Wisconsin : our state, our story / Bobbie Malone, Kori Oberle.
p. cm.
Includes bibliographical references and index.
ISBN 978-0-87020-378-7 (hardcover : alk. paper) 1. Wisconsin--Textbooks. I. Oberle, Kori. II. Title.
F581.3.M35 2007
977.5--dc22
2008001787

Front and back cover photo: *Rolling Harvest* by Richard La Martina

∞ The paper used in this publication meets the minimum requirements of the American National Standard for Information Sciences—Permanence of Paper for Printed Library Materials, ANSI Z39.48-1992.

Publication of *Wisconsin: Our State, Our Story* was made possible by a major grant from the Halbert & Alice Kadish Foundation.

Significant additional funding was provided by the Greater Milwaukee Foundation, Dr. Abraham and Irma F. Schwartz Fund. Funding was also provided by the Hugh Highsmith Family Foundation.

Contents

Acknowledgements

The Wisconsin Historical Society thanks the many individuals who helped create *Wisconsin: Our State, Our Story* including teachers, reading specialists, school administrators, scholars, and Wisconsin Historical Society staff. We also thank the teachers and students in classrooms throughout the state who provided early feedback on pilot chapters of this book.

Advisory Board

John Broihahn, State Archaeologist, Wisconsin Historical Society
Wonza Canada, Assistant Principal, Milwaukee
Sharon Durtka, Social Studies Consultant (former), Milwaukee
Heidi Ebert, 4th Grade Teacher, West Salem
John Hallagan, 4th Grade Teacher, Genesee Depot
Patty Harvey, 4th Grade Teacher (retired), Appleton
J. P. Leary, American Indian Studies Consultant, Department of Public Instruction
Nikki Mandell, American Historian, University of Wisconsin–Whitewater
Philip McDade, Monona School Board
Mike McKinnon, Curriculum Director, Janesville
Susan McLeod, Director, Chippewa Valley Museum, Eau Claire
Sally Michalko, Social Studies Curriculum Director, Waukesha
Susan O'Leary, Reading Specialist, Madison
Barb Rogers, Reading Specialist, Muskego-Norway
Patty Schultz, 4th Grade Teacher, Madison
Angie Vetsch, 4th Grade Teacher, Spring Valley

Wisconsin
Our State, Our Story

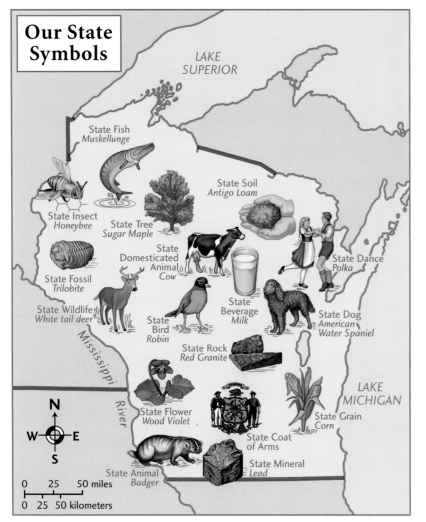

Our State Symbols

LAKE SUPERIOR

State Fish
Muskellunge

State Soil
Antigo Loam

State Insect
Honeybee

State Tree
Sugar Maple

State Domesticated Animal
Cow

State Dance
Polka

State Fossil
Trilobite

State Wildlife
White tail deer

State Bird
Robin

State Beverage
Milk

State Dog
American Water Spaniel

State Rock
Red Granite

LAKE MICHIGAN

State Flower
Wood Violet

State Coat of Arms

State Grain
Corn

State Mineral
Lead

State Animal
Badger

Mississippi River

N
W — E
S

0   25   50 miles
0   25   50 kilometers

Chapter 1:
Connecting to Our State's Story

• How Do We Tell Our State's Story?

• What Does It Mean to Think Like a Historian?

• What Kinds of Evidence Do Historians Use?

• How Do Historians Use Evidence to Write History?

Wisconsin is known for many things. What kinds of stories could you expect from looking at these **symbols**?

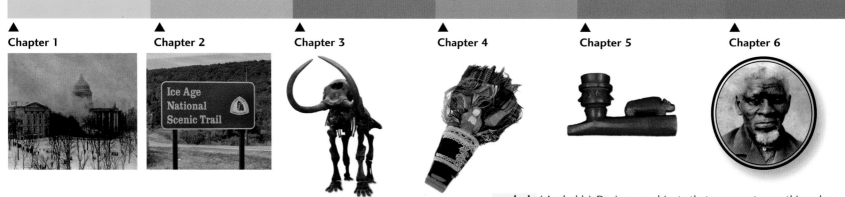

Chapter 1

Chapter 2
Ice Age National Scenic Trail

Chapter 3

Chapter 4

Chapter 5

Chapter 6

symbols (**sim** buhls) Designs or objects that represent something else

Key Words

- artifacts
- Cause and Effect
- Change and Continuity
- document
- evidence
- historian
- interpret
- investigate
- primary sources
- secondary sources
- Thinking Like a Historian
- Through Their Eyes
- Turning Points
- Using the Past

Thinking Like a Historian

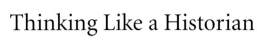 Through Their Eyes

Cause and Effect

Turning Points

Using the Past

Change and Continuity

▲ Chapter 7 ▲ Chapter 8 ▲ Chapter 9 ▲ Chapter 10 ▲ Chapter 11 ▲ Chapter 12

How Do We Tell Our State's Story?

In this chapter, you'll learn what history is all about and how to think like a historian. You'll find out how historians learn about the past. And you'll find out how this book will help you learn to think like a historian while you learn about Wisconsin's past.

What is history?

History is *not* the past, as some people think, but rather, the *study* of events that took place in the past and people who lived in the past. No one can describe every event that took place long ago or just yesterday, even though both long ago and yesterday make up the past.

Historians are people who study and **interpret** the past through the stories they tell. Whether you learn about the past by listening to stories that your parents or older people tell, by visiting a museum, by watching a movie or TV program, or by reading a book, you are learning about what someone thinks is important enough to remember and share. It is not the entire past, but a view of the past.

How do historians choose stories?

Historians are a lot like detectives. They **investigate** the past by asking questions. They need **evidence** to answer their questions. They use the evidence to help them choose what to tell. They also need to be sure that their stories help us get a better idea of what the past was like. At all times, they ask themselves: Does this matter? If so, *why* does it matter?

The photographs on the next page will give you a chance to answer questions. Keep thinking, What matters? Why does it matter?

History (his tuh ree) The study of the past **Historians** (hi **stor** ee uhnz) People who study and tell or write about the past
interpret (in **tur** prit) To explain the meaning of something **investigate** (in **ves** tuh gayt) To find out as much as possible about something
evidence (**ev** uh duhns) Information and facts that help prove something really happened

This photograph of the state capitol was taken in Madison in 1904. What is this photo telling us about what has happened to the capitol? Why is there smoke coming out of the building? Why are there people standing outside? What time of the year was this photo taken?

Someone took this photograph from inside the capitol. Look closely at the photo. Can you tell what part of the capitol this is?

What is this photo telling you about the capitol building?

What is happening in this photo of the capitol? Is the statue *Wisconsin* coming down or going up?

What Does It Mean to Think Like a Historian?

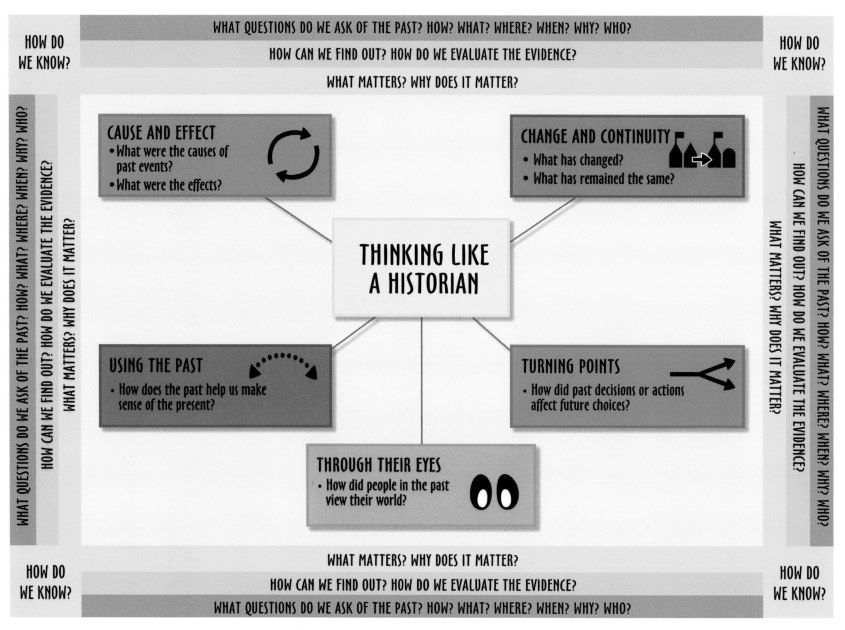

This chart shows the kinds of questions that historians ask when they investigate events and people of the past. As you read this book, you will learn how to use these types of questions to help you think like a historian.

How can I use this chart to help me think like a historian?

Cause and Effect ⟳ Cause and effect questions are the most common questions that historians use. They want to find out what made an event happen. And they want to find out what changes the event created.

Change and Continuity 👣➡👣 Historians also want to know what things have not changed and what things have changed over time. Change and **continuity** help us connect to history.

Turning Points ➤ We call a change a turning point when it is so large that it changes how people live. Turning points might be huge natural disasters like big hurricanes, terrible human tragedies like wars, world-changing events like the discovery of America, or major inventions like automobiles or computers.

Through Their Eyes 👀 It's important to remember that yesterday, last year, and many years ago might have been very different from today. We want to understand events and people's actions as if we are looking through their eyes, not ours.

Using the Past ⤳ Sometimes historians want to know how something in the past shaped something in the present. They are often using the past when they try to understand what caused a current event.

HOW DO WE KNOW? This box reminds you that historians can interpret history only by studying the evidence that they are able to find.

WHAT QUESTIONS DO WE ASK OF THE PAST? HOW? WHAT? WHERE? WHEN? WHY? WHO? You already know the "question words" in the top line of the border on the chart. You'll see that historians use them to ask their questions. And you'll learn to use them to ask your own questions.

HOW CAN WE FIND OUT? HOW DO WE EVALUATE THE EVIDENCE? Historians have to figure out or **evaluate** the evidence they find. They ask themselves, "What does this evidence mean?" in order to understand what they've found. They ask themselves, "Does this evidence help me answer the question I've asked?" or "What story does this evidence help me tell?"

WHAT MATTERS? WHY DOES IT MATTER? Think about all the things that happened in your life yesterday. Now choose one thing about yesterday that you want to tell someone. First you'd have to decide: "What mattered to me the most?" and "Why?" Historians need to think about these same questions in order to understand what happened in the long-ago past. And they use these questions to help them evaluate the evidence they find and to figure out what matters most.

continuity (kon tuh **noo** uh tee) Something that lasts or continues over a long period of time
evaluate (i **val** yoo ayt) To decide how good or valuable something is after thinking about it

What Kinds of Evidence Do Historians Use?

What are sources?

Historians use two kinds of sources of evidence when they investigate. They need **secondary sources** like books to find out what kinds of questions other historians have already explored. They also need to see **primary sources** that supply the real evidence of a past event. The **historic** photographs of the capitol that you saw on page 5 are one example of a primary source.

Historians investigate many secondary and primary sources because they need to study the past event from many points of view. Only then can historians decide how *they* want to explain the past. On this page and the one following, you'll see more examples of primary sources historians used to write the chapters in this book. You'll discover many other primary sources as you read. Primary sources come in many forms—not all are written materials! You'll want to look at all of the sources on the page before you read the text. Looking at the sources will give you lots of clues to the story itself!

A Wisconsin soldier wrote this letter during the Civil War. Letters are primary sources that let us see the exact words of people writing about their experiences at the time they occurred.

These two spear points are **artifacts**. Each was made and used by a different group of early Indians who lived in Wisconsin thousands of years ago. Artifacts are primary sources that give us a chance to look at something made by people who lived in the past.

artifacts (**ar** tih fax) Objects made by people
secondary sources (**sek** uhn dair ee **sor** suhz) Sources having less importance
primary sources (**prI** mair ee **sor** suhz) The most important, original places, people, and things from which information comes   **historic** (his **tor** ik) Important in history

This historic map dates from 1848, the year Wisconsin became a state. A historic map is a really useful primary resource when you compare it with a more recent map of the same area.

This building is St. Augustine's Roman Catholic Church near the town of New Diggings. It was built in 1844—before Wisconsin became a state. Buildings are another kind of primary source. They tell us about the people who built and used them. Sometimes historic buildings are open to the public, so you can visit them.

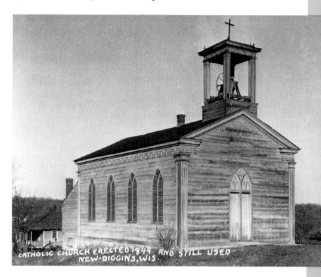

CATHOLIC CHURCH ERECTED 1844 AND STILL USED NEW-DIGGINS, WIS.

This writing is in French from a page in the journal of **Jacques Marquette**. He wrote about his travels in Wisconsin over 300 years ago. He was one of the first non-Indians to travel through Wisconsin. Journals make a perfect primary source. They contain the exact words of people describing events in their lives at the time the events occurred.

CHILD SPONSORSHIP CARD
I.D. No. 23637
Name MAI YA XIONG
Birthdate MAY 22, 1980 F
Age 4 House No. 7,3,12,4,
Came from Laos
Camp Ban Vinai (Loei)
Remarks: Hmong hill tribe from Laos.
Date MAR 1984
INTERNATIONAL CHRISTIAN AID THAILAND

This card belongs to **Mai Ya Xiong**, who came to Wisconsin in the 1980s. The card is an example of a government **document**, another excellent primary source.

This notice for a runaway slave appeared in a Missouri newspaper in 1852. Newspapers from the past are primary sources that tell us what people at the time were thinking about events going on around them.

TWO HUNDRED DOLLARS REWARD.
RAN away from the subscriber, living 4 miles west of the city of St. Louis, on Saturday night last, a negro man by the name of Joshua; about 35 or 40 years of age, about 6 feet high, spare, with long legs and short body, full suit of hair, eyes inflamed and red; his color is an ashly black. Had on when he went away a pair of black sattinet pantaloons, pair of heavy kip boots, an old-fashioned black dress coat, and osnaburg shirt. He took no clothes with him. The above reward will be paid for his apprehension if taken out of the State, and fifty dollars if taken in the State.
May 17, 1852. B. S. GARLAND.
my18 2w

Jacques Marquette (zhok mahr **ket**) **Mai Ya Xiong** (ml **yah** shong)
document (**dok** yoo muhnt) A written or printed paper that contains the original, official, or legal information that can be used as evidence or proof

How Do Historians Use Evidence to Write History?

How do historians—and you—ask questions of primary sources?

On pages 6 and 7, you learned about the Thinking Like a Historian chart. Now, you'll see the way historians use questions to begin to investigate some of the primary sources you saw on the past two pages. Remember, historians are always asking themselves: How can this primary source help me better understand this particular time in the past? You'll probably have more questions of your own to ask. You'll see all of these sources again later in the book. Then you can see if your questions are answered—or if you still want to investigate more on your own.

- **Who made these spear points? When were they made?**
- **How were they made?**
- **Why are they different sizes and different shapes?**
- **What kind of stone are they made from? Are they both made from the same kind of stone?**
- **Where did the stone come from? Did both kinds of stone come from the same place?**
- **Where were these spear points found? Were they both found in the same place?**
- **Who found them?**
- **When were they found?**
- **How old are they? Is one older than the other?**
- **What can they tell us about Wisconsin?**

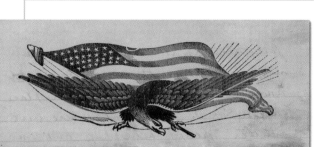

CAMP RANDALL,

Madison 30th 1862.

Mr Charles Palmer Camp Harvey Kenosha
Dear friend - I received your letter this morning and was glad to hear that you and the Berlin boys were held in such high esteem by those on the Camp ground I and the rest of the boys are well Jay Tower has been sick but is pretty well now you wanted to know something about our Camp and how our tents were fixed up and what we had to eat &c. well our camp is about one mile west of the City of Madison the camp ground is any thing but square I should think there is about

- Who is Mai Ya Xiong?
- What is a sponsorship card?
- Why did Mai Ya need this card?
- Why was Mai Ya holding a big card with a number on it?
- What was a "Hmong hill tribe from Laos"?
- What does this card tell us about Mai Ya?
- What does this card have to do with Wisconsin history in 1984?

CHILD SPONSORSHIP CARD

23637

I.D. No.
Name   MAI YA XIONG
Birthdate   MAY 22, 1980   **F**
Age   4   House No.   7,3,12,4
Came from   Laos
Camp   Ban Vinai (Loei)
Remarks: Hmong hill tribe from Laos.

Date: MAR 1984

INTERNATIONAL CHRISTIAN AID THAILAND

- Who wrote this letter?
- When did he write it?
- Where did he come from?
- How old was he?
- Who was he writing to?
- Why was he writing?
- What was he describing in his letter?
- What does this letter tell us about Wisconsin at the time it was written?

TWO HUNDRED DOLLARS REWARD.

RAN away from the subscriber, living 4 miles west of the city of St. Louis, on Saturday night last, a negro man by the name of Joshua; about 35 or 40 years of age, about 6 feet high, spare, with long legs and short body, full suit of hair, eyes inflamed and red; his color is an ashy black. Had on when he went away a pair of black satinet pantaloons, pair of heavy kip boots, an old-fashioned black dress coat, and osnaburg shirt. He took no clothes with him. The above reward will be paid for his apprehension if taken out of the State, and fifty dollars if taken in the State.   B. S. GARLAND.
May 17, 1852.   my18 2w

- Who was B.S. Garland?
- Why did he own a slave named Joshua?
- Where did they live?
- Why was B.S. Garland willing to pay a reward?
- Why did this notice appear in a newspaper?
- How does this newspaper notice help us understand what was going on in Missouri in 1852?
- What does this newspaper notice have to do with Wisconsin history?

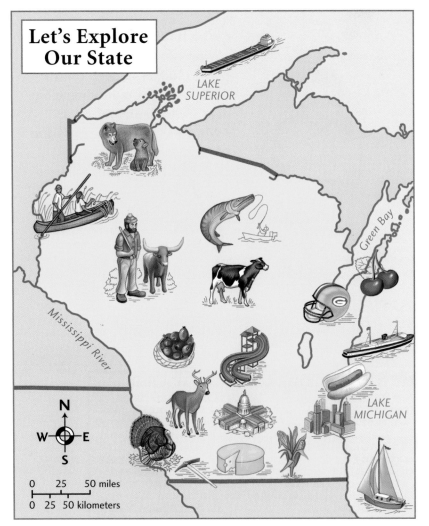

Let's Explore Our State

LAKE SUPERIOR

Mississippi River

Green Bay

LAKE MICHIGAN

N
W E
S

0   25   50 miles
0   25   50 kilometers

How does our state's geography help make us who we are and what we do as people from Wisconsin? How do people from elsewhere see us? How do we see ourselves?

Chapter 2: Wisconsin: A Place with a Past

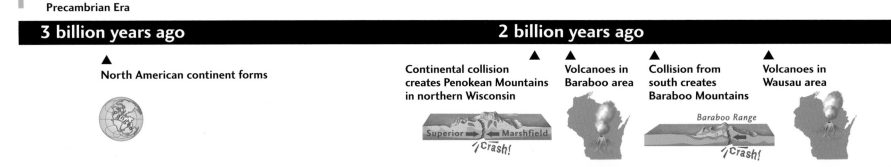

Precambrian Era

3 billion years ago   **2 billion years ago**

▲
North American continent forms

▲
Continental collision creates Penokean Mountains in northern Wisconsin

Superior → ← Marshfield
Crash!

▲
Volcanoes in Baraboo area

▲
Collision from south creates Baraboo Mountains

Baraboo Range
Crash!

▲
Volcanoes in Wausau area

Key Words

- cities
- compass rose
- continent
- country
- county
- elevation
- Equator
- geography
- geology
- glacier
- hemisphere
- Ice Age
- landforms
- latitude
- locate
- longitude
- parallels
- physical boundary
- political boundary
- Prime Meridian
- region
- state
- wetlands

Thinking Like a Historian

 What major turning points shaped the area that we see and live in today?

How does our landscape reflect these changes?

How do our waterways reflect these changes?

How did our waterways influence where people settled and where cities grew?

What features of a Wisconsin region attracted people to settle and live there?

Thinking Like a Geographer

1. How do we locate Wisconsin among neighboring states, in a region, in the United States, in a continent, in a hemisphere, and on a globe?
2. How can reading maps help us learn more about the state, region, nation, and world where we live?
3. In what ways are regions in Wisconsin different from one another? In what ways are they similar?

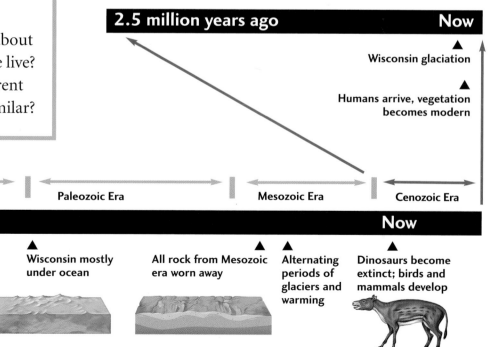

2.5 million years ago — **Now**

▲ Wisconsin glaciation

▲ Humans arrive, vegetation becomes modern

Paleozoic Era — Mesozoic Era — Cenozoic Era

1 billion years ago — **Now**

▲ Continent splits, lava oozes —Lake Superior area

▲ Hardened lava cork pops up —Lake Superior area

▲ Wisconsin mostly under ocean

▲ All rock from Mesozoic era worn away

▲ Alternating periods of glaciers and warming

▲ Dinosaurs become extinct; birds and mammals develop

A Landscape Shaped over Time: The Ice Age Trail

Ice Age
National
Scenic Trail

In this chapter, you'll find all kinds of information about Wisconsin's natural history and **geography**. You'll learn how the land and waterways were shaped over a long, long time. You'll also be amazed at the many new vocabulary words you'll be able to use to describe the natural **features** around you and to place Wisconsin in the United States and in the world.

Have you seen a sign like this near your house or school? Maybe you've seen this sign while traveling or camping in Wisconsin. Have you hiked or snowshoed on the **Ice Age** Trail? If so, then you've seen **landscapes** shaped by **glaciers**. This is what they look like today.

What is the Ice Age Trail?

In this chapter, you'll read about the way the **Ice Age** completely reshaped Wisconsin's **landscape** many thousands of years ago. The Ice Age Trail crosses **features** of the Ice Age's last glacier in Wisconsin. During the Ice Age, **glaciers** covered a large part of the earth.

Geologists have found that as the glaciers slowly moved forward, they pushed all kinds of rock and soil from farther north. **Glacial** movement completely changed the state's landscape. Then, about 14,000 years ago, the glaciers slowly melted when the weather finally warmed.

Even though the glaciers have melted and the Ice Age ended a long time ago, you can see some of the glacial features today if you hike the Ice Age Trail. For example, along the trail you'll find several hundred lakes and ponds created by the glaciers. You'll also find maps and signs along the way to help you understand how the glaciers changed Wisconsin's **topography**.

As you can see on the map on the next page, the Ice Age Trail winds a long way through Wisconsin.

geography (jee **og** ruh fee) The study of the earth, including its people, resources, climate, and physical features
features (**fee** churz) Important parts or qualities of something
Ice Age A period of time, long ago, when glaciers covered much of the earth's surface. The last Ice Age was more than 10,000 years ago.
landscapes (**land** skaypz) The shapes and forms of the land such as hills, plains, and valleys
glaciers (**glay** shurz) Giant sheets of ice formed in mountain valleys or near the North or South poles
Geologists (jee **ol** uh jists) Scientists who study the earth's layers of soil and rocks   **Glacial** (**glay** shuhl) Having to do with glaciers
topography (tuh **pog** ruh fee) The detailed description of the physical features of an area, including hills, valleys, mountains, plains, and rivers

Why is the Ice Age Trail in Wisconsin?

Wisconsin is not the only state in the United States that was mostly covered by glaciers during the Ice Age. So why is Wisconsin one of only two states that have an Ice Age trail? In the 1950s, a man from Milwaukee, Ray Zillmer, shared his idea of a hiking trail that would wind through Wisconsin. Its path would trace along the southern edge of the last glacier in the state. Soon a group of people formed to help plan the trail. Many interested people cooperated to make the trail a reality.

The Ice Age happened long ago and lasted thousands of years. But the Ice Age Trail is still being built. You and your family may volunteer to help build a part of the trail near where you live. Check with the Ice Age Trail volunteer chapter in your area. You'll be learning about Wisconsin's geography while helping the trail tell its story about glaciers and the Ice Age. You'll become part of a group of people who care about the state's **environment** and history. As you read this book, you'll learn more about other people who care enough about Wisconsin to take care of its land and water.

The Ice Age Trail is still being built. Today about 600 miles of the trail are completed. When it is finished, it will be 1000 miles long. As you read Chapter 2, you'll find out more about Wisconsin's glaciers and you'll learn more about the state's geography and **geology**.

Ray Zillmer worked to create the Ice Age Trail to protect Wisconsin's glacial landscape.

geology (jee **ol** uh jee) The study of the earth's layers of rock and soil   **environment** The natural world of lands, waters, and air

Locating Wisconsin in the United States

Where are you in Wisconsin?

Think of telling someone where you live. You might give your home address, and next describe your neighborhood or some nearby landmarks. Or you might start with your **county**, then tell about your community or city, and finally get to your neighborhood and home. Either way, you are describing **location**. Maps are the best way to show location. Different kinds of maps help you **locate** Wisconsin, along with its neighboring **states**, in its Midwestern region and then among the other states in this country.

Use the **compass rose** to help you describe the part of the state where your county is **located**. If your county is between two points, use both of those—northwest, northeast, southwest, or southeast—to describe where it is. If it's close to the middle, then it's in central Wisconsin. Practice by describing the location of these counties: Chippewa, Sheboygan, Racine, Rock, Ashland, Portage, Florence, Buffalo, and Grant.

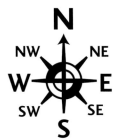

---

compass rose A map feature that shows the basic or cardinal directions (North, South, East, West) and often, shows those in between, such as southwest and northeast.
located Found   **county** (**kown** tee) One of the parts into which a state is divided
location The place or position where something is found   **locate** To find where something is
states One of the parts into which the United States is divided. Wisconsin, Illinois, Michigan, Minnesota, and Iowa are all states.

Our Neighbors

MINNESOTA

CANADA

Lake Superior

WISCONSIN

Lake Michigan

Lake Huron

MICHIGAN

Lake Erie

Mississippi River

IOWA

INDIANA

OHIO

ILLINOIS

MISSOURI

N W E S

0 ⎯ 150 miles
0 ⎯ 150 kilometers

Take a look at Wisconsin's location. Our state is nearly surrounded by water. It has Lake Superior to the north, Lake Michigan to the east, and the Mississippi River to the west. These waterways form natural **physical boundaries**. Can you find Wisconsin's **political boundaries**? Our neighboring states lie on the other side of these physical and political boundaries.

Regions of the United States

0 ⎯ 300 miles
0 ⎯ 300 kilometers

CANADA

Plains Wisconsin Great Lakes

WEST

NORTHEAST

MIDWEST

Mississippi River

SOUTHWEST

SOUTHEAST

PACIFIC OCEAN

ATLANTIC OCEAN

MEXICO

N W E S

Gulf of Mexico

The Midwest **region** of our **country** forms the northcentral part of the United States. The Midwest is the only region that has two separate groups of states: the Plains states and the Great Lakes states. In what ways do you think Wisconsin is more similar to its Great Lakes neighbors than it is to most of the other states in the region?

---

physical (**fiz** uh kuhl) **boundaries** (**bown** da rees) Natural features like rivers, lakes, or mountains that separate counties, states, or countries
political (poh **lit** uh kuhl) **boundaries** Boundaries that governments create to separate counties, states, or countries
region (**ree** jun) A defined area of a place (state or country, for example) that has common features, such as a similar landscape
country (**kun** tree) An area of land that has boundaries and a government that are shared by all the people living there; a nation.

Locating Wisconsin in the World

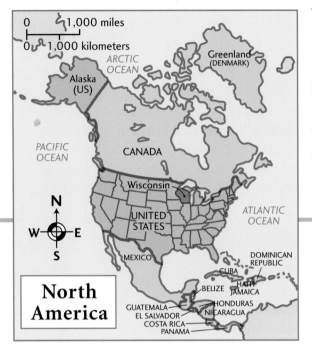

How would you describe Wisconsin's location in North America?

Where in the world is Wisconsin?

Maps that show the "big picture" help us locate Wisconsin in a larger world. Mapmakers do their best to make flat maps to represent the **sphere** that is the Earth. The maps on these two pages help you see Wisconsin's place in the world. The new vocabulary words will help you describe what you are seeing. And they will introduce you to the language that geographers and **cartographers** use.

Prime Meridian
An imaginary line that divides the globe into two equal halves, from North to South.

Equator
An imaginary line that goes around the middle of the globe like a belt from East to West.

The globe in your classroom is in the shape of a **sphere**, just like the shape of the Earth. In fact, a globe provides a small model of the Earth. On some smaller globes the individual states of the United States may be too small to be labeled. Try to locate Wisconsin on your classroom globe. Start by finding the land immediately south of Lake Superior and west of Lake Michigan.

sphere (sfeer) A round solid shape like a basketball where all sides are the same distance from the center   **cartographers** (car **tahg** ruh phurs) Mapmakers

How is the globe divided?

The globe is divided into different parts to help people locate and describe places on Earth. The Equator separates the globe into two parts: a top half and a bottom half. The top half above the equator is known as the Northern Hemisphere. The bottom half south of the equator is known as the Southern Hemisphere. You can remember the word **hemisphere** by remembering that **hemi** means half, so the word "hemisphere" means "half a sphere." What **continents** do you find in the Northern Hemisphere? In the Southern Hemisphere? Use the compass rose to help.

The Prime Meridian also separates the globe into equal parts from the North Pole to the South Pole. The half to the west of the Prime Meridian is known as the Western Hemisphere. The half to the east of the Prime Meridian is known as the Eastern Hemisphere. What continents do you find in the Western Hemisphere? In the Eastern Hemisphere? Use the compass rose once again. How do you describe Wisconsin's location using the words "continent" and "hemisphere?"

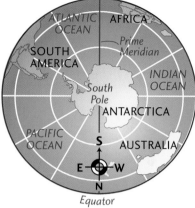

Northern Hemisphere
Above the Equator

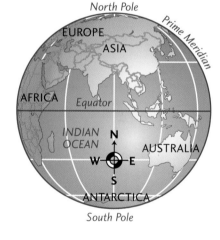

Southern Hemisphere
Below the Equator

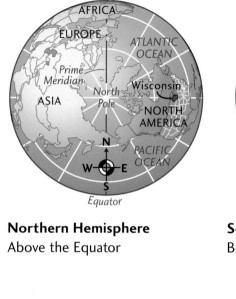

Western Hemisphere
The half of the globe to the west of the Prime Meridian

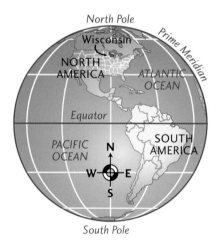

Eastern Hemisphere
The half of the globe to the east of the Prime Meridian

hemisphere (**heh** mis feer) Half a sphere   **hemi** (**heh** mee)
continents The seven large landmasses of the Earth. They are Africa, Antarctica, Asia, Australia, Europe, North America, and South America.

Using Longitude and Latitude

How do lines of longitude help describe locations on Earth?

Two sets of imaginary lines help people describe exact locations on the Earth.

Lines of **longitude,** called meridians, run north to south from the North Pole to the South Pole, just like the Prime Meridian. The lines of longitude are measured in degrees (you'll see the degree symbol ° next to the number). The lines of longitude begin with 0° at the Prime Meridian. In this example, each line is 30° east or west of it. Lines of longitude that are west of the prime meridian have a "W" for West after them. Lines of longitude east of the Prime Meridian have an "E" for East after them.

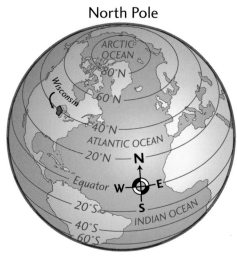

North Pole

Longitude

How do lines of latitude help describe locations on Earth?

Lines of **latitude,** called **parallels,** run from east to west around the globe, both north and south of the Equator. The parallels begin with 0° at the Equator. In this example, each line is 20° away from the one to the north or south of it. Lines of latitude that are north of the Equator have an "N" for North next to them; those south of the equator have an "S" for South next to them.

North Pole

Latitude

longitude (**lon** juh tood) Lines, or meridians, that run from the North Pole to the South Pole on the globe
latitude (**lat** uh tood) Lines, or parallels, that run from east to west around the globe   **parallels** (**pair** uh lehls)

Latitude and longitude in Wisconsin

- The North Pole is at 90° N, and the South Pole is 90° S.

- Half of 90° is 45°, and 45° N runs right through Wisconsin.

- The Prime Meridian is at 0° longitude; 90° W also runs right through Wisconsin!

- These two lines cross in Marathon County. Can you find them meeting on the map? That spot is halfway between the Equator and the North Pole.

- Between which parallels do you live? Between which meridians do you find most of Wisconsin?

What Does Wisconsin Look Like Today?

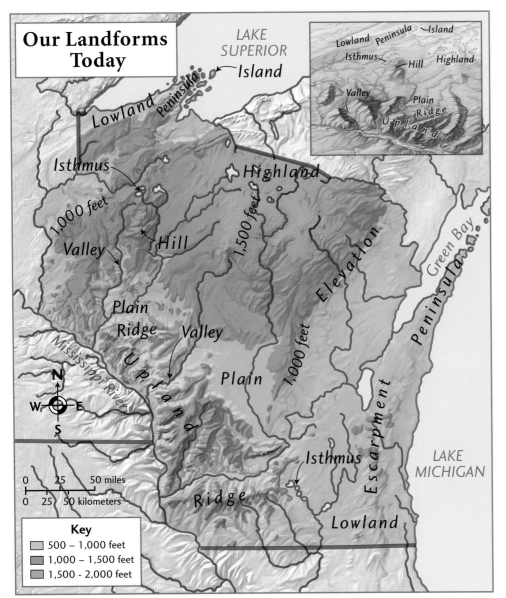

Our Landforms Today

LAKE SUPERIOR

Island

Lowland

Peninsula

Isthmus

1,000 feet

Valley

Hill

Highland

1,500 feet

Plain
Ridge

Valley

Upland

Plain

1,000 feet

Mississippi River

N
W E
S

0   25   50 miles
0   25   50 kilometers

Isthmus

Elevation

Green Bay

Peninsula

Escarpment

LAKE MICHIGAN

Ridge

Lowland

Inset map labels: Lowland, Peninsula, Island, Isthmus, Hill, Highland, Valley, Plain, Ridge, Upland

Key
- 500 – 1,000 feet
- 1,000 – 1,500 feet
- 1,500 - 2,000 feet

This photo shows the isthmus between Lake Mendota and Lake Monona in Madison. Isthmuses are one of Wisconsin's many landforms. Look for Wisconsin's state capitol building in this photo.

This map shows many **topographical** features of Wisconsin's landscape.
How many of these **landforms** have you seen?

topographical (top uh **graf** uh kuhl) Showing details of the physical features of an area, including hills, valleys, mountains, plains, and rivers
landforms Features of the Earth's surface, such as hills, valleys, and prairies

How do maps and the language of maps help describe Wisconsin?

Like the rest of the Midwest region, Wisconsin has a variety of interesting features, with many different landforms. The vocabulary below describes what you are seeing. As you learn the words for the different landforms, you'll be thinking like a geographer and sounding like one, too!

isthmus (**iss** muhss) A narrow strip of land that lies between two bodies of water and connects two larger land masses

plains Level or nearly level lands

uplands (**uh** plundz) Rocky cliffs and steep valleys

hills Raised areas of land that are less than 2000 feet above the surrounding land

ridges Long and narrow chains of hills

elevation (eh leh **vay** shun) The height of land above sea level

lowlands (**low** lundz) Fairly flat lands that are lower in elevation than the lands around them

peninsula (peh **nin** suh luh) A piece of land that sticks out from a larger land mass and is nearly surrounded by water

escarpment (ess **carp** munt) A steep, rocky cliff or long slope of land that is higher than the lands on either side of it

islands (**ɪ** lundz) Areas of land completely surrounded by water

highlands (**hy** lundz) Hilly lands that are higher in elevation than the lands surrounding them

valleys Areas of low ground between two hills

Reshaped by a Long-Ago and Very Cold Past

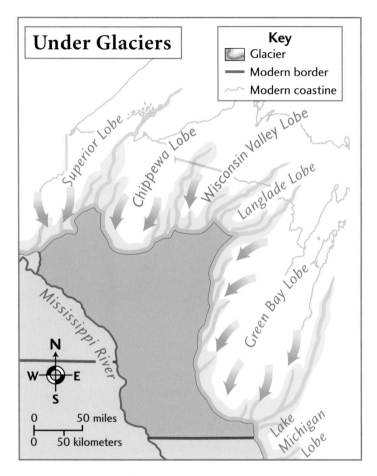

Under Glaciers

Key
- Glacier
- Modern border
- Modern coastline

Superior Lobe

Chippewa Lobe

Wisconsin Valley Lobe

Langlade Lobe

Green Bay Lobe

Mississippi River

Lake Michigan Lobe

N W E S

0   50 miles

0   50 kilometers

Over thousands of years during the Ice Age, the weather changed from colder to warmer and back again. During colder periods, the edge of ice moved very slowly. It was like a cold, thick syrup that covered much of Wisconsin. During warmer periods, the glaciers melted back.

How did the Ice Age reshape Wisconsin?

About a million years ago, the weather was warmer than it is today. Then the climate grew colder. To the north of Wisconsin, more snow fell in the long winters than melted during the short summers. The snow piled deeper and deeper. The lower layers of snow turned into ice that got thicker and thicker—more than a mile thick in some places. This thick ice is known as glaciers. The glaciers slowly flowed south. They scraped down the highest places on the landscape. Glaciers scraped away the rock beneath them and picked up large amounts of sand and rock. Glaciers carried this mix with them as they moved.

The weather grew warmer. The ice melted. The edges of the glaciers melted back. This happened over and over again. Finally, the weather warmed permanently. **Moraines** show how far glaciers moved and stayed over time. The last glacier's melting ice dumped its load of rock, **silt**, and clay on the land. This mix of ice, sand, and rocks melted out and is called **till**. It filled in the lowest spots in the landscape. The melting and dumping created the gently rolling landscape that forms much of the **glaciated** area of Wisconsin that we see today. You'll find those glacial features on the maps on the next page.

Moraines (muh **rains**) Ridges or long hills that were once the side or edge of a glacier
silt Fine particles of soil washed along by flowing water to settle at the bottom of a river or lake
till A combination of clay, silt, pebbles, and larger rocks   **glaciated** (**glay** shee ay tuhd) Once covered by glaciers

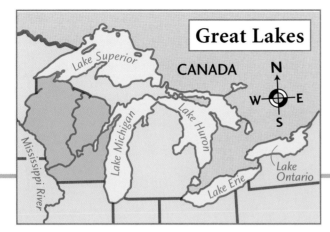

Great Lakes

CANADA

Lake Superior

Lake Michigan

Lake Huron

Lake Erie

Lake Ontario

Mississippi River

Did you know that glaciers created the Great Lakes?

How do glacial features appear on maps?

The maps on this page show how glaciers reshaped the land and waterways in and around Wisconsin. Glaciers also created the Great Lakes. The Great Lakes are so large that they are sometimes known as "inland seas." The scraping away of rock beneath glaciers made the **basins** of what are now lakes Superior, Michigan, Huron, Erie, and Ontario even deeper. These great basins funneled the flow of ice into the lowest parts of the landscape.

The southwestern part of Wisconsin and neighboring areas in Iowa, Illinois, and Minnesota were not covered by glaciers. This part of the region is known as the **Driftless Area**. The Driftless Area has no glacial deposits or "drift." It has no glacial features and few lakes or **wetlands**. Instead, the Driftless Area has steep and twisting valleys and ridges that are several million years old.

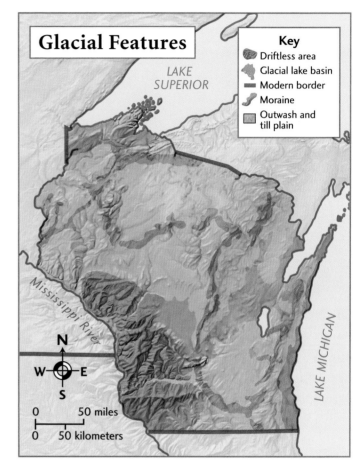

Glacial Features

LAKE SUPERIOR

Mississippi River

LAKE MICHIGAN

0   50 miles
0   50 kilometers

Key
- Driftless area
- Glacial lake basin
- Modern border
- Moraine
- Outwash and till plain

Look at this map and then back at the topographical map on page 22. Can you find the **Driftless Area** on that map? Can you find the moraines?

Driftless Area Southwestern Wisconsin and parts of the neighboring areas of Iowa, Illinois, and Minnesota that were never covered by glaciers
basins Low areas   **wetlands** Areas covered with water for all or part of the year

Glacial Landforms Today

What kinds of landforms that glaciers made can we still see today?

Kettle

A scooped-out area that was filled with a large block of ice. When the ice melted, it left a low area. If the area filled with water, it became a kettle lake.

Esker

A long, snake-shaped hill formed of rounded sand and gravel. Eskers were formed by melting streams that flowed through tunnels at the base of a glacier.

Moraine

A ridge or long hill that was once the side or edge of a glacier. Moraines show how far glaciers reached and stayed over some time. Glaciers formed moraines by pushing and dumping piles of many kinds of dirt and rocks.

Kame

A steep, rounded hill formed by streams of melting glacial ice pouring down a hole and depositing their load of dirt and rocks into a large pile.

Drumlin

A long hill that looks something like an overturned canoe or a teardrop. Drumlins were formed in the same direction as the glaciers flowed. They often occur in groups known as drumlin fields.

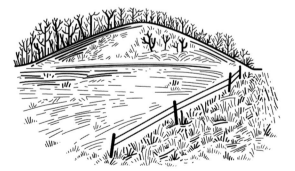

Connected by Water: Wisconsin's Waterways

How do Wisconsin's waterways work?

Water drains from the land into the nearest wetland and **waterway**—whether it's a marsh, pond, lake, stream, or river. The area of land that drains into the same waterway forms a **watershed.**

As a smaller stream flows into a larger waterway, the land drains. The smaller stream is called a **tributary.** Each tributary that flows into the larger waterway increases that waterway's size. On a map, the larger rivers are darker and wider. That makes it easy for you to follow a tributary from its source (where it begins) to its mouth (where it enters a larger waterway).

Most of Wisconsin's major watersheds flow into the Mississippi River. One watershed flows into Lake Michigan. By looking at the map on this page, you can see that many smaller rivers flow into Lake Superior and Lake Michigan. These rivers drain a much smaller area.

Wisconsin's watersheds and waterways worked well to help Native People **navigate** their canoes and to trade with people who lived elsewhere. Later, these same waterways were helpful to the settlers who came here in the 1800s and became Wisconsin's miners, lumbermen, **manufacturers,** and farmers. Waterways helped them get their goods to markets in this country and other countries. Waterways helped them receive the goods they needed from other places around the world. Our larger waterways are still major shipping lanes. You'll read about them later in this book.

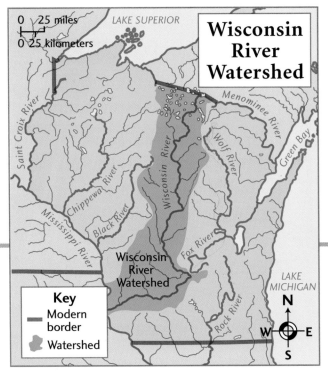

Wisconsin River Watershed

This **watershed** map shows smaller streams and rivers draining into the Wisconsin River. Where do Wisconsin's largest rivers drain? How do you think that has helped Wisconsin connect to the rest of the world?

watershed The area of land that drains into the same waterway   **waterway** River, lake, or other body of water on which ships and boats travel
tributary (**trib** yuh tair ee) A stream that flows into a larger waterway
navigate (**nav** uh gayt) To travel in a boat, aircraft, or other vehicle using maps, compasses, the stars, and other devices to guide you
manufacturers (man yuh **fak** chur urz) People who manufacture or make things, often with machines

Why are Wisconsin's waterways so important?

Wisconsin has many large and small waterways. Some are deep and wide enough for people to navigate. Smaller waterways such as streams or ponds might be large enough for only a canoe or a small boat. But large boats and **barges** travel on the Great Lakes and the Mississippi River. For thousands of years, people have used waterways of all sizes to travel and move their goods. Wisconsin's waterways have kept us connected to the rest of the world. Ours is the only state that sits between two Great Lakes and the Mississippi River. That's one reason why people have always used our location as a crossroads—a place that brings many kinds of people together.

Waterways also provide **habitats** for **waterfowl,** fish, insects, and **aquatic** plants and animals that live below the surface of the water. Some ponds and lakes were so shallow that aquatic plants slowly filled them. Over time, these areas became wetlands.

Wetlands themselves are important to our environment. Horicon Marsh in Dodge County and other wetlands welcome many wild creatures. Wetlands play another really important role in protecting our natural environment. They act like sponges. They soak up water and slow runoff, which prevents flooding. They also soak up harmful **pollutants** to keep them from **polluting** our waterways. In the past, wetlands covered twice as much area in Wisconsin as they do today. People over the last 200 years have drained land for farming, road building, and other uses. Now many wetlands are protected by law.

Wisconsin is nearly surrounded by water, and this map shows Wisconsin's most important waterways. Our state has thousands of inland lakes and thousands of miles of rivers and streams. In fact, a quarter of Wisconsin lies under water. No matter which direction we travel, there's a waterway nearby!

barges (**bahr** juhz) Long, flat boats   habitats (**hab** uh tats) Places and natural conditions where plants and animals live
waterfowl Birds, like ducks and geese, that spend their lives on or near water   aquatic (uh **kwat** ik) Living or growing in water
pollutants (puh **loot** uhnts) Things that pollute or make dirty   polluting (puh **loot** ing) Making dirty

Exploring Wisconsin's Five Regions: Identifying the Regions, Lake Superior Lowland

What are the five physical regions of Wisconsin?

Geologists and geographers use five physical regions to describe Wisconsin's geology and geography. These five regions are: 1) the Lake Superior Lowland; 2) the Northern Highland; 3) the Central Plain; 4) the Western Upland; and 5) the Eastern Ridges and Lowlands. The state's five regions each have unique features. They also have similar features. Read on to discover how the regions are the same and how they are different. Learn to recognize the state's five regions and try to remember as much about them as you can. As you read the rest of this book, you'll be exploring how people, over time, have interacted with these regions.

Our Five Physical Regions

LAKE SUPERIOR

MINNESOTA

LAKE SUPERIOR LOWLAND

MICHIGAN

NORTHERN HIGHLAND

Green Bay

Mississippi River

WESTERN UPLAND

CENTRAL PLAIN

Lake Winnebago

EASTERN RIDGES AND LOWLANDS

LAKE MICHIGAN

IOWA

N
W E
S

0   25   50 miles
0   25   50 kilometers

ILLINOIS

This photo shows some of the 21 Apostle Islands in the Lake Superior Lowland. You can explore them by camping, canoeing, and kayaking. Along the shoreline, you will see caves and bluffs created by Lake Superior.

Which region is named after the largest of the Great Lakes?

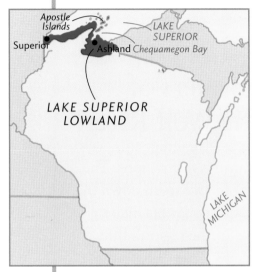

The Lake Superior Lowland region is the smallest of the state's regions. It occupies portions of Douglas, Bayfield, and Ashland counties on the northern tip of Wisconsin. The region is called a lowland because the land is lower in elevation than the Northern Highland to the south. The bottom of Lake Superior is even lower, more than 300 feet below sea level in places.

The region is flat near Superior and Ashland. But it slopes gently toward the southern shore of Lake Superior, the largest of the Great Lakes. Farther from the lake, swift-running rivers once cut deep **ravines** and **gorges** through the region. These rivers contain rapids and waterfalls that tumble down **volcanic** rock. Volcanic rock is so hard that it erodes slowly.

One of the most striking features of this region is Lake Superior. It is also known as "the Big Lake" by some people. In many places, the Lake Superior shoreline has steep escarpments that rise high above the water. The Apostle Islands lie right off the Bayfield Peninsula in **Chequamegon** Bay. These islands form the northernmost tip of the state.

The Lake Superior Lowland has outstanding natural resources. Pine and birch forests cover much of this region. Lake Superior has supplied people with lake trout and whitefish. The region's rivers and streams are home to trout, walleye, and northern pike. Neighboring wetlands have **sloughs** of wild rice. About 100 years ago, **quarries** in this region provided brown sandstone for building construction. The Apostle Islands were logged. All of these resources are important to the people who call this region home and to those who visit.

Did you know that Lake Superior is the largest body of fresh water in the world?

The Amnicon River created this waterfall over **volcanic** rock. Both features are now part of the Amnicon Falls State Park. You can hike the trails along the river to see more of this region's landscapes.

volcanic (vol **kan** ik) Having to do with volcanoes
ravines (ruh **veenz**) Deep, narrow valleys with steep sides   **gorges** (**gor** juhz) Deep valleys with steep, rocky sides
Chequamegon (shuh **waw** muh guhn)   **sloughs** (slooz) Marshy or swampy areas with slow-moving or standing water
quarries (**kwor** eez) Places where stone is dug or cut

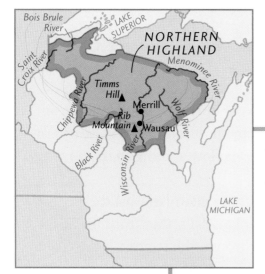

Exploring Wisconsin's Five Regions: Northern Highland, Central Plain

Which region contains the headwaters of both the Wisconsin River and the Wolf River?

The Northern Highland region is the largest of Wisconsin's five regions. The region is made up of mountains nearly two billion years old and worn down by weather and water. About one billion years ago, other natural changes made some of the land dome up. No wonder "highland" is part of the region's title. Geologists have studied fossils from the Northern Highland. They believe that these mountains are among the oldest in the world. The state's highest point, Timms Hill, is found in this region. It measures 1951 feet above sea level and is located in Price County.

This hilly region has upland plains, ridges, and deep valleys. You can also find moraines and glacial soil in areas of the Northern Highland once covered by glaciers. Forested lands are much more common than farmland. The lumber industry has provided many jobs for people in the region for more than 100 years.

Waterways are an important part of the Northern Highland. The region's many lakes and **swamps** provide water for the region's rivers. These include the **headwaters** of the Wisconsin and Wolf rivers as well as the **St. Croix** and **Chippewa** Rivers. Rapids, waterfalls, marshes, and **peat** swamps also form a large part of this region. Both the forests and bodies of water attract hunters, fishermen, and vacationing families year round. In Vilas and Oneida counties alone, there are almost 2500 lakes!

The St. Croix River comes so close to the **Bois Brule** River that Wisconsin's Native People made this an important water highway between Lake Superior and the Mississippi River. They walked and carried their canoes the short distance between the two smaller rivers.

Rib Mountain, which rises 800 feet above the Wisconsin River, is about five miles southwest of Wausau. Some say the mountain is over one billion years old! Rib Mountain is the key feature in Rib Mountain State Park.

---

swamps Wet, soft lands   **headwaters** The place where a stream starts before it flows into a river
peat Dark brown, partly decayed plant matter found in bogs and swamps   **St. Croix** (saynt kroi)   **Chippewa** (**chip** uh wuh)   **Bois Brule** (bwah brooll)

Which region is home to Wisconsin Dells?

The Central Plain region stretches across the middle of the state. It is bordered by the Northern Highland on the north, by the Western Upland on the west and south, and by the Eastern Ridges and Lowlands on the east. Think of the Central Plain as a very long field in the shape of a "V" or a backward check mark. Glaciers created much of this region's plain.

Much of this low-lying region long ago lay at the bottom of a lake—Glacial Lake Wisconsin. As the glaciers melted at the end of the Ice Age, they filled this low area with a huge lake that spread over one million **acres**. Eventually, the water dried up and left the sandy plain for us to see today. The region's soil is not like the rich, black dirt in the neighboring Eastern Ridges and Lowlands.

The Central Plain also contains tall cliffs made of sandstone. With their rough and rocky walls and flat tops, they look like castle towers rising out of the sandy plain that surrounds them. Glacial Lake Wisconsin's waters long washed up against their sandstone sides. The fast-moving waters carved some of the sand away, leaving these jagged natural towers. The height of these rock walls near Baraboo and Wisconsin Dells shows how high the lake's water once stood.

The Wisconsin River flows through the middle of the Central Plain region. The Black, Chippewa, Fox, and Wolf rivers are other major waterways in this region.

You can hike and camp at the **Roche-A-Cri** State Park. Be sure to check out its large rock bluff. It has wooden steps that you can climb to the top. It stands about 300 feet above the plain. From the top of it, you can see many other sandstone towers that stood in Glacial Lake Wisconsin, such as Mosquito Mound, Bear Bluff, and Rattlesnake Mound.

acres Measurements of area equal to 43,560 square feet. An acre is almost the size of a football field. **Roche-A-Cri** (ro shuh kree)

Exploring Wisconsin's Five Regions: Western Upland, Eastern Ridges and Lowlands

Which region includes the place where the Wisconsin River flows into the Mississippi River?

The Western Upland region is the only one of the state's five regions that was not covered by the glaciers. That's why the region is part of the Driftless Area. Look back at the glacial map on page 25 to see how far the Driftless Area extends. And remember, when you explore here, you're discovering how Wisconsin looked before the Ice Age!

You'll find that high ridges and deep valleys called **coulees** fill the Western Upland. Over millions of years, streams cut into the limestone and sandstone there to create these features. These coulees can be seen from country roads in Buffalo, Jackson, La Crosse, Monroe, Trempealeau, and Vernon counties.

The western border of this region is the Mississippi River. It flows through a large gorge that lies more than 500 feet below the top of the region's ridges. The gorge's bottomlands measure almost seven miles wide at some points. Steep bluffs border the gorges.

The hills of the Baraboo Range, in Sauk and Columbia counties, form one of the oldest rock **outcrops** in North America. The Baraboo Range also contains forests, prairies, marshes, and Devil's Lake. Did you know that the Military Ridge is the dividing line between the creeks and rivers that flow north into the Wisconsin River and the creeks and streams flowing south to the Rock and Mississippi rivers?

You can stand on top of a bluff in Grant County to see where the Wisconsin River flows southwest into the Mississippi River.

coulees (**koo** leez) Deep, narrow valleys, often with streams
outcrops Groups of rocks above the surface of the ground

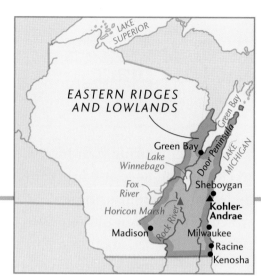

Just south of Sheboygan, Kohler-Andrae State Park shares its sand dunes and Lake Michigan shoreline with horseback riders, hikers, campers, swimmers, and skiers.

Which region has Lake Michigan as its eastern border?

The Eastern Ridges and Lowlands region gets its name from the three limestone ridges that run through the region from north to south. Wide lowlands separate these three ridges from each other. In some parts of the region, the ridges are only two miles wide. In other places they are 20 miles wide. The lowest place in the region—and in the state—is along the shoreline of Lake Michigan. Lake Michigan forms most of this region's eastern border.

Remember that glaciers shaped the lake's basin, or bottom. Glaciers also shaped this region's landscape and waterways in other ways. Glaciers **eroded** areas that became rivers that we see today: the Milwaukee River, the Fox River, and the Rock River. As glaciers melted, they created the many kettles that make the Kettle Moraine, which is one of the most beautiful parts of this region. Some kettles filled with water to become lakes. Other kettles became wetlands and marshes, like Horicon Marsh, the largest freshwater cattail marsh in the United States.

Glaciers left more than a thousand drumlins in the Eastern Ridges and Lowlands region. They range in length from 30 feet to two miles. Some are only five feet high. Others are as high as 140 feet. These drumlins contain clay, gravel, sand, and silt left behind by the glaciers. They also include **igneous** and **metamorphic** rocks.

The Eastern Ridges and Lowlands region contains Wisconsin's two largest **cities**: Milwaukee and Madison.

Did you know that this region includes five islands off the tip of the Door County peninsula? They are Washington Island, Rock Island, Detroit Island, Pilot Island, and Plum Island. Washington Island is the largest of the five islands. Rock Island is a state park. No cars or bikes can be used there. You can take a ferry to Rock Island, but then you must explore on foot.

---

eroded Worn away by wind and water   **igneous** (ig nee uhs) Created by great heat or by a volcano   **metamorphic** (met uh mor fik) Changed by heat and pressure
cities (sit eez) Large, important centers of population and business

Favorite Places in Wisconsin to Visit

Not only can you see waterfalls at Copper Falls State Park, but you can also hike, ski, swim, fish, and camp here in the Lake Superior Lowland!

What have you learned about this place called Wisconsin?

Wow! You have traveled all over Wisconsin in this chapter. During your travels, you've learned how to find Wisconsin on maps and globes. You have also learned many words that geographers and geologists use to describe the state's physical features. You read about the glaciers that covered much of Wisconsin thousands of years ago and the waterways they helped to create. You also learned about the state's five physical regions. Maybe you even started a list of places around Wisconsin that you will want to read more about, or visit with your family and friends. Perhaps some of these new places will become some of your favorite places!

In the next chapters, you will read about many different groups of people that have made their homes in Wisconsin. You'll discover how they built their homes and what kinds of work they have done here. Now that you know something about Wisconsin's geography and geology, you will better understand how people have lived here and why they made the choices they did. This knowledge will help you make your own choices about how you live in Wisconsin, and how you care for the land, water, and air around you.

Governor Thompson State Park is near the Peshtigo River State Forest in Marinette County, in the Eastern Ridges and Lowlands region. There are several lakes within this protected forest, including Wood Lake and Huber Lake.

Maple trees, like these in New Glarus Woods State Park, add color to the Western Upland landscape in fall.

More Places to Visit in the Five Regions

- Apostle Islands National Lakeshore near Bayfield in the Lake Superior Lowland
- Granddad Bluff east of La Crosse in the Western Upland
- Henry S. Reuss Ice Age Interpretive Center in the Kettle Moraine State Forest in the Eastern Ridges and Lowlands
- Nicolet National Forest near Laona in the Northern Highland
- Wisconsin Dells in the Central Plain
- Weis Earth Science Center in Menasha in the Eastern Ridges and Lowlands

Some Things to Read

- *Learning from the Land: Wisconsin Land Use* by Bobbie Malone, Chapter 1
- *Working with Water: Wisconsin Waterways* by Bobbie Malone and Jefferson J. Gray, Chapter 1

You'll see places like this in Black River State Forest in the Central Plain. You can also swim and fish in the Black River!

You can canoe on the Flambeau River and camp and fish alongside it at the Flambeau River State Forest in the Northern Highland region.

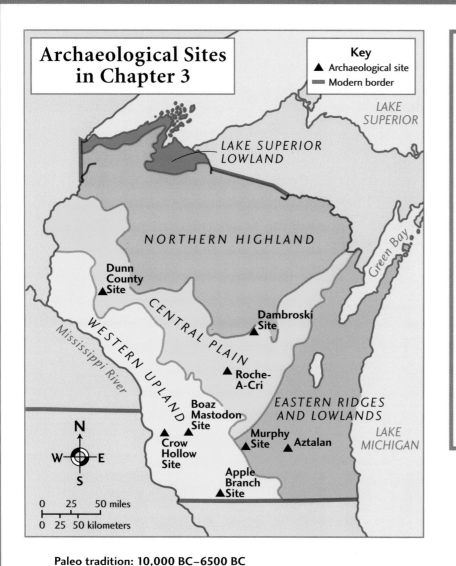

Archaeological Sites in Chapter 3

Key
▲ Archaeological site
— Modern border

LAKE SUPERIOR

LAKE SUPERIOR LOWLAND

NORTHERN HIGHLAND

Green Bay

Dunn County Site ▲

CENTRAL PLAIN

Dambroski Site ▲

WESTERN UPLAND

Mississippi River

▲ Roche-A-Cri

Boaz Mastodon Site ▲

EASTERN RIDGES AND LOWLANDS

Murphy Site ▲ ▲ Aztalan

LAKE MICHIGAN

▲ Crow Hollow Site

Apple Branch Site ▲

N W E S

0 25 50 miles
0 25 50 kilometers

Chapter 3: Wisconsin's First People

- Native People Today Celebrate Their History and Traditions
- Ways to Discover the Long-Ago Past
- Mammoths, Mastodons, and Earliest People
- Inventions for a New Age: The Archaic Tradition
- People of the Woodland: New Ways of Living and Viewing the World
- The Mysterious Mississippian Tradition
- Early Wisconsin Farmers: The Oneota Tradition
- Communicating in Many Forms
- Changes over Thousands of Years

Paleo tradition: 10,000 BC–6500 BC

Archaic tradition: 6500 BC–800 BC

| 10,000 BC | 9000 BC | 8000 BC | 7000 BC | 6000 BC | 5000 BC |

▲ **Boaz mastodon** 9000 BC–8700 BC

Key Words

- adapted
- adaptation
- Archaic
- ceremonies
- communicate
- cultivate
- excavate
- Mississippians
- Oneota
- Paleo-Indians
- resources
- survived
- Woodland Indians

Thinking Like a Historian

👀 How did the earliest people in Wisconsin live?

🔁 How did the lives of Wisconsin Indians change as the climate warmed?

⤙ What kinds of changes in the lives of Wisconsin Indians were so large that archaeologists see them as turning points?

🏺→🏺 What kinds of things did Wisconsin Indians do thousands of years ago that we still do today?

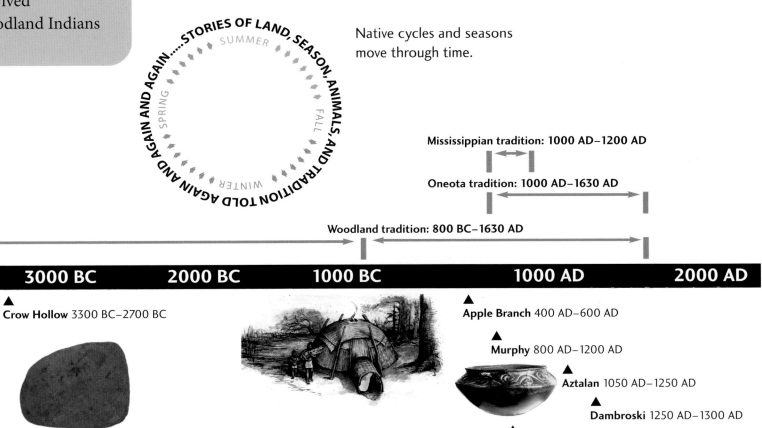

STORIES OF LAND, SEASON, ANIMALS, AND TRADITION TOLD AGAIN AND AGAIN AND AGAIN AND AGAIN...

SPRING SUMMER FALL WINTER

Native cycles and seasons move through time.

Mississippian tradition: 1000 AD–1200 AD

Oneota tradition: 1000 AD–1630 AD

Woodland tradition: 800 BC–1630 AD

| 4000 BC | 3000 BC | 2000 BC | 1000 BC | 1000 AD | 2000 AD |

Crow Hollow 3300 BC–2700 BC

Apple Branch 400 AD–600 AD

Murphy 800 AD–1200 AD

Aztalan 1050 AD–1250 AD

Dambroski 1250 AD–1300 AD

Roche-A-Cri 800 AD–1300 AD rock carvings; 1400 AD–1600 AD red painting

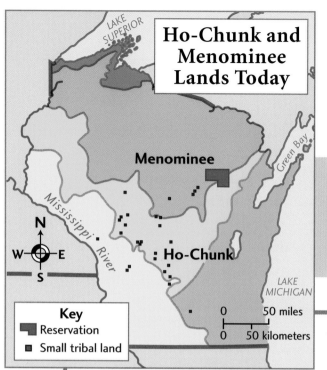

Ho-Chunk and Menominee Lands Today

LAKE SUPERIOR

Menominee

Green Bay

Mississippi River

N W E S

Ho-Chunk

LAKE MICHIGAN

0   50 miles
0   50 kilometers

Key
■ Reservation
▪ Small tribal land

Native People Today Celebrate Their History and Traditions

In this chapter, you will read about different groups of Indians who lived in Wisconsin thousands of years ago. As the climate warmed up, plant and animal life changed. The ways people lived changed, too. You will recognize these changes as you read through the chapter.

Who are Wisconsin's First People?

Native people have lived on the North American continent for thousands and thousands of years. Many different groups of Native people lived in the area that we now know as Wisconsin. Native people are also known as the First People.

For example, the **Menominee** and the **Ho-Chunk** people are two of the Indian nations in Wisconsin today. They tell stories of their **ancestors** who lived here thousands of years ago. Other Indian nations in Wisconsin today arrived here much later.

The earliest Wisconsin Indians **adapted** or changed their way of living as the land and weather changed. This **adaptation** happened very slowly, as you can tell by looking at the timeline on pages 38 and 39. You'll learn just how people's homes, foods, hunting, and ways of living adapted to the changes in the land and weather. Indian nations in the state today continue to adapt. Yet they still honor the stories and memories of their ancestors.

Each nation has its own language, history, and traditions. Each nation also has its own creation story that tells of the tribe's beginning. Tribal **elders** have passed down the nation's history and culture in stories, art, and songs to the next generation. You'll read a Menominee story on the next page.

Menominee (muh **nah** muh nee) and **Ho-Chunk** American Indian nations   **ancestors** (**an** ses turz) Family members who lived long ago
adapted (uh **dap** tuhd) Changed or adjusted to fit different conditions   **adaptation** (ad ap **tay** shuhn) Act of changing to fit different conditions
elders (**el** durz) Older people

How did the Menominee people come into being?

A Menominee **sacred** legend tells of the tribe's beginning along the shores of the Menominee River. First the Creator made the world and all living things. He made the lakes, rivers, rocks, mountains, hills, and valleys of Grandmother Earth.

Then a light-colored bear traveled alone along the banks of the river. He spoke with the Creator. The bear explained that he was lonely. He wanted to change his form. The bear wished to be a human being. The Creator agreed, and changed the bear into the first Menominee.

The first Menominee continued walking along the riverbank until he spied a golden eagle circling high in the sky. He called the eagle down and asked it to be his brother. The Creator also permitted the eagle to change form. Now there were two Menominee brothers. Each became the head of a **clan,** and their **descendants** became the clan.

The two brothers came upon other animal spirits. One by one, these also became brothers. Each clan has its own story of joining the first two Menominee brothers. Together the clans form the Menominee people. Today the Menominee people live along the banks of the Wolf River in Menominee County. The Menominee knew this land as "The Place Where Everything Is Good."

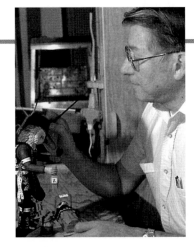

This is Menominee sculptor James **Frechette** at work. As a child, he listened to tribal elders tell stories of Menominee traditions. As an adult, he carved the Light Colored Bear to the right. You can see the Menominee clan story on display at the University of Wisconsin-Stevens Point Library.

Frechette (fre **shet**)　**sacred** (**say** krid) Holy; deserving of respect
clan A group of Native people with the same ancestor
descendants (dee **sen** dunts) Family members who are born after their ancestors

Ways to Discover the Long-Ago Past

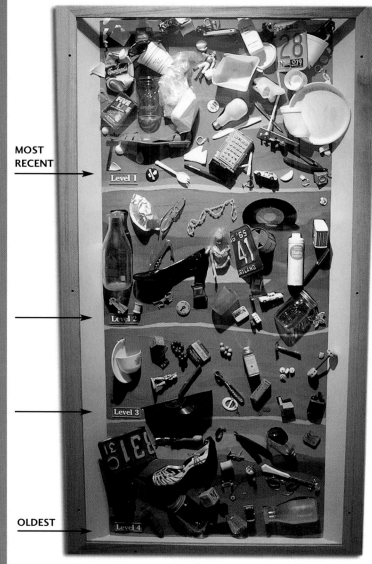

MOST RECENT

Level 1

Level 2

Level 3

OLDEST

Level 4

The deeper you dig, the older the artifacts and features you find. Can you identify any of the oldest objects in this garbage dump exhibit from the Wisconsin Historical Museum?

How do we know about people who lived long ago?

To study the past, you need the "stuff" of the past. Historians study newspapers, diaries, buildings, and other things from the past. These documents and artifacts help us learn what really happened long ago.

But there's a problem. People who lived thousands of years ago did not leave us documents. How can we learn about them? One way is known as **oral tradition.** Tribal stories like the Menominee legend you just read were passed down from one person to another without ever being written. They connect people to this land.

Archaeology is another way to learn about the long-ago past. Almost none of those objects and buildings from the long-ago past still exist as they did when they were made! So, how do archaeologists find evidence of the way people lived?

Archaeologists learn about past people by studying artifacts and **features** like house foundations found at a particular site. Archaeologists learn about the way people lived at a **site** at a particular time in the past. Sometimes a site is named for its location or for the landowner. If a site was found in the Dells, for example, it might be called the Dells Site, or maybe the Waterslide Site!

oral tradition The passing down of stories by telling them over and over without writing them down
Archaeology (ahr kee **ol** uh jee) The study of past people based on the things they left in the places where they once lived   **features** Immovable human-made things
site A place where people lived, worked, and worshipped; where archaeologists find artifacts and features

As archaeologists sift dirt through a screen, they find small artifacts that they otherwise might not see. When they study this evidence later, they will understand more about the way people lived at a site like Apple Branch.

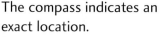

The compass indicates an exact location.

Archaeologists use trowels to carefully scrape dirt.

How do archaeologists study a site?

Once archaeologists discover a site, they may decide to **excavate** portions of it to see how people once lived at the site. Archaeologists have to carefully keep track of exactly where they find all artifacts and features as they dig.

The work you see on this page took place at the Apple Branch Site in **Lafayette** County in the Western Uplands. The artifacts and features archaeologists found led them to believe that Indians lived at Apple Branch between 400 AD and 600 AD.

Archaeologists carefully map and take notes about all the evidence they find. Many objects rot away before any archaeologist finds them. So an archaeologist's work is like trying to solve a giant jigsaw puzzle. But the archaeologist has to work without having most of the pieces and without knowing what the final picture is supposed to look like.

WESTERN UPLAND

Apple Branch Site

Archaeologists found these two spear points at Apple Branch. They are both the actual sizes.

excavate (ek skuh vayt) To dig carefully   **Lafayette** (lah fee **et**)

Mammoths, Mastodons, and Earliest People

What is the Boaz Mastodon?

A bit more than one hundred years ago, two young boys from the Dosch family found a couple of bones belonging to this **mastodon**. They found the bones on their family's farm near **Boaz** in Richland County in the Western Upland region. Soon after, the boys and their families excavated the rest of the bones. They also found two spear points. Through their hard work, the Dosch family preserved one of Wisconsin's most important historical discoveries. You can visit the preserved skeleton of the Boaz Mastodon in the Geology Museum on the University of Wisconsin–Madison campus.

Mastodons and mammoths are relatives of today's elephants. By studying their skeletons, scientists can tell us that the adults were from 8 to 10 feet tall at the shoulder. They were close to 16 feet long, weighed about 9 tons, and were covered with long fur.

Boaz (**boh** az)   **Mastodons** (**mas** tuh dons) Large, hairy mammals, related to the elephant, that died out thousands of years ago

Who were the Paleo people?

Archaeologists call the earliest people in Wisconsin **Paleo-Indians.** They lived here as hunters and gatherers between 10,000 and 6500 BC. Archaeologists have found artifacts like the spear points on this page at about 750 sites in what is now our state. The points' large and easily recognized shape tells us that the Paleo-Indians were hunters who made these points. They were skilled hunters and craftsmen who are the ancestors of Native people today in Wisconsin and elsewhere.

Many tribes and groups of Paleo-Indians lived in Wisconsin during this period. The climate was much colder then. Few edible plants were growing. Paleo people had to travel far and wide to find enough food to survive. They lived in small family groups most of the time.

Paleo-Indians traveled on foot to hunt mammals such as deer, elk, mammoths, and mastodons, and they gathered berries and nuts in the forests. They also crossed lakes and rivers in boats they made of skins and other materials. Because these people lived so long ago, few of the things they made and used have **survived.** These few artifacts, however, do tell us important information about how Paleo-Indians actually lived.

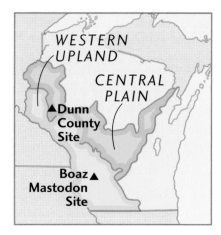

This map shows some **Paleo** sites that archaeologists have found in Wisconsin.

Archaeologists found this spear point in Dunn County. Glaciers were still shrinking north when this point was made.

People in the Paleo **era** often made their homes in a **rock shelter** like this one.

This is the size of one of the two spear points that the Dosch boys found near the mastodon bones. In 1962 a professor learned that the boys had found these spear points. This discovery helped scientists realize that American Indians at this site had killed and butchered the mastodon for food, clothing, and tools. Mastodons became **extinct** not long after the First People arrived here in Wisconsin. Spear points in this shape are known as Gainey points. This spear point's style tells archaeologists that the Boaz Site is one of Wisconsin's earliest sites.

extinct No longer existing   **Paleo** (**pay** lee oh) Old   **era** A period of time in history   **rock shelter** Shallow cave
Paleo-Indians The first people in Wisconsin, who lived here between 10,000 BC and 6500 BC   **survived** Continued to exist or live

Inventions for a New Age: The Archaic Tradition

How was life different for Archaic Indians?

About 9000 years ago, the climate in Wisconsin became much warmer and drier—even warmer and drier than it is today. Oak trees began to replace pine forests in the southern part of the state. Mammoths and mastodons disappeared forever. Deer and smaller animals increased in numbers in the new oak forests.

Indian communities adapted to this new environment. They hunted and gathered new foods. They made new tools to do new tasks. Archaeologists use the name **Archaic** to describe the different groups of people who used these new tools. They also lived in one place for longer periods of time.

More food helped Archaic people survive, so their communities grew larger. Together, such changes in ways of living mark a **turning point** in history.

Over the next 6000 years, Native communities continued to feed, educate, and protect themselves as the world around them slowly changed. Many separate groups of Archaic Indians lived in different parts of Wisconsin. They survived by using many of the same tools and living much the same way, even though they were not related to one another.

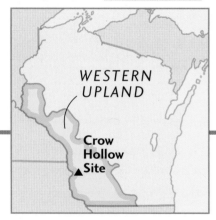

WESTERN UPLAND

Crow Hollow Site ▲

In 1997 archaeologists from the Wisconsin Historical Society excavated the Crow Hollow Site in Crawford County in the Western Upland region. Indians lived there 5000 years ago. All artifacts and features you see on these two pages were used by people living at Crow Hollow.

In warmer weather, people at Crow Hollow needed less shelter. They probably lived in wigwams something like this one. They made their wigwams of branches, hides, and bark.

When archaeologists excavate, they find animal bones. This evidence tells us that **Archaic** peoples hunted animals such as deer, elk, rabbits, and birds. They also fished and gathered clams from the water. They killed or caught what they needed to survive.

Archaic (ahr **kay** ik) Old; Indians who lived in Wisconsin between 6500 and 800 BC   **turning point** Major change

How did Archaic people live?

Families and friends formed communities at different places at different times of the year. They knew when food **resources** would be most **abundant** at certain places. They moved from one campsite to the next, depending where the resources were best at a particular time or season of the year.

Archaic communities moved to sheltered areas when the weather turned cold. Sometimes they used rock shelters. At other times, they built warm houses at the bottom of tall ridges away from the wind.

During summer, the Archaic Indians wanted to be near a wetlands area. Wetlands gave them plenty of fish to catch and wild rice and other plants to gather. The Indians dried and stored the food that they didn't eat right away.

In the summer and early fall, Archaic people lived at a site like Crow Hollow. Crow Hollow is in a hilly area with plenty of deer and other game. Crow Hollow also has nut-bearing trees like hickory, oak, and walnut. And the site is near a creek with fish and good drinking water.

Archaic Tools from Crow Hollow

Why do you think this spear point is much smaller than a Paleo point? Think of the size of the animals each group hunted!

Archaic Indians began making many different stone tools to help them survive. They sharpened spear points on a sharpening stone like this one. Some Archaic peoples also made copper tools. None were found at Crow Hollow.

Archaic people used this scraper to scrape hides. It is about as large as a computer mouse. They used the hides for clothing and blankets. Archaic Indians also made containers from hides and used hides as a building material for their houses. So you can see why scraping hides and keeping spear points sharp were important skills that helped Archaic people survive.

People at Crow Hollow split open and roasted nuts. Then they used the nutshells as fuel for the fire. Archaeologists store them in a bottle to protect them.

---

resources (**ree** sors sez) Things that are useful or valuable   **abundant** (uh **buhn** duhnt) More than enough

People of the Woodland:
New Ways of Living and Viewing the World

Who were the people of the Woodland tradition?

Archaic Indians did not disappear or move away. They changed the way they made a living and the way they viewed the world. Indian people changed enough by 800 BC that archaeologists refer to them as **Woodland Indians**. Woodland ways of living were different from those of Archaic Indians in three important ways. First, the climate began to warm, and this made it easy for Woodland people to **cultivate** crops. Second, Woodland people began to make **pottery**. Third, they also built special burial mounds. These changes did not happen everywhere or all at once.

One group of Woodland Indians made their homes in the rich wetlands in the Eastern Ridges and Lowlands just northwest of where the city of Madison would later be built. Today the location of this community is known as the Murphy site. All the features and artifacts you see on these pages are from the Murphy Site. They tell us about the way people lived during the Woodland era.

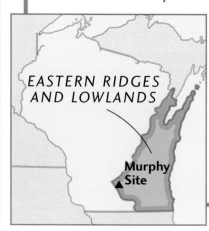

EASTERN RIDGES AND LOWLANDS

Murphy Site

This style house at the Murphy Site is known as a keyhole house because it had a long tunnel-like entrance to keep out the winter's chill.

Archaeologists uncovered the remains of small keyhole-shaped houses like this one at the Murphy Site. The photograph was taken from above. It shows you how the shape of the house appeared on the ground.

Woodland Indians Groups of Indians who lived in Wisconsin between about 800 BC and 1630 AD   **cultivate** (**cuhl** tuh vayt) To plant, grow, and harvest
pottery Pots and other containers made from clay

What was life like for Woodland Indians?

Woodland families spent their time hunting, gathering, and cultivating corn, squash, and other plants along the edge of the wetlands. Families harvested their gardens in the late summer. Then they celebrated with community dances and feasts.

In the fall, Woodland families gathered wood for fuel and nuts from hickory, oak, and walnut trees in the woods and wild rice from the wetlands. Adults also developed new tools for hunting. Their bows and arrows replaced spears. Older children probably helped make these tools.

Woodland families still hunted for food, fur, and hides. They built storehouses above ground and dug storage pits in the ground where they kept the food safe. Woodland people were the first to make pottery. Pottery came in handy for preparing, cooking, and storing food.

Even though Woodland Indians still moved from season to season, they spent more time at places like the Murphy Site. There they found many resources, and they cultivated gardens that helped them survive.

This piece of pottery was all that survived from a cooking and storage pot. Using pots made cooking foods, especially corn, easier for Woodland People.

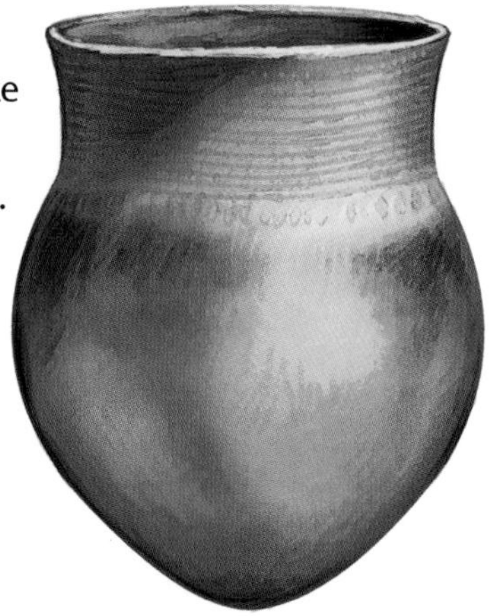

This is how the complete pot would have looked.

What are effigy mounds?

Woodland Indians built mounds where they held **ceremonies** and buried their dead. Many people had to cooperate to build **effigy mounds**. People living at the Murphy Site could easily walk to a nearby effigy mound group known today as Pheasant Branch. This group included two bird mounds like these.

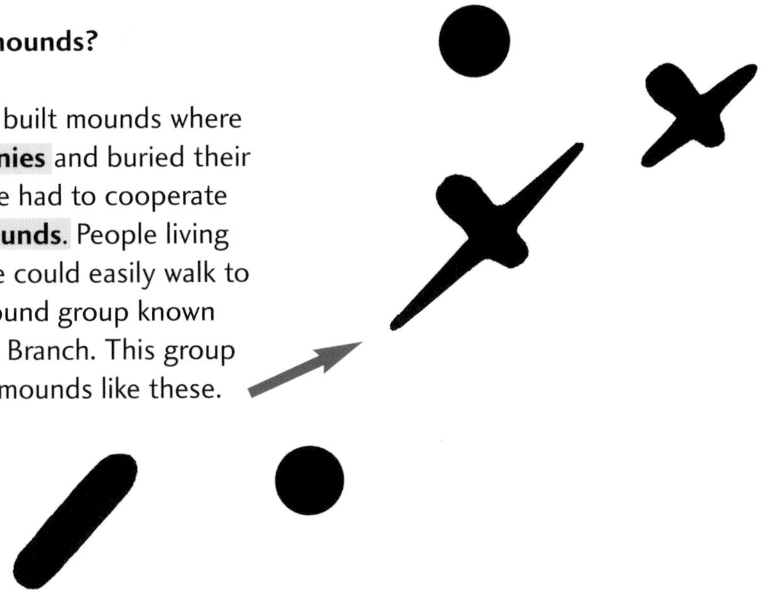

This grinding stone was used for grinding corn and is about as big as a donut.

Woodland people living at Murphy attached this triangular point to an arrow to hunt for deer and other animals. The point shown here is the actual size.

ceremonies (**ser** uh moh neez) Important acts done at special times and places   **effigy** (**ef** uh jee) **mounds** Human-made mounds created in shapes such as animals

The Mysterious Mississippian Tradition

EASTERN RIDGES AND LOWLANDS

Aztalan ▲

Aztalan ▲

Cahokia ▲

For just about 200 years, the Mississippians lived at Aztalan, then the largest city in Wisconsin. Many people lived there year-round. People could have traveled back and forth between Aztalan and Cahokia by paddling their canoes on rivers that connected the two sites.

What makes the Mississippians mysterious?

Woodland peoples lived all over what is now Wisconsin for more than 2400 years. Then, about 1000 AD, different groups of people began living in the southern part of the area. These groups had their own traditions, and they brought new ideas to Wisconsin. Their settling in Wisconsin marked another turning point. Archaeologists call one of these new groups **Mississippians**, because they built many of their villages along the Mississippi River.

The Mississippians lived very differently from their Woodland neighbors. No one knows why Mississippians came into Wisconsin, and no one knows why they later disappeared. Only a few Mississippian sites have been found in Wisconsin. **Aztalan** is the largest of these. Aztalan is on the west bank of the Crawfish River, near Lake Mills in Jefferson County in the Eastern Ridges and Lowlands.

Perhaps people from **Cahokia,** in what is now southern Illinois, moved to Wisconsin. Or people from Wisconsin traded with Cahokians and brought new ideas north. Like Cahokia, Aztalan was located on a river and surrounded by walls. Perhaps those living there needed to defend themselves from their neighbors.

Mississippian Tools from Aztalan

This copper tool is an awl for sewing animal skins.

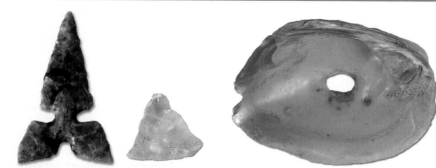

These two points are the actual sizes. Mississippians attached them to arrows rather than spears.

This clamshell could be attached to a bone or wooden handle. Then it became a garden tool used in cultivating crops.

Mississippians (mis uh **sip** ee uhns) Groups of Indians who lived in Wisconsin between 1000 and 1200 AD
Aztalan (**az** tuh lan) A Mississippian site in Jefferson County near the Crawfish River
Cahokia (kuh **ho** kee uh) A large Mississippian site in southern Illinois near the Mississippi River

Today, you can visit this temple mound built at Aztalan. Perhaps dance ceremonies, like the one pictured here, took place on top of this mound or one of the two others there. What do you think the dancer represents?

What was life like at Aztalan?

People lived at Aztalan all year, so they needed food to survive the long winters. Mississippians still hunted animals like deer and fished. They were also good farmers and depended even more on the crops they grew and stored, like corn and squash.

Just like cities today, Aztalan had to be very well organized to keep things running smoothly. People had special skills and jobs to do. For example, there were farmers, hunters, potters, and builders. Mississippians built three large, flat-topped temple mounds at Aztalan. A few powerful leaders may have lived in houses on top of the mounds. These leaders also conducted ceremonies on the temple mounds.

This photograph shows an Aztalan house re-created on the second floor of the Wisconsin Historical Museum in Madison. You can actually walk into it!

Mississippians at Aztalan made their pots by grinding up clamshells to add to their clay. The ground-up clamshells made the clay easier to mold into large pots.

Early Wisconsin Farmers: The Oneota Tradition

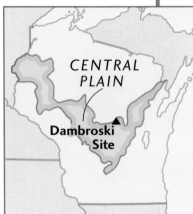

One group of **Oneota** people lived along the **Waupaca** River in Portage County in the Central Plain. Archaeologists call their village the **Dambroski** Site.

Who were the early Wisconsin farmers?

Other groups of Indians began living in Wisconsin a little later than the Mississippians. Archaeologists named them **Oneota**. The Oneota were the ancestors of the Ho-Chunk and other Indian nations. Archaeologists identified a group of Indians living differently from both the Woodland and the Mississippian peoples along the Oneota River Valley in Iowa. See how many differences you can find between the Oneota and the other Indians, and you'll be thinking like an archaeologist!

Archaeologists have found more Oneota sites than Mississippian sites in Wisconsin. The Oneota settled in large villages in the southern part of our state. They often built their villages near large waterways like the Mississippi River and Lake Michigan. They also lived along smaller rivers. The **Dambroski** Site is one of several small Oneota villages that archaeologists have found along the **Waupaca** River.

At least some of the people lived at the site year-round, just as the Mississippians did at Aztalan. All the artifacts and features on these two pages were found at the Dambroski Site.

The Oneota people were excellent farmers. They cultivated corn, beans, and squash—three vegetables that many Native people of the Americas later called the "three sisters." These three sisters grew well together and made for a very well balanced diet.

Oneota Tools from the Dambroski Site

This shaped piece of turtle shell was once part of a bowl. Resources from the marsh—fish, shellfish, and turtle—were used by the Oneota both for food and as material to make useful objects.

Oneota hunters like those at Dambroski attached points like this one to arrows.

This point is the actual size.

Oneota (oh nee **oh** tuh) Native people living in Wisconsin between 1000 AD and 1630 AD
Waupaca (waw **pak** uh)   **Dambroski** (dam **brah** skee)

Archaeologists discovered this longhouse at Dambroski by carefully excavating a large area and recording patterns of postholes. This line of postholes was all that was left of a wall of the longhouse. The holes you see in this photo would have held posts like those in the drawing on the left.

The side of the house has been cut away to show how people lived in a **longhouse** where several families lived under one roof. Can you see how the walls were layered with grass between the posts?

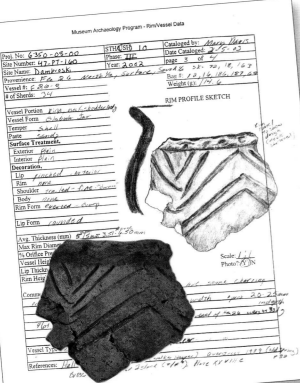

What was life like for the Oneota?

The Oneota houses were different from those of the Mississippians and the Woodland groups. Some houses at Dambroski and elsewhere were just large enough for one family. These houses didn't have long, low entrances like those at the Murphy site. At Dambroski, the Oneota people also built **longhouses**. Sometimes grandparents and aunts and uncles and other family members all must have lived there together. Other families lived in smaller groups.

People at Dambroski ate a wide variety of foods. They planted crops like the three sisters: corn, beans, and squash. They caught turtles, sturgeon, catfish, and perch in the river. People also gathered wild rice in the wetlands. People hunted animals like deer and bobcats in the nearby woods. No wonder the Oneota spent more of the year at this site on the Waupaca River!

The Oneota made pottery with different patterns than the Mississippian and Woodland people used. In some ways, however, their traditions were similar. Like the Mississippians, they added crushed clamshells to the clay when they made pots. Compare the design on this pot fragment to the pot found at Aztalan. Do you think it looks more like the Mississippian pot on page 51 or the Woodland pot fragment on page 49?

longhouse A long, narrow wigwam built large enough to hold multiple families

Communicating in Many Forms

Archaeologist Increase Lapham mapped this Kenosha County effigy mound in 1850 and named it a lizard mound. Ho-Chunk people have always understood that this effigy symbolizes a water spirit. You can see that a road was already cut through the body when Increase Lapham made his map.

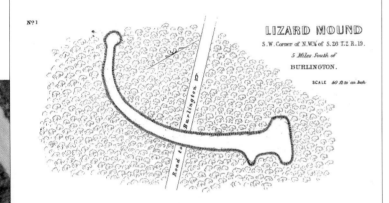

How did early people communicate?

How do you share ideas or **communicate** with people you know? Do you talk to, email, text message, or telephone your friends? Not so long ago, most people mailed postcards and letters to friends and family who lived far away. Over 1000 years ago in Wisconsin, some Native people used the sides of cliffs to leave messages for others. Other groups around Wisconsin carried load after load of dirt to create huge animal- or spirit-shaped effigy mounds. The designs that potters carved into clay pots were another form of communication.

People also communicated with one another in ways that are familiar to us today. They tattooed their bodies, added designs to their clothes, or changed their hairstyles. We are not always sure what these past people were trying to say. But we know that they were telling others something about themselves and the way they lived. The large and small things that early Wisconsin Indians created also communicated ideas about what they believed.

This 1927 photograph of the same mound was the first photograph of an archaeological site in Wisconsin taken from an airplane. What changed in the 77 years between the drawing and the photograph?

From earliest times to the present, Indian groups used many ways to communicate messages and ideas about their history and traditions.

This basket was made by 20th-century Ho-Chunk artist Ruth Cloud, Baraboo.

You can see this beaded-cloth Ojibwe bag, on the left, and this Woodland pot, on the right, in the Wisconsin Historical Museum collection.

communicate (kuh **myoo** nuh kayt) To share ideas

Where can you see rock art in Wisconsin?

CENTRAL PLAIN

▲ Roche-A-Cri

You can visit one of the largest sites for rock art at **Roche-A-Cri** State Park in the Central Plain in Adams County. Long ago, Indians at Roche-A-Cri carved messages into the sandstone of the large cliff there. They also painted small figures on it. Other people who came later added their names and drawings. But you can still see the work done by the early Indians.

These Indians may have come to Roche-A-Cri on a **spiritual** journey. What were they trying to say? Perhaps their drawings and carvings told important stories or were used in ceremonies. We are very lucky that we can still see their work, even after all these years.

As you see in the black and white drawing, to the left, there is a figure of a person with a head like a bird. To its right is a figure with outstretched wings. The spot on this figure's chest may show where its heart is. The yellow arrow shows where this design is on the rock. The initials "J.S.F." were carved by someone much later and are not part of the design. Such carving is now against the law because it destroys the sacred Indian images.

Roche-A-Cri (ro shuh **cree**)   **spiritual** (**spir** ih choo ul) Having to do with the soul and the spirit

Changes over Thousands of Years

What have you learned about Wisconsin's early Indian groups?

In this chapter, you've looked at the way the First People lived on land that later became Wisconsin. You've learned that Native people tell about their own past in stories and in images. You've found that archaeologists learn about the past in a different way. They are interested in Native stories, but they also use clues from artifacts and features to find out about how people lived in the distant past.

You've seen how the First People in Wisconsin slowly changed their ways of living over thousands of years. The earliest Paleo people lived on the edge of glaciers and hunted huge mammals, now extinct. The warming climate created different turning points in the way people lived. Archaic people adapted to using more plant and animal resources. By the end of that time period, more groups of people lived in Wisconsin.

The Woodland, Mississippian, and Oneota were groups that lived in Wisconsin at about the same time. These groups lived somewhat differently from one another. Some cultivated corn, beans, and squash. Others survived mainly by hunting and gathering. But the animals they hunted and the weapons they used had changed from earlier times.

The Woodland, Mississippian, and Oneota also had tools just for cultivating and gathering plants. The pottery they made and the homes they built were different in style.

In the next chapters, life seems to speed up. When non-Indians arrived in Wisconsin, they brought more changes. Wisconsin's Indian people had to adapt more rapidly. We continue to adapt to change today.

What do the changes in tool technology tell you about the differences in the way people hunted from the Paleo people to the Oneota?

Some Places to Visit

- Aztalan State Park in Jefferson
- Chippewa Valley Museum in Eau Claire
- Geology Museum at the University of Wisconsin–Madison
- Kenosha Public Museum
- Menominee clan story display at the University of Wisconsin–Stevens Point Library
- Milwaukee Public Museum
- Mississippi Valley Archaeology Center at the University of Wisconsin–La Crosse
- Wisconsin Historical Museum in Madison

Some Things to Read

- *Digging and Discovery: Wisconsin Archaeology* by Diane Holliday and Bobbie Malone, Chapters 1–5
- *Native People of Wisconsin* by Patty Loew, Chapter 1
- *Learning from the Land: Wisconsin Land Use* by Bobbie Malone, Chapter 2
- *Working with Water: Wisconsin Waterways* by Bobbie Malone and Jefferson J. Gray, Chapter 2

Compare the houses—from the Paleo rock shelter at top left to the Mississippian house at bottom right. What do we learn about the differences in the groups of early Indians in Wisconsin?

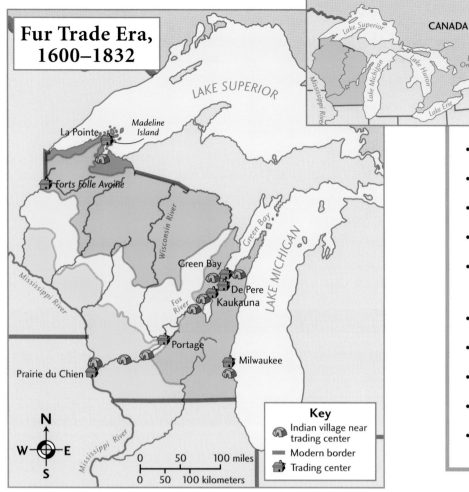

Fur Trade Era, 1600–1832

LAKE SUPERIOR

CANADA

Lake Superior

Lake Michigan

Lake Huron

Lake Ontario

Lake Erie

Mississippi River

Madeline Island

La Pointe

Forts Folle Avoine

Wisconsin River

Mississippi River

Green Bay

Green Bay

De Pere

Fox River

Kaukauna

LAKE MICHIGAN

Portage

Prairie du Chien

Milwaukee

Mississippi River

N W E S

0   50   100 miles

0   50   100 kilometers

Key

Indian village near trading center

Modern border

Trading center

Chapter 4:
The Fur Trade Era: Exploration and Exchange in Wisconsin

- Exploring and Learning Today
- Native People near the Close of the Old Time
- Explorers from Europe Arrive in Wisconsin
- Missionaries and Mapmakers
- Beavers Mean Business: The French Fur Trade in Wisconsin
- Bringing Cultures Together: The Métis Experience
- From French to British Control
- Same Trade, New Leaders: Americans Take Over
- From Forts to Settlement
- Changes over Two Hundred Years

The Old Time: Before people from Europe arrive

1634–1763: French control of Great Lakes fur trade

1600	1620	1640	1660	1680	1700

1634 Jean Nicolet arrives at Red Banks near Green Bay

1673 Father Marquette and Louis Jolliet find the Mississippi River

1684 French set up fort and trading post at La Baye (Green Bay)

1685 French set up fort and trading post at Prairie du Chien

Key Words

- American Revolution
- British
- Europeans
- exchange
- French and Indian War
- fur trade
- Jean Nicolet
- Jesuit missionaries
- Métis
- portage
- War of 1812

Thinking Like a Historian

 How did early explorers find their way in Wisconsin?

 How did the lives of Wisconsin Indians change because of the fur trade?

 What kinds of changes in the fur trade in Wisconsin were so large that historians see them as turning points?

 How are exploration and exchange still part of what we do today?

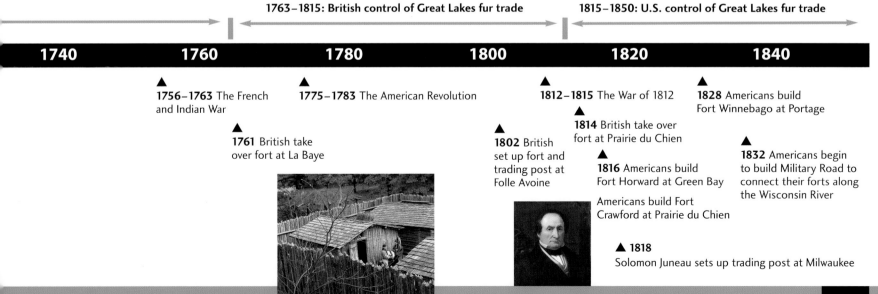

1763–1815: British control of Great Lakes fur trade

1815–1850: U.S. control of Great Lakes fur trade

| 1740 | 1760 | 1780 | 1800 | 1820 | 1840 |

1756–1763 The French and Indian War

1761 British take over fort at La Baye

1775–1783 The American Revolution

1802 British set up fort and trading post at Folle Avoine

1812–1815 The War of 1812

1814 British take over fort at Prairie du Chien

1816 Americans build Fort Horward at Green Bay

Americans build Fort Crawford at Prairie du Chien

▲ **1818** Solomon Juneau sets up trading post at Milwaukee

1828 Americans build Fort Winnebago at Portage

1832 Americans begin to build Military Road to connect their forts along the Wisconsin River

EASTERN RIDGES AND LOWLANDS

Wade House ■

Old World ■
Wisconsin

Wade House is between Sheboygan and Fond du Lac in Sheboygan County. Old World Wisconsin is outside of Eagle. Both of these historic sites are in the Eastern Ridges and Lowlands.

At Old World Wisconsin, visitors learn about the past by taking part in the work of the past. This boy is grooming one of the horses, just as he might have done if he had lived on a Wisconsin farm 100 years ago.

Exploring and Learning Today

Are you an explorer?

Exploration is the act of looking into or studying something or someplace unknown. Are you curious? Do you like to learn new things? Do you ask a lot of questions? Do you like to use library books or search the Internet to find answers to your questions? Do you and your family and friends like to travel to new places? Perhaps you and your family will travel out of state to explore a national park like Yellowstone or the Grand Canyon next summer. Or maybe you will visit a state park like Wyalusing near **Prairie du Chien**. There you can see where the Wisconsin River flows into the Mississippi River.

In Chapter 3, you learned about the work that archaeologists do to uncover artifacts and learn about the past. After reading this chapter, you may decide that archaeologists and explorers have similar jobs. Archaeologists use tools such as spade shovels, trowels, and screens to discover artifacts and features at a site. Then they use tape measures and notebooks to describe what they've found. Explorers use maps to travel to and discover new places. Both archaeologists and explorers work with land and waterways. Archaeologists dig or dive down to explore different layers of history. Explorers travel out over the land and water to discover new and different places.

Europeans (yur up **pee** uhns) People from Europe   **exchange** (iks **chanj**) Act of giving one thing for another   **Prairie du Chien** (prair ee du **sheen**)

Hiking in the Wisconsin woods is a great way to explore the beauty of our state.

At Wade House, this young girl learns how to make an S-hook from the blacksmith there. What equipment do you see in this picture that would not have been there 150 years ago? Why do you think it's there now?

What do explorers hope to find in Wisconsin?

In this chapter you'll soon be reading about explorers who came 400 years ago from as far away as Europe to travel through and learn about Wisconsin. Some of these explorers came looking for rivers and routes to the west. Others came looking for fur-bearing animals such as beaver, mink, and otter. Some explorers stopped their exploring and stayed put. They lived with Indian people and learned their languages and their traditions. Many, many things have changed in Wisconsin since then, but there is still plenty of exploring to do here today.

You can also explore and find out about new places at the library.

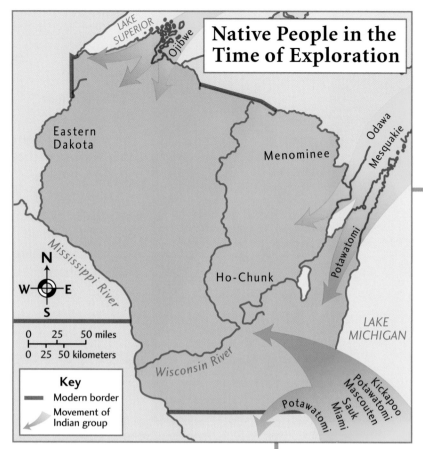

Native People in the Time of Exploration

Key
— Modern border
↘ Movement of Indian group

Many groups of Eastern Woodland Indians moved to Wisconsin in the early 1600s. What events pushed them here? What kinds of resources pulled them to the area?

Native People near the Close of the Old Time

How did Indian people live in the Old Time?

The time before Europeans and other new groups arrived is known as the Old Time among Indian people. Toward the end of the Old Time, Ho-Chunk people lived in villages on the open prairies and in stands of oak trees in the southern part of Wisconsin. They farmed and hunted for food. They also gathered wild rice and caught fish.

Farther north, Menominee people lived in a large village near what is now called Green Bay. They hunted bear and deer and they grew corn, beans, and pumpkins. They gathered wild rice and caught fish, too. Sometimes Ho-Chunk and Menominee people hunted together for buffalo.

Ojibwe people lived still farther north. The short growing season made successful gardening in the north difficult. The Ojibwe people traveled from season to season to hunt and gather enough food to live. Many of the Indian groups traded tools and jewelry with each other and with other Indian groups living outside of what we now call Wisconsin. The Old Time came to a close when people from Europe began exploring the Great Lakes areas. All Indian groups in Wisconsin had to adapt greatly in order to live with non-Indian ways. Life became more and more complicated for everyone.

Frances Mike, an **Ojibwe** woman, harvests wild rice.

Ojibwe (o **jib** way) An American Indian nation

What Indian People lived here when explorers arrived?

Around 1500, Europeans started traveling to North America. They first arrived on the East Coast. Along with new trade goods, these newcomers also carried their diseases that killed many Indians. Different groups of Europeans fought one another and Indians over land. Many Indians were pushed west to avoid these conflicts. Some Eastern Woodland groups from the Northeast came to Wisconsin.

You learned in Chapter 3 that ancestors of the Ho-Chunk and Menominee people lived here for thousands of years. By the early 1600s, the Santee **Sioux** Indians also lived in Wisconsin. Eastern Woodland Nations arrived later. They were pushed into Wisconsin by conflicts in the Northeast. The Ojibwe, Potowatomi, and **Odawa** have stories that tell of their beginnings here, journeys to the east, then returning.

With so many different groups of Indian people now living in Wisconsin, life was changing in big ways for everyone. Some groups got along with each other. These groups shared ideas, tools, and traditions. Other groups didn't get along so well. More fighting took place in this land where they all wanted to live. This land was where Indian people had gathered berries and wild rice, hunted deer and moose, caught fish, and cultivated corn, beans, and squash for thousands of years.

Ojibwe Indian Marvin Defoe built this birchbark canoe in the late 1990s. He built it just as his ancestors built their canoes.

Menominee, Ho-Chunk, and other Indian groups hunted for buffalo, which are also called bison. These bison are part of a captive herd that lives in the Sandhill Wildlife Area in Wood County.

Sioux (soo)　　**Odawa** (oh **dah** wah)

Explorers from Europe Arrive in Wisconsin

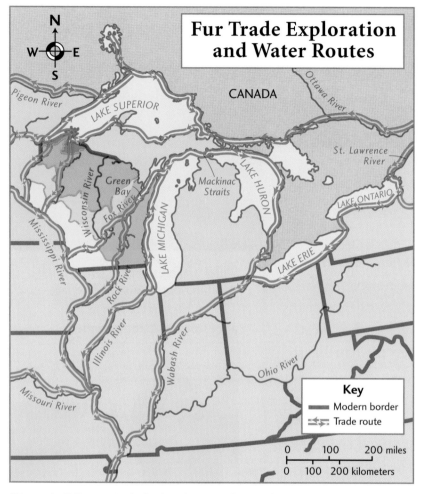

Fur Trade Exploration and Water Routes

CANADA

Pigeon River
LAKE SUPERIOR
Ottawa River
St. Lawrence River
Green Bay
Fox River
Wisconsin River
Mackinac Straits
LAKE HURON
LAKE ONTARIO
Mississippi River
LAKE MICHIGAN
Rock River
LAKE ERIE
Illinois River
Wabash River
Ohio River
Missouri River

Key
Modern border
Trade route

0   100   200 miles
0 100 200 kilometers

Rivers in Wisconsin link the Great Lakes with the Mississippi River. After traveling south from Green Bay on the Fox River, Indian people then carried their canoes and goods overland a short distance to reach the Wisconsin River. They traveled the Wisconsin River until it flowed into the Mississippi River near Prairie du Chien. With your finger, trace the water-highway routes yourself and imagine traveling those distances by canoe about 400 years ago. How might the water and the landscape have looked? What would be very different today?

How did explorers travel to Wisconsin?

Some historians believe that explorers such as **Jean Nicolet** may have traveled with some Huron Indians by canoe through the **Straits** of **Mackinac**. The Straits connected Lake Huron with Lake Michigan. Indian peoples living in Wisconsin in the 1600s traveled on foot and by canoe. They had no horses or cars or trucks. So there were no highways, motor vehicles, or stoplights here when people from Europe began exploring the area. However, the Midwest was rich in lakes and rivers that were used like water-highways. Indian peoples had been traveling these water-highways for thousands of years by the time the first explorers from Europe arrived.

Jean Nicolet (zhon nik oh **lay**) The first European explorer generally believed to have landed in Wisconsin
Straits A narrow channel connecting two bodies of water   **Mackinac** (**mak** uh naw)

Who was Jean Nicolet?

Members of the Menominee, Ho-Chunk, and Potawatomi Nations met the explorer Jean Nicolet when he visited them near Green Bay in 1634. Nicolet was born in France. As a young man he traveled to New France. Today New France is known as Canada. Nicolet went there to work for a French trading company. He lived with several different Canadian Indian groups and learned their languages and traditions.

Nicolet was about 36 years old when he began to explore and travel into new lands where he had never been. He met and made friends with groups of Native people living at a place now called Red Banks, near Green Bay. Nicolet had traveled by canoe about 700 miles. In these travels he met many different people. He saw parts of the Midwest that only Indians knew about.

After Nicolet's visit he returned to Canada. Although he wrote notes about his explorations in Wisconsin, none of his records have survived. We know about this trip through the writings of a priest who knew Nicolet. There are no photographs of Nicolet or his explorations because cameras had not yet been invented.

EASTERN RIDGES AND LOWLANDS
Red Banks
Green Bay

Explorer Jean Nicolet wore a robe of Chinese silk when he landed somewhere near Green Bay in 1634. But no one is sure what the robe or Nicolet looked like when he arrived. The paintings on these two pages were created around 300 years later. What differences can you find in these two paintings?

Missionaries and Mapmakers

Why did more French explorers and priests come to Wisconsin?

Some of the French explorers brought **Jesuit missionaries** with them on their trips to study Wisconsin. Both the explorers and missionaries were sent by the government of French Canada. The Jesuits came to teach their religion to different groups of Indian people living here. Father **Jacques Marquette** was a missionary from Canada who had lived with different Indian groups. First he went to **Chequamegon** Bay and then near Green Bay. Some of the tribal people told him about the big river that we now call the Mississippi. In 1673, the Jesuits' leader sent Father Marquette off to find the big river. He was 36 years old at the time. A trader named **Louis Jolliet** who was 28 joined him.

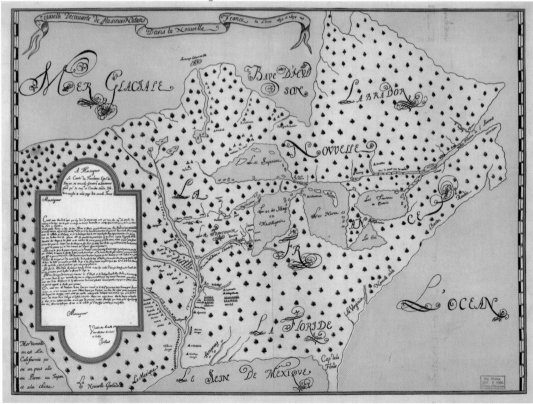

Explorers **Jacques Marquette** and **Louis Jolliet** arrived at the Mississippi River in June 1673. Indians living in the area helped them. Jolliet drew this map from memory the year after their journey.

Jolliet's maps caused a turning point in history. They showed new routes to the Mississippi River Valley. With new maps, new people from France and French Canada began coming to this area.

Jacques Marquette (zhok mahr **ket**) A Jesuit missionary. He and **Louis Jolliet** (loo **wee** zho lee **et**) were the first Europeans to find and travel down the Mississippi River.
Jesuit missionaries (**jezh** yoo wit **mish** shuh nair eez) Catholic priests who try to teach others to become Christians **Chequamegon** (shuh **wah** muh guhn)

ole que nous avons trouuée gi joie bonne et tres abondante,
ole est Couuerte de trois pieds de bonne terre, assez proche d'une
haine de rocher, dont le bas est plein de fort beau bois, apres —
20 lieües sur Cette mesme route, nous arriuons a l'embou=
hure de nostre Riuiere et [nous trouuant a 42 degrez et
demy d'Eleuation, Nous entrons heureusement dans Missisipi
le 17e Juin auec vne joye que je ne peux pas Expliquer.]

Section. 4.eme

De la grande Riuiere appellée Missisipi ses
plus notables particularités, de Diuers —
Animaux et particulierement des Pisikious
ou Bœufs Sauuages, Leur figure et Leur
Naturel, des premiers Villages des
Jlinois ou les françois arriuent.

Nous voyla donc sur cette Riuiere si renommée dont jay taché
d'en remarquer attentiuement toutes les Singularités; Sa Riuiere
de Missisipi tire son origine de diuers Lacs qui sont dans le païs
des peuples du Nord, elle est Estroitte a Sa décharge de Miskous;

Both Marquette and Jolliet kept journals during their trip, but Jolliet's journal was lost. Here you see a part of page 11 of Father Marquette's journal. He was writing about seeing the Mississippi River for the first time. Here is a **translation** of his description:

"...we arrived at the mouth of our river and we found it at 42 ½ degrees of elevation, we entered happily into [the] Mississippi on the 17th of June [1673] with a joy that I cannot explain."

Can you find Marquette's spelling for the Mississippi? *Riviere* is the French word for "river." Why do you think Marquette was so happy to find this river?

Just as with Nicolet, we do not know how Marquette and Jolliet looked. German-born Milwaukee artist Frank H. Zeitler made this painting in 1921.

translation (tranz **lay** shuhn) A change from one language to another

Beavers Mean Business: The French Fur Trade in Wisconsin

What was the fur trade?

The **fur trade** was an important early business throughout the Great Lakes. When explorers from France and French-speaking Canada began showing up in Wisconsin in the 1600s, they discovered that Indians were hunting beaver, mink, and otter for both food and clothing. The **pelts** from these animals made especially warm clothing.

Soon French traders started arriving here to buy such pelts. They did not pay for the pelts with money. Instead they traded Indian people things like blankets, **brass**, cooking pots, metal axes, woolen fabric for clothing, and glass beads. They traded French goods for Indian goods. Historians named this exchange system the fur trade.

Indians traded more than furs. They also traded wild rice, maple sugar, fish, venison, canoes, and information about travel routes. Indians showed the traders how to use snowshoes and moccasins. Indians taught traders how to survive the cold winters outdoors.

French traders wanted lots of beaver pelts. But when their food supplies ran out during the winter, they needed the wild rice and maple sugar to keep going. Indians wanted metal cooking pots because they lasted longer than homemade birchbark and clay pots. Trading for iron axes and steel knives meant Indians didn't have to make stone tools anymore. Who do you think made the best trade? Why?

Who would have guessed that Europeans' desire for this small furry animal would be a turning point in the history of the Native people of North America?

Why did the French and Canadians trade for beaver pelts? Because back home, hats made of beaver-fur felt and coats trimmed with beaver fur were very popular. Everybody wanted one, so French traders made a lot of money selling the **pelts**.

This recent photo shows a Montreal canoe at a museum. The Montreal canoe was like the semi truck of the fur trade because it carried hundreds of pounds of furs from the Great Lakes to the East Coast. From there, the furs went to Europe.

pelts Animal skins with the fur or hair still on them
fur trade The process of exchanging European trade goods for Indian goods, such as pelts or wild rice   **brass** A yellow metal made from copper and zinc

Why were trading posts important to the fur trade?

As the fur trade grew, French traders created a gathering spot, or an **entrepôt** in the French language, on Madeline Island. Madeline Island is in Lake Superior just off the northern tip of Wisconsin. The French named it La Pointe, and it became a place for both French and Indian traders to meet and exchange goods. Traders could also get food and travel supplies at this trading post. Soon, the French built a second trading post called La Baye near what is now Green Bay.

The French built a trading post they named **Prairie du Chien** where the Wisconsin River flows into the Mississippi River. It was an important entrepôt for both Indian and French traders. They came every spring when the ice broke and water-highways were ready for traffic again. The French named this annual gathering event the **Rendezvous**. Trading took place at the Rendezvous, but it was also a time to have fun. French and Indian traders exchanged customs, language, and ideas about how to live, as well as trade goods.

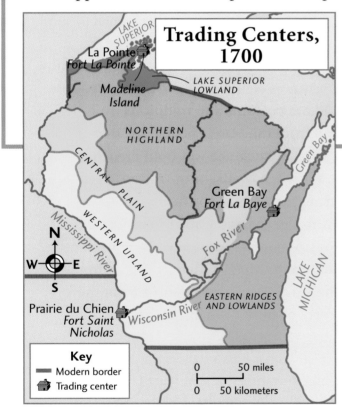

Trading Centers, 1700

La Pointe
Fort La Pointe

Madeline Island

LAKE SUPERIOR
LOWLAND

NORTHERN
HIGHLAND

CENTRAL PLAIN

WESTERN UPLAND

Green Bay
Fort La Baye

Fox River

LAKE MICHIGAN

Green Bay

Mississippi River

Prairie du Chien
Fort Saint Nicholas

Wisconsin River

EASTERN RIDGES
AND LOWLANDS

Key
— Modern border
🎒 Trading center

0 — 50 miles
0 — 50 kilometers

The French trading posts grew into **forts** to protect their goods. These forts controlled important nearby water-highways.

I Go back to the Planes of the Dogs— this Plane is very Handsum one ... on the Pint of Land Betwene the Mouth of the Wisconstan where it Emties in to the Masseppey & the Last River. ... All the traders that Youseis [use] that Part of the Countrey & all the Indians of Several tribe Meat fall & Spring where the Grateist Games are Plaid Both By French & Indians. The French Practis Billiards—ye latter Ball ... These Amusements Last three or four weakes in the Spring of the Year.

Peter Pond was a trader from Connecticut who wrote the following description about the Rendezvous at Prairie du Chien in about 1772.

forts Buildings built strong enough to survive attacks. Sometimes they were surrounded by walls or tall fences.   **entrepôt** (**awn** truh poh) Gathering spot
Prairie du Chien (prair ee du **sheen**) An important city and trading center located where the Wisconsin River flows into the Mississippi River
Rendezvous (**rahn** day voo) Place for meeting

Bringing Cultures Together: The Métis Experience

Places Elizabeth Lived

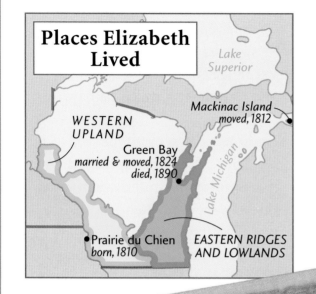

Lake Superior

WESTERN UPLAND

Mackinac Island
moved, 1812

Green Bay
married & moved, 1824
died, 1890

Lake Michigan

Prairie du Chien
born, 1810

EASTERN RIDGES
AND LOWLANDS

What was life like for Elizabeth Therese Fisher, a Métis girl?

In 1810, toward the close of the fur trade in the Great Lakes region, a girl named Elizabeth **Therese** Fisher was born in Prairie du Chien. Her father, Henry Fisher, was a fur trader. Some of her mother's family had come from France by way of Canada. Her mother's great-grandfather, **Kwenaquot**, was an Odawa Indian.

As Elizabeth grew up, her mother taught her how to speak French as well as English. Elizabeth also learned Odawa customs and traditions from her family and from the Native people she met at the trading post. Because she was both French and Odawa, she was a **Métis**, or of "mixed" heritage.

During the years of the fur trade, some of the men from Europe and Canada who came to Wisconsin married Indian women. Their children were Métis. Often these children learned languages and customs from the cultures of both of their parents.

Elizabeth's mother or aunt taught her how to embroider this **sampler**. Making samplers of different embroidery stitches was an important skill for girls growing up in the 1800s.

sampler Hand-stitched cloth designed to show the skills of the person who stitched it
Therese (tuh **rees**)   **Kwenaquot** (**kwen** uh kot)
Métis (may **tee**) Of mixed blood or traditions

What happened when Elizabeth grew up?

In 1824, Elizabeth married Henry Baird. Henry was born in Ireland and came to the United States as a young boy. At that time, some women from American Indian families married men from Europe or the eastern United States. Elizabeth and Henry moved to Green Bay, where they lived for many years.

Henry was a lawyer. He worked with the Ho-Chunk and Menominee Indians during the sale of their lands to the U.S. government. Elizabeth helped Henry with his work by **interpreting** for his French clients. Before she died in 1890, Mrs. Baird wrote down her memories of growing up at the close of the fur trade era. These **memoirs** are now part of the Wisconsin Historical Society's collections. Many artifacts from Elizabeth's childhood are also part of these collections.

Elizabeth Therese Fisher Baird as an adult

Elizabeth learned how to make the doll in this toy cradleboard. She also added the beads and ribbons according to Odawa custom.

interpreting (in **tur** pruh ting) Translating   **memoirs** (**mem** wahrz) Memories written by someone after the event or events occurred

From French to British Control

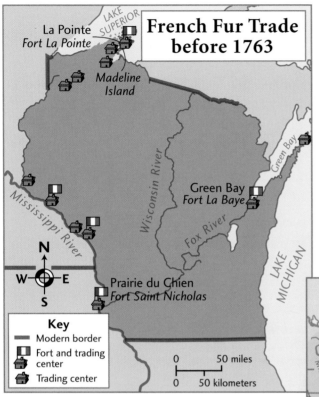

French Fur Trade before 1763

The French controlled the Wisconsin fur trade before 1763, as you can tell by the French names on this map.

What was the French and Indian War?

The Indians and the French had been successful partners in the fur trade here for many **decades** when the **British** began arriving. The British also were looking for furs. They wanted to take control of the French trading forts and posts. The British wanted to be in charge of what is now Wisconsin. Most Wisconsin Indians were comfortable with the French as trading partners and wanted to continue trading with them. Trading with the French had helped the Indians and their families survive.

For seven years, between 1756 and 1763, the French and the British fought for control of the trading forts and water-highways in Wisconsin, the Midwest, and Canada. Historians call this series of battles the **French and Indian War.** The French didn't have enough soldiers and supplies. In 1763, the last of the French forts surrendered to the British. Many Indians fought *against* the British. But now the British controlled the fur trade. Indians had to adapt once again.

The Burnett County Historical Society rebuilt Forts **Folle Avoine** to look very much like it did 200 years ago. Did you know that Folle Avoine is French for "wild rice"? Today you can visit and get a good idea of how the trading post looked.

Folle Avoine (ful ah **vwan**)   **decades** (dek aydz) Periods of 10 years
British People from the island of Great Britain, which includes the countries of England, Scotland, and Wales
French and Indian War (1756–1763) The seven-year-long battle between the French and the British for control of the trading forts and water-highways in Wisconsin, the Midwest, and Canada

What happened to the French forts after the war?

After 1763, French soldiers and leaders left their forts and posts and returned to France. However, many French and French-Canadian traders stayed in Wisconsin. They continued to work with the different Indian groups to trap and trade animal pelts. They shipped bundles of furs on the same water-highways as before, but they were now selling the bundles to British trading companies.

During the war, French and British soldiers had traveled through Wisconsin and occupied the forts. Some Wisconsin Indian groups had traveled east from Wisconsin to fight for the French. The fighting during the French and Indian War did not take place in Wisconsin. But the war caused soldiers and others to move about to fight or protect forts. Word about the rich forests, prairies, and water-highways spread. Sharing this information, in turn, brought other newcomers to Wisconsin.

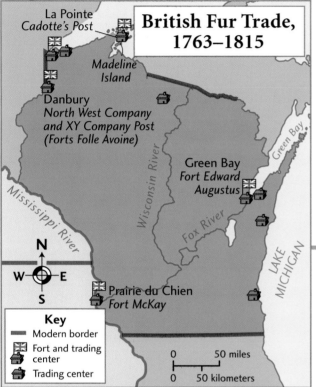

British Fur Trade, 1763–1815

La Pointe
Cadotte's Post

Madeline Island

Danbury
North West Company and XY Company Post (Forts Folle Avoine)

Green Bay
Fort Edward Augustus

Mississippi River

Wisconsin River

Fox River

Green Bay

LAKE MICHIGAN

Prairie du Chien
Fort McKay

Key
— Modern border
⚑ Fort and trading center
🏠 Trading center

0   50 miles
0   50 kilometers

BRITISH INFLUENCE

Mississippi River

ATLANTIC OCEAN

After 1763, the British took control of the fur trade in what is now Wisconsin. Indian, French, and Métis people still lived in the area. But they were no longer in charge.

The North West Company and the XY Company were two British trading companies that both had posts at Forts Folle Avoine in 1802–1803. XY **merged** with North West in 1804. Here you see an Indian **interpreter** explaining Native life outside the fort.

Inside the fort at Folle Avoine today, you can see a man dressed as a trader. He displays the kind of trade goods that Indians could select in exchange for furs.

merged (murjd) Joined   **interpreter** (in **tur** pruh tur) Someone who explains the meaning of something

Same Trade, New Leaders: Americans Take Over

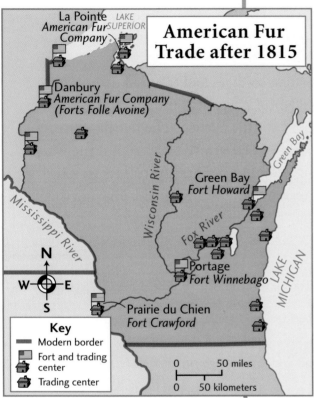

American Fur Trade after 1815

La Pointe
American Fur
Company
LAKE SUPERIOR

Danbury
American Fur Company
(Forts Folle Avoine)

Mississippi River

Wisconsin River

Fox River

Green Bay
Fort Howard

Green Bay

Portage
Fort Winnebago

LAKE MICHIGAN

Prairie du Chien
Fort Crawford

N
W E
S

Key
— Modern border
🏴 Fort and trading center
🏠 Trading center

0   50 miles
0   50 kilometers

Mississippi River

AMERICAN CONTROL

ATLANTIC OCEAN

How did the American Revolution affect the fur trade?

In the early 1600s, the British were some of the first Europeans to send people to settle permanently in the northeastern part of our country. Then, some 150 years later, the British-American settlers or **colonists** wanted to form an independent country. Between 1775 and 1783, British troops fought against the **colonial** forces. This fighting became known as the **American Revolution**. When the colonial forces won, the British lost control of the colonies and the fur trade. The newly formed United States of America controlled both.

The fighting during the American Revolution had little effect on the fur trade in Wisconsin, however. Trading between the Indians, French, Métis, and British continued much as it had before.

After the revolution, the new U.S. leaders were busy setting up a federal government in Washington, D.C. They didn't send people to Wisconsin to stop the British from controlling the fur trade. The British were supposed to leave the trading posts in Wisconsin by 1796, but some of them remained here. Because of the great distance between Washington, D.C., and Wisconsin, the new U.S. government could not force the British to leave. American control of the fur trade began after 1815, following the War of 1812.

colonists (**kol** uh nists) People (or their ancestors) who left their country to live in newly settled areas called colonies
colonial (kuh **loh** nee uhl) Of or about a colony
American Revolution (rev uh **loo** shuhn) (1775–1783) The war in which the American colonies won their independence from Great Britain

How did the War of 1812 affect the fur trade?

The American Revolution was not the last time that British and U.S. troops fought each other. They fought again in the **War of 1812**. During this war, British troops asked some of the U.S. trading forts outside of Wisconsin to surrender.

In 1814, U.S. troops quickly built a fort at Prairie du Chien. British forces demanded surrender of the fort, but the United States refused. This refusal started the only battle between the United States and the British in Wisconsin during this war. After three days of shooting, the United States surrendered the fort.

By the following year, 1815, the war was over. Finally the British agreed to leave Wisconsin. They either returned to Britain or moved to Canada and continued working in the fur trade. The Indians, French, and Métis fur traders once again adapted to work with the United States.

We know about what happened to Fort Shelby when the British arrived from the account given by **Augustin Grignon**. He was a fur trader who fought for the British and later became a U.S. citizen. This photograph of Augustin was taken 30 or 35 years after the Fort Shelby battle. He is holding an axe that also could be used as a pipe. Why do you think Augustin had his photograph taken with it?

American and British troops fought for control of the fort you see in this picture during the War of 1812—in Prairie du Chien on the banks of the Mississippi River. It was called Fort Shelby by the Americans and renamed Fort McKay by the British. Why do you think both armies wanted a fort located on a large river like the Mississippi?

Augustin Grignon (aw gus **tahn gree** nyoh)
War of 1812 (1812–1815) The war in which troops from the United States fought British troops for control of American land claims in North America. When the United States won, the British no longer had any real power over trade and other businesses.

From Forts to Settlement

Why did the U.S. government build military forts at Prairie du Chien, at Green Bay, and at Portage?

When the War of 1812 ended, the U.S. government quickly took over the fur trade business in Wisconsin. The government built two military forts in Wisconsin. These forts protected two important trade locations: Fort Crawford near Prairie du Chien and Fort Howard at Green Bay. A few years later the United States built Fort Winnebago at the **portage** between the Fox and Wisconsin rivers. Each fort had a hospital nearby.

The U.S. soldiers stationed at these forts were responsible for keeping control of Wisconsin's water-highways for fur trade business. They also chopped down trees and built roads. The first road was known as the Military Road. It was built to connect the three forts by land as well as by the Fox–Wisconsin waterways. You can bike on part of the Military Road today. The 40-mile Military Ridge State Trail in Iowa and Dane counties connects Dodgeville and Madison.

This modern map shows the route of the Military Road between Fort Howard at Green Bay to Fort Winnebago at Portage and on to Fort Crawford at Prairie du Chien.

Juliette Magill Kinzie was the first woman to write about life on the Wisconsin frontier in her book, *Wau-Bun*. In the early 1830s, Juliette Kinzie lived near Fort Winnebago with her husband, John. He was the Indian agent at Portage. He worked to protect the interests of the Ho-Chunk people in the area.

Juliette Kinzie painted this view of Portage and Fort Winnebago in 1831.

portage (por tidj) A location on a river or lake where things are carried from one shore to the other

Solomon **Juneau** was a French-Canadian fur trader. In 1818, he took over his father-in-law's trading post at Milwaukee. Soon after, he became the first non-Indian person to plan a village in Milwaukee. Later, Solomon Juneau served as Milwaukee's first mayor, its first postmaster, and its first newspaper editor.

How did the U.S. government cause conflict with the cultures already living in Wisconsin?

The U.S. government built and ran three military forts in Wisconsin. The government also affected the lives of the different Indian groups living in Wisconsin. First, the government appointed **agents** to work with the Indians. Some of the agents' work was helpful. Some was harmful to Native cultures. These Indian agents were hired to work with the Indian people. The government wanted the Indians to become more like non-Indians.

Second, the U.S. government also ran trading houses for the Indians so they would be less likely to trade with any French or British traders in the area. Finally, the U.S. government created new fur trade rules and local governments run only by white men.

Many of the Indian nations and some of the Métis, French, and French-Canadian people **resented** the way that the U.S. government treated them. The new government's rules and decisions did not reflect the same values and customs of those who had been living here, marrying, raising families, and working together. The Métis, French, and French-Canadians felt that the newcomers did not respect their trading traditions or their knowledge and feelings for the forests, prairies, and water-highways.

This is an early drawing of the home where Solomon Juneau and his family lived. He and his wife, Josette, had 17 children!

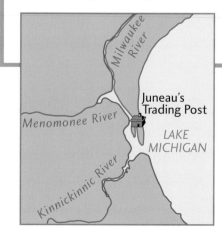

On this map, you can see that Juneau's early settlement was between the Milwaukee River and Lake Michigan. Why was this a good location for a trading post?

Juneau (**ju** noh)
agents (**ay** juhnts) People who have the power to act for others
resented (ri **zen** tuhd) Felt hurt or angry by actions done to them

Changes over Two Hundred Years

What have you learned about exploration and exchange in Wisconsin?

In this chapter you've explored some of Wisconsin's major water-highways. You've learned how explorers from France and Canada found their way to and through Wisconsin with the help of Indian travel guides. You've seen how the earliest fur traders in Wisconsin, the Indian peoples, began exchanging beaver, mink, and otter furs with traders from France and Canada.

The exchange of furs for metal tools and cooking pots changed the Indian ways of life forever. The need to trap more and more fur pelts took some Indian men farther away from their family camps and villages. The longer they were away from home, the more work the Indian women and children had to take on. Their work roles and their family roles slowly began to change. Because Indians could trade for metal items, they spent less time crafting traditional stone tools or birchbark and pottery containers.

Exploration and the fur exchange in Wisconsin caused many new peoples to move here. At first the newcomers were Indian groups from the east coast and traders from France, Canada, and Britain. Then, after the War of 1812, people from the United States began arriving.

In the next chapter, you'll read how the story of Wisconsin continued to change. While some people still made their livings through the fur trade, others were drawn here by rich deposits of lead ore. Others came to Wisconsin to buy land and work for the U.S. government. The conflicts continued over values and ideas about land. You'll discover that change is still part of everyday life in Wisconsin.

Europeans brought many goods to trade with the Indians, such as the powder horn and the earrings you see here. Why do you think the Indians wanted them?

Some Places to Visit

- Forts Folle Avoine: a reconstructed 1802–1803 British trading post and Ojibwe Village in Burnett County near Webster
- The Fur Trade Exhibit at the Wisconsin Historical Museum in Madison
- Villa Louis Historic Site in Prairie du Chien
- Madeline Island Museum Historic Site in La Pointe
- Waswagoning: a re-created Ojibwe village near Lac du Flambeau in Vilas County

Some Things to Read

- *Digging and Discovery: Wisconsin Archaeology* by Diane Holliday and Bobbie Malone, Chapter 6
- *Learning from the Land: Wisconsin Land Use* by Bobbie Malone, Chapter 2
- *Native People of Wisconsin* by Patty Loew, Chapter 2
- *Working with Water: Wisconsin Waterways* by Bobbie Malone and Jefferson J. Gray, Chapter 2

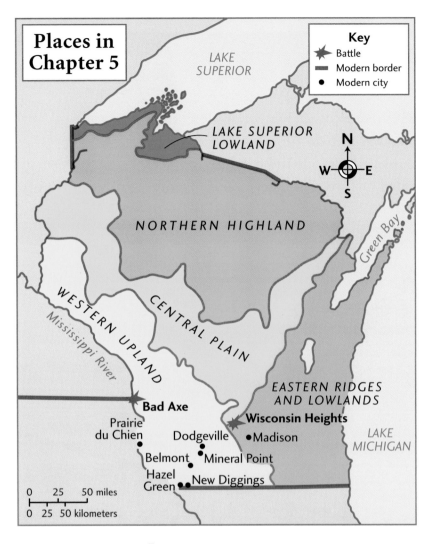

Places in Chapter 5

Key
- ✦ Battle
- — Modern border
- • Modern city

LAKE SUPERIOR

LAKE SUPERIOR LOWLAND

NORTHERN HIGHLAND

Green Bay

Mississippi River

WESTERN UPLAND

CENTRAL PLAIN

EASTERN RIDGES AND LOWLANDS

LAKE MICHIGAN

✦ Bad Axe

Prairie du Chien

✦ Wisconsin Heights

Dodgeville • Madison

Belmont • Mineral Point

Hazel Green • New Diggings

0   25   50 miles

0   25   50 kilometers

Chapter 5:
Becoming Wisconsin: From Indian Lands to Territory to Statehood

- Wisconsin Lands Change Hands
- Treaty Making
- Living on the Lead Frontier
- The Black Hawk War
- Measuring and Mapping Land to Sell
- Wisconsin Becomes a Territory
- Wisconsin Becomes the 30th State
- What Happens at the Wisconsin Capitol?
- Looking Back at Our State's Beginnings

1804–1854 Treaties with Wisconsin Indian nations

| 1800 | 1810 | 1820 |

▲ **1804** Treaty between the Sauk and Mesquakie Nations and the U.S. government

▲ **1825** Treaty of Prairie du Chien

Key Words

- Black Hawk War
- capital
- capitol
- cede
- citizens
- executive
- federal
- frontier
- governor
- judicial
- legislators
- legislature
- massacred
- militia
- representatives
- survey
- territory
- treaties

Thinking Like a Historian

How did Native peoples' ideas about land use affect their understanding of treaty-making?

How and why did lead mining in the early 1800s change life in Wisconsin?

In what ways was the Black Hawk War a turning point for Wisconsin?

How did the signing of treaties affect Wisconsin Indians?

How did the signing of treaties affect new settlers?

Why did Wisconsin become a territory?

How did Wisconsin become a state?

How did our state constitution define the way our government still works today?

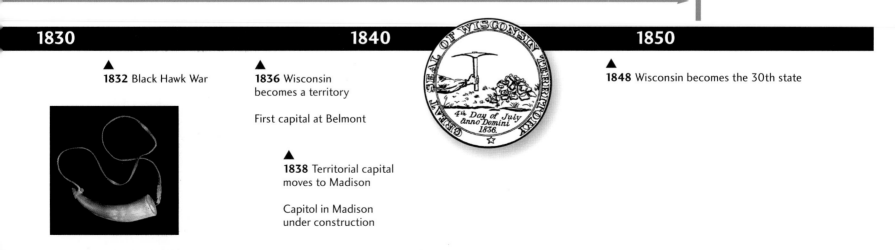

1830

▲ **1832** Black Hawk War

1840

▲ **1836** Wisconsin becomes a territory

First capital at Belmont

▲ **1838** Territorial capital moves to Madison

Capitol in Madison under construction

1850

▲ **1848** Wisconsin becomes the 30th state

Wisconsin Lands Change Hands

In this chapter, you might be surprised by the many ways Wisconsin changed in the first half of the 1800s. At the beginning of that time, all land belonged to Indian nations. By 1848, most Indian nations had to give up much of their land, and Wisconsin became the 30th state in the United States. By 1854, the Ojibwe had also **ceded** most of their land. You'll find out why and how these changes took place. You'll also learn how these changes changed the lives of all who lived in Wisconsin.

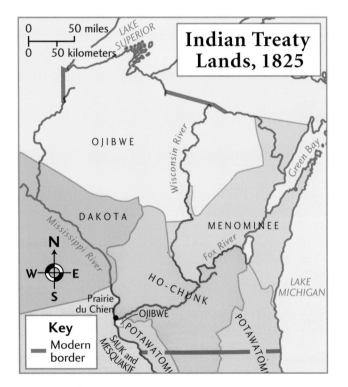

Indian Treaty Lands, 1825

Key
— Modern border

In 1825, the U.S. government invited **representatives** from all Indian nations then living in Wisconsin to meet at Prairie du Chien. The government wanted to set up official boundary agreements to keep relations peaceful among the Indian nations and the early non-Indian traders and settlers.

Whose land is it?

How would you feel if your neighbors started building a garage in your backyard? "Not fair! That's our property!" That's the way your family would probably feel. You would let your neighbors know right away that they couldn't build on your family's land. Boundary or property lines separate and protect private land use today in the United States.

In contrast, most Indian nations in the early 1800s believed that land was a gift from the Creator. People could use the land and its resources, but the land itself could not be owned. It could not be bought or sold, although one nation might control its use and resources. The fur traders used the land very much as Indians did, just taking fur and other resources from the land. But at that time, new settlers coming to Wisconsin wanted more than resources. They wanted to own both the land and its resources because they were coming to stay. New questions arose: Whose land was it, anyway? Who had the rights to its resources? The answers to such questions became another turning point in Wisconsin history.

ceded (**seed** uhd) Given up
representatives (rep pri **zen** tuh tivz) In general, people chosen to speak or act for others. Some people elected to public offices are also known as representatives.

What happened to Indian lands in the early 1800s?

Some Indian nations that had settled in Wisconsin during the fur trade period remained here. Others had moved on. Still, at the beginning of the 1800s, all of Wisconsin remained Indian land. All members of a tribal group shared land as a community, but they did not think of land as something that could be bought or sold.

From the early to mid-1800s, however, Indian lands in Wisconsin became American lands. Non-Indian people gained control of waterways and land where Native ancestors had lived for centuries. Through **treaties** signed with the United States, Wisconsin Indians had to cede their land to the new U.S. government.

The **Sauk** and **Mesquakie** became the first Indians to cede land in Wisconsin when they signed the Treaty of 1804. It called for removing the Sauk and Mesquakie from their homelands in Wisconsin and Illinois sometime in the future. By removing Indians from the same lands that non-Indians would one day buy and settle, the treaty set off a string of events that changed Wisconsin forever.

About 5000 members of Indian nations gathered in Prairie du Chien in 1825.

treaties Official written documents between nations   **Sauk** (sawk) and **Mesquakie** (mes **kwaw** kee) Two American Indian nations

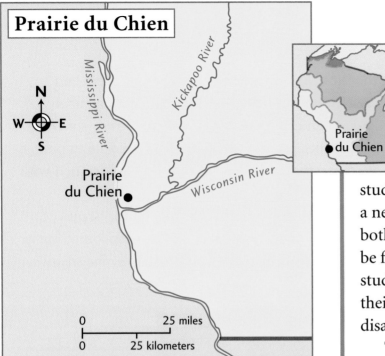

Prairie du Chien

N W E S

Mississippi River

Kickapoo River

Prairie du Chien

Wisconsin River

0   25 miles
0   25 kilometers

You learned in Chapter 4 that Prairie du Chien had been an important gathering place for thousands of years. What natural features made it such a good choice for groups to meet one another?

THE PIPE DANCE   and   THE TOMAHAWK DANCE
of the Chippeway tribe.

translate To turn one language into another

Treaty Making

Why was treaty making difficult for Indian nations?

What if you and your classmates met a group of students from another country who wanted to teach you to play a new game? You would need someone who knew how to speak both languages to **translate** the rules. The rules would already be familiar to those who invited you to play with them. These students would also know some of the best plays because it was their game. You and your classmates would already be at some disadvantage before the game even started.

Treaty making between American Indians and the U.S. government was something like that, only it wasn't a game. Tribal groups had no experience in making treaties. Treaty making was conducted and written in English, which put Native people at a disadvantage. Sometimes, no one at the treaty signing was able to translate between English and the Indian languages. More importantly, Indian nations' very different ideas about land use led to later misunderstandings. Most tribal groups did not realize that signing a treaty meant giving up their own rights to use the land forever. And most tribal groups expected the U.S. government to deliver on its promises, which didn't always happen.

Ceremonies such as this Ojibwe pipe dance took place at the tribal gathering at Prairie du Chien in 1825. The peace pipe was adapted to become an important ceremonial part of treaty making.

How did treaty negotiating and signing affect Indian nations?

U.S. government officials did not always look for tribal leaders to **negotiate** treaties. Instead, the government wanted people who would rather negotiate than fight against the U.S. government. Once treaties were signed, however, all members of that Indian nation had to live with the results.

In the Treaty of 1804, for example, the U.S. government paid the Sauk $2,234.50 for their land east of the Mississippi River in Illinois and Wisconsin. The Sauk Nation was also supposed to receive a yearly payment. The government understood that the treaty gave it the right to open this land to future non-Indian settlers. Many Sauk people did not want to give up or cede their lands at all. Many did not understand that the treaty would force them to move from their homelands someday.

The United States did not always live up to the promises made in its treaties. Sometimes the government failed to deliver the money or goods in exchange for Indian lands. Sometimes the government promised the tribes land west of the Mississippi—but other Indian nations already lived on the land there. Sometimes these new lands did not have the natural resources necessary for the tribes to survive. Tribal members lost their homelands and the ability to provide for their families as they had in the past. Many Indian people were disappointed and angry.

Can you read the beginning of the Treaty of Prairie du Chien on this page? Some tribes had different names then. The Chippewa are now known as the Ojibwe, and the Winnebago are now known as the Ho-Chunk.

negotiate (ni **goh** shee ayt) To discuss something in order to come to an agreement

Living on the Lead Frontier

Indian women were the miners. They picked up the lead that lay just under the surface or dug tunnels and shafts where they could mine larger amounts of lead. When the lead became too difficult to remove, the Indians left their "diggings" behind.

What was the Wisconsin Lead Rush?

When gold was discovered in northern California in 1848, it started what became known as the California Gold Rush. People from all over the world rushed to California to look for gold. The Wisconsin Lead Rush was similar, though smaller and earlier. People began to move to the hilly areas of northwestern Illinois, northeastern Iowa, and southwestern Wisconsin after 1815. This region was then considered the **frontier**. They hoped to get rich by mining for lead. It's easy to understand why people wanted gold, but what was it about lead that made it valuable then?

Native People who lived in the area had mined and collected lead for thousands of years. They used the naturally formed cubes of **galena** they found to make jewelry and other kinds of decoration. When the French and, later, the British arrived in Wisconsin, Indian people began to realize the value of galena to the Europeans. Then Indian groups began to mine galena in large quantities to trade with these non-Indians.

Remember that these lead-rich areas were still Indian lands in the early 1800s. That's when the demand for lead was beginning to pull non-Indians into Wisconsin. These new settlers manufactured lead **shot** for guns. Lead shot was especially important for settlers in need of defending themselves and their land. Lead had many other uses. It could make things like water pipes, weights, paint, and toys. As lead—and the land in which it was deposited—became important to non-Indians, more and more new settlers arrived in Wisconsin.

The southern part of the Driftless Area of Wisconsin was rich in lead.

frontier (fruhn **teer**) The far edge of a country where few people live
galena (guh **lee** nuh) A shiny gray mineral used to make lead   **shot** Small balls or pellets to be fired from a gun

Northwestern Illinois, northeastern Iowa, and southwestern Wisconsin made up most of the Lead Mining Region of the Upper Mississippi Valley. Can you find names of communities that reflect how important lead mining was to the area? Mineral Point was the largest community in Wisconsin during the lead boom.

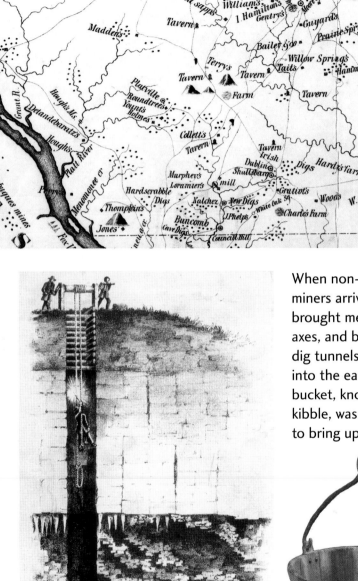

Who were the first Wisconsin "badgers"?

The Lead Rush brought many newcomers from the northeastern and southern United States. Daniel M. Parkinson, an early white settler, moved his family to New Diggings in 1827. He explained that men worked so hard at mining that they didn't have time to build real homes for themselves. "Instead of houses," he wrote, "they usually lived in dens or caves: a large hole or excavation being made in the side of a hill, or bluff, the top being covered over with poles, grass and **sod**. A level way from the edge of the hole at the bottom was dug out, some ten or twelve feet . . . forming a sheltered entrance to the 'dug-out,' as such places were usually called." Many families lived like this for years!

Some thought that the miners burrowed in these dugouts like badgers. This is the origin of Wisconsin's nickname, the Badger State.

When non-Indian miners arrived, they brought metal picks, axes, and buckets to dig tunnels deeper into the earth. This bucket, known as a kibble, was one used to bring up lead.

sod The top layer of grass and soil

The Black Hawk War

Black Hawk was a Sauk warrior and leader. What can you see in this portrait to tell you that he was already an older man by the early 1830s?

How did the Treaty of 1804 lead to conflict?

The Treaty of 1804 warned the Sauk people that the U.S. government expected them to move sometime in the future. By the mid-1820s, lead was pulling more and more non-Indians into the lead-mining areas of Illinois, Iowa, and Wisconsin. In 1829, the government ordered the Sauk people to leave behind their homelands and move across the Mississippi River. Black Hawk and his band of Sauk did not want to leave their village, but they did.

The government promised the Sauk people that it would provide them with corn for the winter. The corn never arrived. In the summer of 1832, Black Hawk and some of his followers were angry. They thought that the treaty negotiations had been unfair. About 1200 Sauk men, women, and children crossed the Mississippi with Black Hawk. They planned to return to their homes in Illinois. When they arrived, they found non-Indian settlers already living on their homelands and harvesting their fields.

Settlers feared that Black Hawk and his people would attack them. Black Hawk saw Illinois **militia** troops guarding the settlers. He knew that his people were outnumbered and unprepared to fight. Unfortunately, when he sent scouts to **surrender,** some men in the militia killed them. Other Indians fired back in self-defense. The U.S. Army arrived to help the militia. What became known as the Black Hawk War had begun.

militia (muh **lish** uh) A volunteer army trained to fight only in an emergency   **surrender** (suh **ren** dur) To give up

What happened to Black Hawk and his people?

Black Hawk wanted to lead his people back across the Mississippi, but the militia blocked the way. He knew he had to avoid the lead-mining district that was full of settlers. The band traveled east, up the Rock River. For the next few months, Black Hawk tried to keep his band safe as the army followed them.

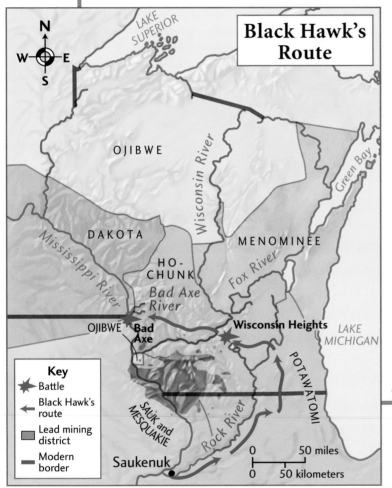

Black Hawk's Route

Key
- Battle
- Black Hawk's route
- Lead mining district
- Modern border

0   50 miles
0   50 kilometers

Black Hawk knew he had to get his people back across the Mississippi River. In this map of their journey, can you see how he and his people had to travel so far east of the river? You can find out why by reading this page.

Many Sauk people died of hunger or **exhaustion**. Some died in battles, like that at Wisconsin Heights. Those followers of Black Hawk who survived finally reached the Mississippi at the mouth of the Bad Axe River. Black Hawk attempted to surrender again. Again, the army ignored him and kept firing on his people.

Finally, as men, older people, women, and children tried to swim across the river, soldiers on a gunboat **massacred** many of them. Only about 150 people survived. Black Hawk himself escaped but later surrendered. He spent several months in prison and finally returned west across the Mississippi to join the other Sauk people who had resettled there.

The U.S. government used the Black Hawk War as an opportunity to get land for non-Indian settlers. It pressured other Indian nations in southern Wisconsin to cede their lands, too, whether or not they helped Black Hawk. Indian lands were now open to new settlers.

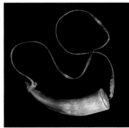

An unknown member of the militia carried this powder horn in the Black Hawk War during the spring and summer of 1832. The powder inside would have been used to fire his rifle. He may have made the powder horn himself by hollowing out a cow horn.

exhaustion (eg **zaws** chuhn) The state of being completely worn out   **massacred** (**mass** uh curd) Fiercely attacked and killed

Measuring and Mapping Land to Sell

What did the U.S. government do with the Wisconsin land that it got through treaties?

The same event can be bad for one group and good for another. When Indian nations had to cede their homelands, non-Indians moving to southern Wisconsin had the opportunity to move, buy land, and begin new and better lives in southern Wisconsin. Some people wanted to buy land even before they moved here. They needed to know some answers to their questions: What land is available? Where is it located?

The U.S. government had planned ahead. In 1785, the government had passed a law that set up an orderly way to **survey** and sell land to settlers moving west. Would they have guessed that lead would draw large numbers of newcomers to Wisconsin 50 years later?

Large bodies of water have often been used to create natural boundaries. Lakes Michigan and Superior and the Mississippi River are all natural boundaries of our state. People working for the U.S. government created our southern state boundary and the northern border with Michigan. They also created boundaries within our state. But how did they decide where and how to draw these lines that show us where counties, cities, and **townships** are located on maps?

The U.S. General Land Office hired surveyors to measure and describe land. Each surveyor had to walk the land in order to do his job. From the notes, a mapmaker drew rectangular grids like a checkerboard to mark off that land on a map.

Once the surveyor and the mapmakers had done their work, the land could be sold—even to people who had never seen it.

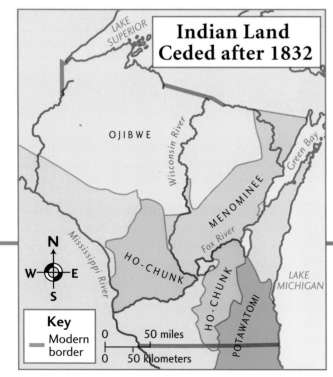

Indian Land Ceded after 1832

LAKE SUPERIOR

OJIBWE

Wisconsin River

MENOMINEE

Green Bay

Fox River

HO-CHUNK

Mississippi River

HO-CHUNK

POTAWATOMI

LAKE MICHIGAN

N W E S

Key
— Modern border

0　　50 miles
0　　50 kilometers

Treaties made before and immediately following the Black Hawk War forced tribal people to cede lands in southern Wisconsin. The U.S. government could now survey the land, divide it, and sell it cheaply to new settlers.

survey (**sur** vay) To measure an area to make a map　　**townships** Square-shaped pieces of land, six miles on each side, divided into 36 sections

What can we find out from studying a lead-mining community?

Just the name New Diggings tells you something about this community. People went there to mine lead. The photograph and map on this page are the kinds of documents historians use to learn about life in the 1800s.

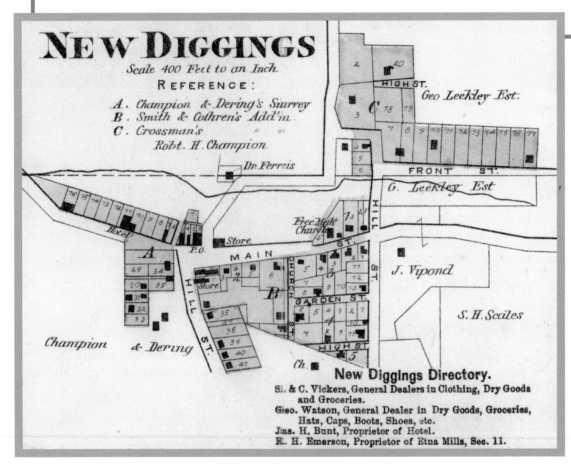

NEW DIGGINGS
Scale 400 Feet to an Inch

REFERENCE:

A. Champion & Dering's Survey
B. Smith & Cothren's Add'm
C. Crossman's   "   "
   Robt. H. Champion

New Diggings Directory.

S. & C. Vickers, General Dealers in Clothing, Dry Goods and Groceries.
Geo. Watson, General Dealer in Dry Goods, Groceries, Hats, Caps, Boots, Shoes, etc.
Jas. H. Bunt, Proprietor of Hotel.
R. H. Emerson, Proprietor of Etna Mills, Sec. 11.

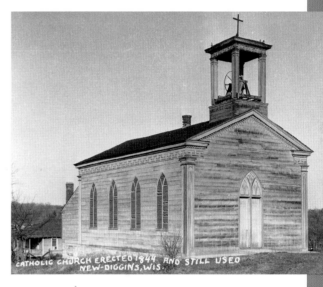

CATHOLIC CHURCH ERECTED 1844 AND STILL USED NEW-DIGGINS, WIS.

You can still visit St. Augustine's Church near New Diggings. Father Samuel **Mazzuchelli** designed and built it in 1844. He came from Italy to southwestern Wisconsin. He wanted lead-mining families to have real family-centered communities.

On this map of 1874, see if you can find the following:
• The three main areas of New Diggings
• The kinds of stores where lead miners and their families could shop
• The names of three streets

The Wisconsin survey began at the Point of Beginnings, near Hazel Green, just above the Illinois border in Grant County.

Mazzuchelli (mat zoo **kel** ee)

Wisconsin Becomes a Territory

This is Wisconsin's first territorial seal, the official mark of the government of the Wisconsin **Territory**. Can you tell what mattered most to those living in Wisconsin at that time?

How did Wisconsin become a U.S. territory?

Once the land was surveyed and ready to be sold, people began pouring into southwestern Wisconsin. At the time, Wisconsin was part of the Michigan Territory. By 1835, enough non-Indian people were living in Wisconsin for the U.S. government to recognize it as a new **territory**. James Duane Doty was a territorial judge and the leader who worked hardest to make sure Wisconsin would become its own territory.

On July 4, 1836, the U.S. Congress created the Wisconsin Territory. President Andrew Jackson appointed General Henry Dodge as governor. One of his responsibilities was calling a meeting of Wisconsin's first territorial **legislature**. The **legislators** met in Belmont, the place he selected as the territorial **capital**. The non-Indian settlers were the people who formed Wisconsin's territorial government. No Native people were part of that government. Many legislators weren't happy with Belmont, however. They wanted the capital to be moved, but where? You'll find out on the next page.

In 1836, Wisconsin's first territorial government met near Belmont in the Western Upland region. Today Belmont is the First **Capitol** Historic Site, which you can visit.

Before Wisconsin became the Wisconsin Territory, it was part of three other territories: first, Indiana, then Illinois, and finally Michigan. This map shows the large area that was the Michigan Territory between 1818 and 1836.

territory (**tair** ih toh ree) An area of land that belongs to the United States, but is not a state
Capitol The building in which lawmakers and other important government officials meet
legislature (**lej** uh slay chur) An elected group of people who have the power to make laws for the state
legislators (**lej** uh slay turz) Lawmakers who make up the legislature   **capital** The city or town where the government of a country or state is located

James Duane Doty came to Wisconsin as a judge. As he traveled the area on horseback and canoe, he got to know Wisconsin better than most people. He used his knowledge to make money buying and selling land. He owned the land that became downtown Madison where the capitol now stands.

This shows James Doty's plan for Madison. He hoped the capitol would be built on a hill at the very center of the city.

Why didn't James Duane Doty and Henry Dodge get along?

Henry Dodge and James Duane Doty were the two most important leaders in the Wisconsin Territory. They had very different talents, viewpoints, and personalities. They didn't like each other. Yet each shaped Wisconsin in his own way.

In the 1820s, Henry Dodge moved with his family to southwest Wisconsin to mine lead near what is now Dodgeville. He led a militia during the Black Hawk War. Being a miner and a military man made him a hero, especially to people living in lead-mining country. Perhaps that's why President Jackson appointed him the first territorial governor.

Dodge had picked Belmont as the capital because it was in the lead-mining district. Yet many lawmakers thought Belmont was too far from Green Bay and Milwaukee. James Duane Doty agreed. He wanted to find a more central location.

Doty dreamed of building cities. He bought land and developed the cities of Neenah, Menasha, and Fond du Lac. He also bought land between two of four lakes in southcentral Wisconsin. Then he had a surveyor plan a city, which he named Madison. He convinced the territorial leaders to make Madison the capital—even though there was no city there at all! He served as territorial governor from 1841 to 1845, although there were many people who didn't trust him. They thought he was too interested in making money.

Henry Dodge looked like a frontiersman. People said he was more comfortable wearing **buckskins** and a knife than wearing a shirt and tie.

buckskins Clothing made from the skin of a buck (deer)

Wisconsin Becomes the 30th State

Why did people in Wisconsin want the territory to become a state?

Use this map to tell where most people lived in 1848 when Wisconsin became a state.

The settlers in the Wisconsin Territory had a very limited say in the way they were governed. They elected representatives to a territorial assembly. These representatives met every year to make laws for the territory, but people could not elect a **governor.**

Those living in the Wisconsin Territory also had no real say in the national government in Washington, D.C. Only *states* had a voice in the houses of the **U.S. Congress.** Territories could elect delegates to Congress. But they had no vote. The **federal** government felt that territories needed time to attract more settlers and to "grow into" being a state.

Becoming a state meant that Wisconsin could raise its own money through **taxes.** By paying taxes, each person helped pay for the government that they elected. As a state, Wisconsin could spend the money on whatever the people there thought needed to be done.

governor The person elected as the head of the state to represent all the people in the state

U.S. Congress The part of government where laws are made. Congress is made up of the House of Representatives and the Senate.

federal (fed ur uhl) Referring to a type of government where its smaller divisions —such as states—are united under and controlled by one government

taxes Money paid to the government

How did Wisconsin become a state?

What did people in the Wisconsin Territory have to do to become a state? First, the population had to grow. Second, Wisconsin **citizens** had to write a **constitution**, and third, the U.S. Congress had to approve statehood for Wisconsin. These steps took time.

In the 1830s, the Lead Rush drew many settlers into the Wisconsin Territory. Wisconsin's population grew from about 30,000 in 1840 to 300,000 in 1848! The Wisconsin Territory had reached that first step on its way to statehood. Writing a constitution and getting people to vote to accept it proved to be more difficult.

A constitution defines the rights and responsibilities of citizens. In 1846, Wisconsin voters elected 124 men to go Madison to write a constitution. For many different reasons, more Wisconsin citizens voted against this constitution than for it. It took another two years before another group of men met to write a state constitution that people would accept. That was also step two.

Step three occurred when the Congress approved statehood. Finally, on May 29, 1848, President James K. Polk admitted Wisconsin as the 30th state in the United States.

In this drawing of Madison in 1852, can you find the capitol with its dome and columns?

citizens (**sit** uh zuhns) Members of a particular country or state who have the right to live there
constitution (kon stuh **too** shuhn) In the United States, a written document that contains the rights and responsibilities people have and describes how government works

What Happens at the Wisconsin Capitol?

Why do we have three branches of government, and what are their responsibilities?

In a **democracy** like ours, the government belongs to the people, because the people choose their leaders. The state capitol serves as the home of our state government. Wisconsin's top elected state leaders have their offices at the capitol.

Remember that our state constitution defines the rights and responsibilities of citizens and the government. The government's most important jobs are to keep us safe and to make sure that government laws are applied fairly.

The state of Wisconsin modeled its organization of government on that of our federal government. That's why we have three branches of state government, each with its own elected leaders. Each has a big name and big responsibilities, and all cooperate to help our state run smoothly. Voting in elections is one way that citizens take part in a democracy.

The Wisconsin state capitol is both a beautiful and very busy building. People from all three branches of state government work there. You can see where the work goes on in the photos and chart on the next page.

The **legislative branch** is the law-making branch of state government. Its responsibility is creating laws for everyone in the state to follow.

The governor is the chief **executive** of the **executive branch**. He or she has the responsibility to **execute** all the laws of the state.

The **judicial branch** has the responsibility to solve the problems that come up as people disagree on what the law means. Their solutions are called **judgments**.

legislative (**lej** uh slay tiv) **branch** The branch of state government that makes laws. The legislative branch has two parts. At the federal level, these are the Senate and the House of Representatives. At the state level, these branches are called the Senate and the State Assembly.
executive (eg **zek** yoo tiv) The head of the state or governor   **executive branch** The branch of government that enforces laws
execute (**ek** suh kyoot) To put into action and enforce
judicial (joo **dish** uhl) **branch** The branch of government that settles arguments about the way laws are carried out or applied
judgments Judges' solutions when people disagree on what a law means
democracy (di **mok** ruh see) A system of government that allows people to choose their own leaders

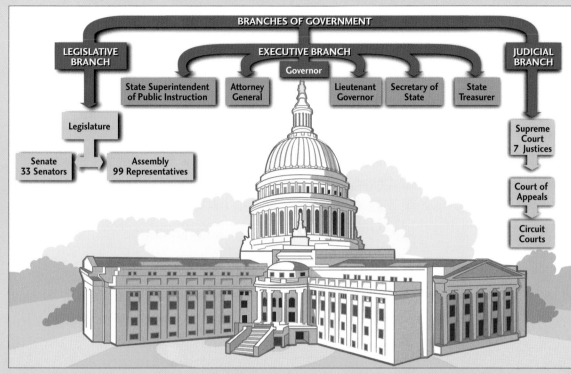

BRANCHES OF GOVERNMENT

LEGISLATIVE BRANCH

EXECUTIVE BRANCH

Governor

State Superintendent of Public Instruction | Attorney General | Lieutenant Governor | Secretary of State | State Treasurer

JUDICIAL BRANCH

Legislature

Senate 33 Senators → Assembly 99 Representatives

Supreme Court 7 Justices

Court of Appeals

Circuit Courts

The judges of the state supreme court meet in this room. As you can see on the chart, this is the most important part of the judicial branch of the government.

As you can tell from this chart, each branch of government has its own responsibilities. Not all of these people work in the capitol itself.

This is the State Assembly chamber where the state representatives meet. From the chart, can you tell how many lawmakers are in the State Assembly? Which branch of government makes laws?

The governor's confence room is used for a variety of meetings and events by the executive branch of the state government. From the chart, can you tell why the governor is so important in heading our state government?

The Senate is part of the legislative branch of state government. Why is it smaller than the State Assembly? You can find the answer in the chart.

Looking Back at Our State's Beginnings

Can you find more than one turning point in Wisconsin history in the first half of the 1800s?

In many ways, the changes that occurred in Wisconsin between 1804 and 1848 were more far-reaching than in any other 44-year period in our state's history. In the early 1800s, few non-Indians lived in Wisconsin, and land belonged to the Indian nations here. As you read earlier in this chapter, over the next three decades, lead drew many new people to the southwestern part of the state. Their communities and farms helped the area attract more and more people. Tensions rose between some settlers and Indians in the area.

Misunderstandings and mistrust over treaties between Indians and the U.S. government led to the Black Hawk War in 1832. After Black Hawk and his followers were defeated by the U.S. troops, the government made treaties with other Indian nations in southern Wisconsin. The Indians were pressured to cede their lands. The government surveyed, mapped, and sold the land that Indians ceded. More treaties ceded more land. New settlements grew. Soon almost all of Wisconsin was open to settlement.

Most nations were able to reserve small amounts of land for themselves as reservations. The Ojibwe managed to reserve some very important rights for all of their bands. All nations had to work hard to adapt their ways of life and still be able to hold onto their traditions.

When enough non-Indians had settled in Wisconsin by 1836, the area became a territory of the U.S. government. The territorial government made its first capital in Belmont and soon moved permanently to Madison. Leaders had to write a constitution that people would accept. It took two tries and two years to make that happen. Then, in 1848, Wisconsin became a state with its own executive, legislative, and judicial branches of government elected by its citizens. Wisconsin citizens at last had a voice in the federal government as well.

In 1844, Tay-che-gwi-au-nee, son of Chief Buffalo of the Ojibwe, presented this pipe to James Duane Doty as a gift from his father. Doty was the territorial governor at the time. The pipe bowl is carved from stone, and it has a two-faced man in a hat on one end and a bison on the other. The pipe was made to be presented as a gift. It is in the collection of the Wisconsin Historical Museum.

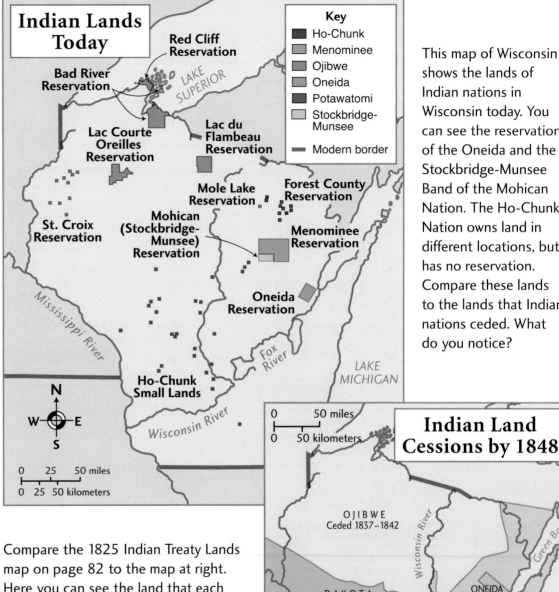

Indian Lands Today

Key
- Ho-Chunk
- Menominee
- Ojibwe
- Oneida
- Potawatomi
- Stockbridge-Munsee
- — Modern border

Red Cliff Reservation
Bad River Reservation
LAKE SUPERIOR
Lac Courte Oreilles Reservation
Lac du Flambeau Reservation
Mole Lake Reservation
Forest County Reservation
St. Croix Reservation
Mohican (Stockbridge-Munsee) Reservation
Menominee Reservation
Oneida Reservation
Mississippi River
Fox River
LAKE MICHIGAN
Ho-Chunk Small Lands
Wisconsin River

This map of Wisconsin shows the lands of Indian nations in Wisconsin today. You can see the reservations of the Oneida and the Stockbridge-Munsee Band of the Mohican Nation. The Ho-Chunk Nation owns land in different locations, but has no reservation. Compare these lands to the lands that Indian nations ceded. What do you notice?

Compare the 1825 Indian Treaty Lands map on page 82 to the map at right. Here you can see the land that each Indian nation ceded to the U.S. government between the end of the Black Hawk War and Wisconsin statehood. In those years, Wisconsin Indian nations ceded most of the lands where their ancestors had lived for hundreds or thousands of years.

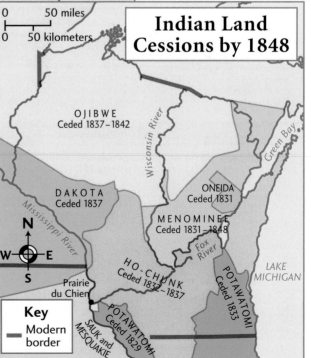

Indian Land Cessions by 1848

OJIBWE Ceded 1837–1842
Wisconsin River
Green Bay
DAKOTA Ceded 1837
ONEIDA Ceded 1831
Mississippi River
MENOMINEE Ceded 1831–1848
Fox River
HO-CHUNK Ceded 1832–1837
LAKE MICHIGAN
POTAWATOMI Ceded 1833
Prairie du Chien
POTAWATOMI Ceded 1829
SAUK and MESQUAKIE

Key
- — Modern border

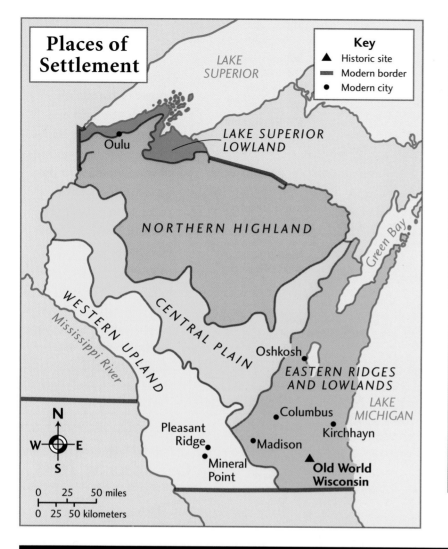

Places of Settlement

Key
▲ Historic site
— Modern border
• Modern city

LAKE SUPERIOR

LAKE SUPERIOR LOWLAND

Oulu

NORTHERN HIGHLAND

Green Bay

WESTERN UPLAND

Mississippi River

CENTRAL PLAIN

Oshkosh

EASTERN RIDGES AND LOWLANDS

LAKE MICHIGAN

Columbus

Pleasant Ridge

Kirchhayn

Madison

Mineral Point

▲ Old World Wisconsin

N W E S

0   25   50 miles
0   25   50 kilometers

Chapter 6: They Came to Wisconsin and They're Still Coming: Immigration and Settlement

- Immigration and Migration: Then and Now
- Making the Journey
- A Stonemason in Cornwall, England, Comes to Mineral Point
- Free at Last
- A German Farmstead in Washington County
- From Finland to Bayfield County
- Lucky to Be in America
- Bringing Texas North to Wisconsin
- Mai Ya's Long Journey from Thailand to Wisconsin
- Looking Back at Immigration and Settlement in Wisconsin

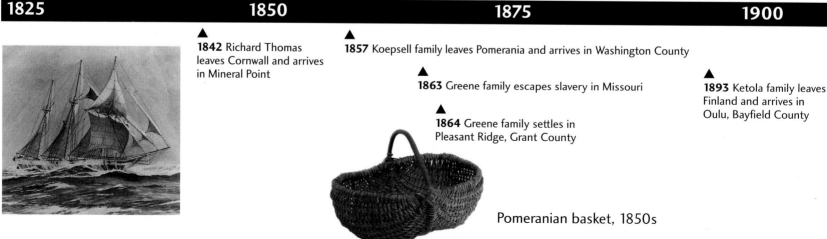

| 1825 | 1850 | 1875 | 1900 |

▲ **1842** Richard Thomas leaves Cornwall and arrives in Mineral Point

▲ **1857** Koepsell family leaves Pomerania and arrives in Washington County

▲ **1863** Greene family escapes slavery in Missouri

▲ **1864** Greene family settles in Pleasant Ridge, Grant County

▲ **1893** Ketola family leaves Finland and arrives in Oulu, Bayfield County

Pomeranian basket, 1850s

Key Words

- emancipated
- emigrate
- Holocaust
- immigrant
- immigration
- integrated
- migrant
- migration
- refugees
- slave
- slavery

Thinking Like a Historian

In what ways did events that were happening where people were living push them to leave or move away? In what ways did opportunities in Wisconsin pull newcomers to the state?

How did newcomers keep traditions they brought with them? How did newcomers adapt to their new homes and environments?

What were the turning points in the lives of the people you read about in this chapter?

How are the experiences of those who moved to Wisconsin long ago similar to those of people who moved here more recently? How are they different?

How did the strengths that people brought with them help them adapt to and survive in Wisconsin?

Typical Hmong storycloth

1925 **1950** **1975** **2000**

1945 Rosa Goldberg is rescued from Germany

1953 Katz family settles in Oshkosh

1957 Cris Plata lives in Wisconsin for the first time

1980 Cris and Ann Plata return to Columbia County permanently

1980 Mai Ya Xiong is born in Thailand

2004 Mai Ya Xiong graduates from the University of Wisconsin–Milwaukee

Immigration and Migration: Then and Now

In this chapter, you'll find out more about people who were not born in Wisconsin but chose to make their homes here. You'll learn why they left their homeland, how they traveled here, and what their lives were like after they arrived. Some people came in the early 1800s. Others came more than 100 years later. How does your family's experience fit into this pattern of stories?

Who is an immigrant?

Have you lived in Wisconsin all of your life? Or did you move from elsewhere? If you came from another country, then you are an immigrant. If you moved here from a different state in the United States, then you are a migrant. Moving from one country to settle and live in another country is called immigration. Moving from one region to another in the United States is called migration.

Maybe you have lived in Wisconsin all of your life, but your parents, grandparents, or great-grandparents moved here from another country. *They* are the immigrants in your family. When you read Chapter 3, you learned that the ancestors of the Ho-Chunk and Menominee Nations have lived in Wisconsin for thousands of years. Other people—or their parents or ancestors who arrived here in the last 400 years—either immigrated or migrated here.

What is immigration?

Why do people leave their homeland and settle in another country? Not every immigrant or migrant chooses to leave home. Sometimes events *push* or force people from their homes in one country or some region of this country. Sometimes people cannot find work to help their families survive. They must move to find good jobs. Sometimes a war makes it impossible for people to continue to live in their home country. They must leave for their own safety. Sometimes, a terrible storm like Hurricane Katrina in 2005 pushes thousands of people from their homes. After the storm, many people lost everything and had to start over elsewhere. People who leave to escape harm are refugees as well as immigrants.

Some people choose to leave to be closer to family or friends who have already moved. Others leave to take better-paying jobs or to buy land that they couldn't buy in their homeland. Opportunities for a better life tend to *pull* people from their home country. In this chapter, you'll read about immigrants, migrants, and refugees who settled in Wisconsin.

---

homeland A country where someone was born or has lived   **immigrant** (**im** uh gruhnt) A person from one country who moves to settle permanently in another country
migrant (**mI** gruhnt) A person who moves from one state or region of a country to another   **immigration** (im uh **gray** shuhn) Moving from one country to settle and live in another country   **migration** (my **gray** shuhn) The process of moving from one region to another within the same country
ancestors (**an** ses turz) Members of your family who lived a long time ago, usually before your grandparents
refugees (ref yoo **jeez**) People forced to leave home to escape harm after disaster or war

What is it like to be an immigrant?

You'll discover in this chapter the real stories of seven people who came to Wisconsin. Some came alone. Others came with their families. They each came from different parts of the world. They came at different times in history. And they settled in different parts of the state. Some were *pushed* from their homes. Others were *pulled* to Wisconsin.

However, they all left familiar places. They all traveled through new, unknown places. They all made new lives in a new land. For some newcomers, this meant learning English. For others, it meant learning new skills. Some felt sad because they had to leave family members behind. Others felt happy because they had escaped from very difficult and dangerous situations. If you are an immigrant, you may recognize some of these experiences. If your ancestors were the immigrants in your family, this chapter may help you understand more about *their* immigration experiences.

Immigration, migration, and settlement in Wisconsin have been going on for thousands of years. Remember reading in Chapter 3 about when the different Indian groups began arriving here to live? Many different groups of people have been arriving here ever since. More people will probably continue to arrive in the future. Immigration and settlement are a big part of Wisconsin's past, present, and future.

These children are celebrating **Ethnic** Pride Day at Our Savior Lutheran Church in Milwaukee. Laotian, African, Hmong, Indian, Hispanic, and American Indian cultures are all celebrated here. Have you ever been to a celebration like this? Are there special things you do with your family to celebrate your **heritage**?

Ethnic Having to do with a group of people sharing the same home country or culture
heritage (**hair** uh tij) Valuable, important traditions handed down from generation to generation

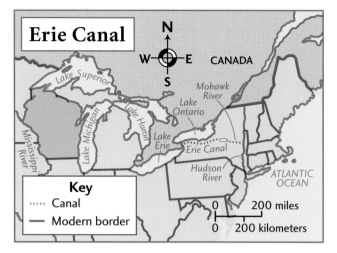

Erie Canal

Key
..... Canal
— Modern border

0   200 miles
0   200 kilometers

Large numbers of people did not begin to settle in Wisconsin until after the Erie Canal was completed in 1825. Many early settlers came from New York state. These settlers included the European immigrants who landed in the port of New York City. People could travel up the Hudson River, go through the Erie Canal, reach Lake Erie, and sail to a Wisconsin port without having to travel over land.

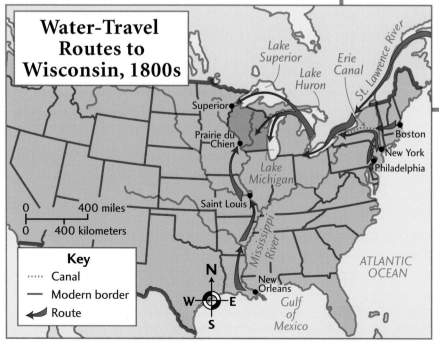

Water-Travel Routes to Wisconsin, 1800s

0   400 miles
0   400 kilometers

Key
..... Canal
— Modern border
◄ Route

Making the Journey

How has travel changed over time for people moving to Wisconsin?

Until the past 50 years, most people traveled by water across the Atlantic or Pacific oceans to reach the United States from other countries. The building of railroads in the mid-1800s was a turning point in overland travel. Two other turning points—the invention of the automobile and the creation of airplanes—came early in the 1900s. People didn't start driving on interstates or flying as passengers from Europe or Asia until the mid-1900s.

Early journeys to Wisconsin took a great deal of time and effort. Now people can move much more rapidly to Wisconsin from another country or from another place in the United States. When did members of your family come to Wisconsin? How did they get here? Where did they settle first?

Waterways connected people and land separated them before railroads, automobiles, and planes. People traveling to Wisconsin during most of the 1800s from distant parts of the United States crossed the Great Lakes or came up the Mississippi River. It was the easiest and cheapest way to reach the state.

This photo shows a ship of people **emigrating** from Queenstown, Ireland, and heading to the United States. In the mid-1800s, most people in Ireland were poor farmers who grew potatoes. When a potato **blight** ruined potato crops in the mid-1840s, nearly one million people died. Another one million left Ireland. Those lucky enough to leave emigrated on ships like this one. Many were starving and died on the journey. Some of those who survived traveled on to Wisconsin.

The Harrell family, at right, got off the train in Beloit at the Chicago & North Western **Depot**. The depot is shown in this postcard from the early 1900s.

This is a photo of children in the Harrell family in 1942. The Harrell family worked as **sharecroppers** in Mississippi. Then they moved to Memphis, Tennessee, where their father, William, got a job making baseball bats. In 1943, the Harrells took the train to Beloit, Wisconsin, where William could make more money working in a **foundry**. Many other African American families had similar experiences. They also moved north in the 1900s for better-paying **industrial** jobs. This was called the Great Migration.

In July 2004, members of the Madison area **Hmong** community gathered at the Dane County Regional Airport to welcome Lor family members who were emigrating from **Thailand** to Wisconsin. The Lors were joining other family already living in Madison.

emigrating (em uh gray ting) Leaving one's own country to settle in another   **blight** Disease
Depot (dee poh) A railroad station building where people arrive and depart on trains   **Hmong** (mong) A language and group of people from Southeast Asia
Thailand (tI land) A country in Southeast Asia
sharecroppers Farmers who were so poor that they had no money to rent the land they farmed. To live on the land, they gave the landowner a "share" of what they produced.
foundry A factory where metal is melted and shaped   **industrial** Having to do with factories

A Stonemason in Cornwall, England, Comes to Mineral Point

In 1842, **stonemason** Richard Thomas **emigrated** from Cornwall, England, to Mineral Point. This photo of him was taken many years after he arrived. He died when he was 69 years old. His **obituary** read, "He was industrious and kind-hearted, and his memory will long be cherished."

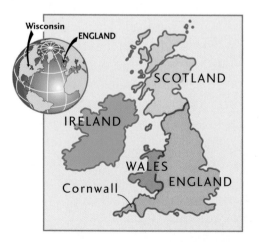

Why did Richard Thomas settle in Wisconsin?

In the spring of 1842, Richard Thomas sailed from Cornwall, England, to New York. He was 25 years old. He grew up in Redruth, a village in the heart of the copper and tin mining area of Cornwall. His father was a stonemason and his mother worked in farm fields as well as at home. Richard's parents' greatest wish was to save enough money for their family to **emigrate** to America. They believed their children would have better opportunities to make a living and own land in the United States than in Cornwall. When he was old enough, Richard became an **apprentice** to a stonemason, and he attended night school.

Richard was the first in his family to emigrate. He traveled from New York to Mineral Point, Wisconsin, where many other Cornish immigrants were settling to work as lead miners. In late 1842 or early 1843, Richard Thomas and his business partner, James Carbis, built a two-story stone house on Hoard Street in Mineral Point. They built it in the same style as those in the villages of Cornwall, with two rooms upstairs and two rooms downstairs. Richard and James built their Hoard Street house of local stone **quarried** nearby.

Cornwall is the most southwestern county of England. Cornish people immigrated to southwestern Wisconsin between about 1836 and 1848. Many came to mine lead ore. Others, like Richard Thomas, came to build houses for the growing population.

stonemason A person skilled in building with stone   **emigrated** (**em** uh gray tuhd) Left one's own country to settle in another
obituary (o **bit** chu air ee) A printed report of someone's death, often in the newspaper   **emigrate** (**em** uh grayt) To leave one's country to settle in another
apprentice (uh **pren** tuhs) A person learning a trade or art   **quarried** (**kwor** eed) Dug out

This is a photo of James Carbis, a second Cornish stonemason who settled in Mineral Point in 1842. He and his wife, Elizabeth, raised five children: James, Susan, John, Sarah, and Fred. They were all born in Mineral Point. As business partners, James Carbis and Richard Thomas built several stone houses there over a 30-year period.

The two-story house on the right in this picture is the first house that Richard Thomas and James Carbis built. Two years later, in 1845, they built the single-story house on the left in this photo. It was a traditional miner's cottage similar to those they had built in Redruth, Cornwall.

Here is a more recent photo of the two houses built by Richard and James. Between 1935 and 1940, Robert Neal and Edgar Hellum restored both buildings. They named the two-story house Trelawny and the single-story house Pendarvis. In the 1960s, the name of Hoard Street was changed to Shake Rag Street to remember the Cornish miners who once worked nearby. Today you can visit the Trelawny and Pendarvis houses between May and October. They are now part of Pendarvis Historic Site, owned by the Wisconsin Historical Society.

What was life like for Richard Thomas in Mineral Point?

Richard married Elizabeth Johns in 1843, but she died three years later. His parents, Sampson and Susanna Thomas, had arrived from Cornwall in 1844, along with his sister, her husband, and their child. They all moved into the house on Hoard Street with Richard, who was now a **widower**. His business partner James and James's wife and son also lived there. The house was now home to seven adults and two children. The neighborhood was also full of Cornish immigrants. By the time Wisconsin became a state in 1848, Richard had been living in Mineral Point for six years. **Census** records show that their neighbors were the Williams, Tregaskis, Uren, Prideaux, Remfrey, and Goldsworthy families. Most of these men worked as lead miners. Eventually the Thomases moved out of the neighborhood to a larger wood-frame house. The Carbis family continued to live in the Hoard Street house until 1862.

As Mineral Point stonemasons and builders, Richard Thomas and James Carbis worked together until about 1870. Occasionally, Richard's father, Sampson, helped them cut, cure, and place the local sandstone. Not only did they build small stone cottages for their neighbors, they also built a large stone **mansion** for Cornish immigrant Joseph Gundry. Mr. Gundry owned and operated a dry goods store on High Street, Mineral Point's main street.

widower (**wid** oh ur) A man whose wife has died   **Census** (**sen** suhs) An official count of all people living in a country or district   **mansion** (**man** shun) A very large house

Free at Last

John Greene and his family became some of the pioneer African American settlers in the Pleasant Ridge community in Grant County in the Western Upland region.

How did John Greene and his family escape slavery to reach Wisconsin?

In 1810, John Greene was born a **slave** in Virginia. As an adult, both he and his wife, Lillie, were slaves owned by the Griffith family in Saint Charles County, Missouri. In 1863, during the Civil War, John and Lillie Smith Greene escaped from the Griffiths' farm. They traveled north to freedom with their children and grandchildren.

Many slave families in the southern United States had been broken up when the slave owners sold one or more family members. The Greene family wanted to escape **slavery** to keep the family together. The Greenes had made one other attempt to escape. But they were captured and brought back before they got very far from the Griffiths' farm. The second time, the Greenes took the little money that they'd saved. Then they started out when it was already dark. The Greenes used some of their savings to buy train tickets. They made at least part of the journey north by rail.

The Greenes spent their first winter in Bloomington, Wisconsin —in Grant County in the Western Upland region. Then, they moved about 10 miles to Pleasant Ridge. There they became farmers. They probably rented land on which to work or helped other farmers. Five years after being the property of the Griffith family, John Greene and his oldest son, Hardy, were able to buy property of their own: farmland in Pleasant Ridge.

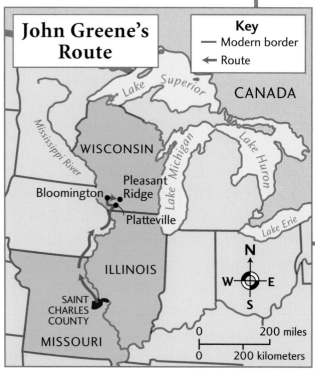

John Greene's Route

Key
— Modern border
← Route

The Greenes' son, Thomas, remembered that the family traveled this route from **slavery** in Missouri to freedom in Wisconsin.

slavery The practice of owning people and making them work
slave Someone who is owned by another person

What was life like for the Greene family and other African Americans at Pleasant Ridge?

The cemetery of the United Brethren Church in Grant County contains the gravestones of many Greene family members. You can see **replicas** of these graves in the church cemetery at Old World Wisconsin. What kinds of things can you learn about a community and the people who have lived there by visiting a cemetery?

In 1874, the European American and African American farm families of Pleasant Ridge built a small log school for all the children of the community when they **established** and **supervised** School District Five. This school was one of the earliest **integrated** schools in the nation.

Everyone who settled in Pleasant Ridge in the last half of the 1800s came for new opportunities for their families. These families were escaped or **emancipated** African American slaves, immigrant Europeans, and European Americans. Both African American and European American families were welcome in the tiny community of Pleasant Ridge.

These farm families worked hard. They needed one another's help to survive. The Greenes did not become wealthy. But they managed to make a living on their own land. They were also well-liked by their neighbors.

All community children attended the **integrated** one-room school of District Five. All the families gathered there for community events such as picnics, sports, and dances.

German immigrant families built their own German-language Methodist church. English-speaking families, both black and white, built their own United Brethren Church with help from the Germans. Families often joined at the church for prayer meetings. They also helped one another take care of the church buildings.

From the 1860s through the 1880s, Pleasant Ridge attracted settlers like the Greenes. All were looking for opportunities to make their lives better. From the late 1880s on, however, children grew up and began to look elsewhere for still better opportunities. Fast-growing cities offered different kinds of work. Pleasant Ridge began to lose many of those who lived there. By the mid-1930s, the entire community had moved to other places.

Mildred Greene was the last person living to have grown up at Pleasant Ridge. In the late 1990s, she remembered what she learned there. "We were taught to love each other and so we did. Most everyone was a farmer and so they relied on each other for help." Perhaps her best memory was that living there, "I never paid any attention to skin color. People were just people."

replicas (**rep** luh kuhz) Exact copies   **established** (ess **tab** lish tuhd) Set up something, such as a school, church, club, or business   **supervised** (**soo** puhr vIzd) Watched over or directed   **integrated** (in tuh **gray** tuhd) Included people of all races   **emancipated** (i **man** suh pay tuhd) Legally freed from slavery

A German Farmstead in Washington County

This is the **Koepsell** farmhouse in Washington County. Friedrich Koepsell cut the logs and built the large house himself in 1859. He used a building style that was traditional to his homeland in **Pomerania**. This type of building is called half-timber.

EASTERN RIDGES AND LOWLANDS

Kirchhayn

In the 1850s, the Koepsell family immigrated to Wisconsin from Pomerania. Pomerania is now part of both Germany and Poland. Between 1839 and 1893, many **Pomeranian** people came to Wisconsin to live.

Why did the Koepsell family move from Pomerania to settle in Wisconsin?

In 1857 **Friedrich** and Sophia **Koepsell** and their three children emigrated from **Pomerania** to Wisconsin. Friedrich was born in a village in Pomerania in north central Europe. He was 38 years old and his wife was 30 years old when they arrived in Quebec, Canada. Then they made their way to Wisconsin. Their two young daughters and son came with them.

Friedrich's brother, Carl, had come to Wisconsin in 1843 with a religious group called the Old Lutherans. They left Pomerania and came to Wisconsin so that they could be free to practice their Old Lutheran religious beliefs. They settled in an area northwest of Milwaukee in Washington County. They called their German-speaking settlement **Kirchhayn**, a word that means "church in the wildwoods."

Perhaps Friedrich also wanted his family to grow up in the Old Lutheran tradition in Wisconsin. As a carpenter, Friedrich would also have more opportunities to build in Kirchhayn where people were moving. Friedrich built his own house in Kirchhayn in 1859 on 40 acres of land. That same year Sophia gave birth to a second son.

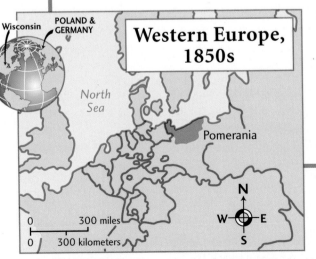

Wisconsin

POLAND & GERMANY

Western Europe, 1850s

North Sea

Pomerania

0   300 miles

0   300 kilometers

N W E S

Koepsell (kep suhl)   **Pomerania** (pom uh **ray** nee uh)   **Pomeranian** (pom uh **ray** nee uhn)
Friedrich (**free** drik)   **Kirchhayn** (keer kIn)

Friedrich and Sophia Koepsell came to Wisconsin in 1857. Together they raised their seven children and farmed 130 acres.

Here's a photo of the Koepsell family's dining room. Today you can visit the Koepsell farmhouse with your family. It has been moved from Washington County and rebuilt at Old World Wisconsin. Sophia and her daughters cooked and baked for the family. They may have eaten apple **kuchen,** traditional German cake baked with apples picked from trees on the farm.

What was life like for the Koepsells in Kirchhayn in Washington County?

Friedrich was both a farmer and a skilled carpenter. He built and developed his own farm. Then he also built houses and farm buildings for people in the Kirchhayn area. During the first ten years, Friedrich enlarged the farm from 40 acres to 130 acres. He farmed some of the land. Perhaps he harvested logs for building from the rest of it. He built barns, a machine shed, and an outhouse for his own family farm. Using one team of horses to farm, he grew hay and raised dairy cows, beef cows, sheep, and pigs. Friedrich also grew a lot of barley. He may have sold it to local brewers to make beer.

Sophia and Friedrich had three more children. The older Koepsell children helped take care of the apple trees, the large vegetable garden, and the large potato field for family eating. They worked on the farm, in the farmyard, and in the farmhouse until they married and moved away. In 1886, when Friedrich was 67 and Sophia was 59, they sold the farm where they had lived for 27 years.

kuchen (koo kuhn)

Take a close look at this detail of the half-timber building style. It is called "half-timber" because it is part wood—or timber—and part brick.

From Finland to Bayfield County

Why did the Ketola family choose to come to Northern Wisconsin?

In the spring of 1889, **Heikki** Ketola left Finland and traveled by steamboat to New York. He was 26 years old. He left his wife, Maria, and their five children at home in Finland when he immigrated to the United States. He wanted to own land and be a farmer. It was nine years before he had saved enough money to bring his family to join him. When Heikki first arrived, he worked at two different Lake Erie ports in Ohio for about three and a half years. Then he learned that other Finns were settling in northern Wisconsin. He left Ohio and moved to the town of **Oulu** in the northwestern corner of Bayfield County, Wisconsin.

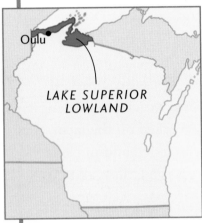

LAKE SUPERIOR LOWLAND

On December 13, 1892, Heikki entered a **homestead** claim to 80 acres of land. The Homestead Act was a national law of 1862 that gave people the opportunity to own land without paying cash for it. In exchange for the **deed** proving ownership, they had to build a house on the land and live there. They had to clear and farm a certain number of acres.

Between 1893 and 1898, Heikki built and lived in a log house that measured 15 by 17 feet on the land that he claimed. That's about as large as today's single-car garages. He cleared trees, stumps, brush, and stones from about seven acres. He also built a log barn for one horse and six cows.

In 1898, he sent enough money to Maria and their children so they could travel from Finland to Wisconsin. He built an addition to the house the same year with logs he had cut. Soon they had three more children and needed more room, so Heikki built on a second addition!

This is the **Heikki** and Maria **Ketola** family outside their log home in Bayfield County. Heikki built the house himself in three sections between 1893 and 1900. The homemade ladders were mounted on the house so Heikki could quickly climb to the roof to put out chimney fires.

Finland is a heavily forested country with small amounts of good farmland. Finnish people immigrated to northern Wisconsin between about 1890 and 1920. Many came to farm. Others worked in the iron mines.

Heikki (**hay** kee)   **Ketola** (**keh** tuh luh)
Oulu (**oo** loo)
homestead A house with its buildings and grounds; farm with all its buildings
deed A document that proves ownership of the land

In this photo, you can see a small log barn that Heikki built. On their growing farm, he also built an outhouse, granary, and **sauna** in which to bathe. Most Finnish farms in northern Wisconsin had saunas. Families used the saunas every Wednesday and Saturday. You can visit the Ketola house and the sauna at Old World Wisconsin near Eagle in Waukesha County. It is preserved there so that visitors can easily see what life was like on a traditional Finnish American farm in Wisconsin.

Maria knit mittens, socks, and shawls from wool provided by their sheep. She fed and milked the cows and worked in the large vegetable garden and potato field. Neighbors described Maria as very kind but very serious.

What was life like for the Ketolas in Oulu?

By 1902, Heikki had been in the United States for 13 years. He had provided a home and farm for his wife, Maria, and their children. He built two hay sheds to store the hay he grew. He also built a large **root cellar** to store **rutabagas** to feed his cows and potatoes to feed his family.

Everyone in the family worked hard, but farming in Bayfield County was difficult. The growing season is short in northern Wisconsin. Enlarging the farm meant more hard work clearing trees and stumps. To help make ends meet, Heikki worked at a different job off the farm a few months every year to earn cash for things they couldn't grow or build. Then he began selling telephones, cream separators, and farm equipment.

The older children married and moved from the farm. The younger children attended school, learned to speak English, and became "Americanized" like the other children at school. Heikki and Maria celebrated their 70th wedding anniversary in 1951. Maria passed away a few months later at the age of 92. Heikki died in 1954 at the age of 91. Their sons, Oscar and Fred, continued to live in the log house on their parents' farm.

Maria and Heikki traveled to their neighbors' farms to attend church services before the church was built. Church records show that Heikki changed his name to Henry Getto. This process is called "Americanizing" immigrant names.

This 2007 photo is of a baked pancake called **pannu kakkuu**. Maria and her daughters baked pannu kakkuu. It tasted good with maple syrup and made good use of the farm's daily supply of milk and eggs.

sauna (**saw** nuh) A Finnish bath that uses dry heat, or a bath where steam is made by throwing water on hot stones   **pannu kakkuu** (**pah** noo **kah** ku)
root cellar A room underground for storing root vegetables   **rutabagas** (**roo** tah bay guhs) Large pale-yellow root vegetables sometimes called "Swedish turnips"
granary (**gran** uh ree) A building for storing grain

Lucky to Be in America

How did Rosa Goldberg Katz survive the Holocaust and come to Wisconsin?

Rosa Katz's Story, 1939–1948

Key
— Border, 1942–1945
■ Concentration camp
▨ Nazi control or occupation, 1941–1945

Wisconsin   POLAND & GERMANY   ATLANTIC OCEAN

SWEDEN
•Vegby
•Malmö
Ravensbrück
Berlin ■   POLAND
GERMANY   •Lodz
Auschwitz ■

Beginning in 1939, Rosa's life in Hitler-controlled Europe was terrifying. The map shows the locations in Poland and Germany, but not the horrors, that Rosa experienced.

In 1924, Rosa Goldberg was born in **Lodz**, Poland, into a wealthy Jewish family. She was the youngest of four children. When Rosa was only 15 years old, **Nazi** German troops **invaded** Poland. A few months later, all of the Jews in Lodz were forced to leave their homes and move into a **ghetto** in the poorest part of the city. The Goldbergs crammed into a tiny apartment with seven other people. This was the beginning of the nightmare that destroyed the world Rosa had known.

Soldiers took Rosa's mother and many Jews away from their families. Their families never saw them again. Finally, the Germans forced all the Jews in the ghetto onto trains. The trains took them to **death camps**, such as **Auschwitz**. That's where Rosa and her remaining family went. Men and boys were immediately separated from women and girls. Rosa never saw her father or brother again.

Rosa was sure that she, too, would soon be killed. But, days later, German soldiers made a mistake that saved her life. They did not realize that she and the other 499 other women in a field were due to be murdered. The soldiers mistook them for French prisoners, pushed them onto another train car, and shipped them to the German city of Berlin. The women had to work in a factory assembling bombs.

Rosa was later shipped to another death camp at Ravensbrück, Germany. Then the Swedish Red Cross freed the prisoners and helped them get to Sweden to recover.

After Rosa regained her strength, she met and fell in love with another refugee and **Holocaust** survivor, Bernard Katz. He emigrated to the United States first. In 1948, Bernard returned to marry her, and the two made their first home in Statesville, North Carolina. That's where Bernard's relatives had helped him find a job. Five years later, in 1953, Bernard's work brought them to Oshkosh, Wisconsin.

Lodz (Looj)   **Nazi** (**not** zee) Describing the followers of Adolf Hitler who wanted to rid Europe of Jews and other peoples of Europe they considered "impure"
invaded Entered by force   **ghetto** A neighborhood in a European city where Jews were forced to live   **death camps** Places designed to kill many Jewish people at one time
Auschwitz (**oush** vitz)   **Holocaust** (**hol** uh kost) The planned murder of the Jews in Europe in the 1940s in which 6 million Jews, and others, were killed

Rosa Goldberg (second from left) was a 10-year-old Jewish girl when this picture was taken. Here she is with her family in 1934. Less than 10 years later, she was the only one in this photograph who had not been killed during the Holocaust. The Holocaust occurred during World War II. That's when the Nazi German government, led by Adolf Hitler, **systematically** destroyed 6 million European Jews and others.

What was life like for Rosa and her family in Oshkosh?

Rosa found that many things helped make the move to Oshkosh successful. The Katzes' closest friends from Statesville also moved to Oshkosh. Oshkosh had a larger Jewish community. The Katzes joined the synagogue right away. By the time they moved to Oshkosh, Rosa's English had improved. Both she and Bernard spoke only English at home. They wanted their children to fit in with the other children they met at school and in the neighborhood.

Rosa did not share her Holocaust story with her own children as they were growing up. "I wanted them to be well-adjusted, happy little kids," she later said. When Rosa told her story to the oral historian who recorded it for the Wisconsin Historical Society in 1980, Rosa had extra copies made for her grown-up children. "God forbid something like this should happen to anybody, especially my own children. It should never happen again."

In 1994, Rosa took part in a video, *We Must Never Forget: The Story of the Holocaust*, made to be used in classrooms. Her last lines in the video expressed her deepest feelings: "And I just want to point to all of us—how lucky we are to be in a country like America."

In 1979, the Katz family celebrated younger daughter Marilyn's **bat mitzvah** at their **synagogue** in Oshkosh. From left to right, you see Ruthie, Rosa, Marilyn, and son Arthur's wife, Sue. Bernard and Arthur are standing behind them. Rosa said, "We are proud to be Jewish . . . Since I am the only one to survive, I ask, 'Why did I survive?' And then I am blessed with four beautiful children, and I think, that's why I survived . . . I want to pass my religion on."

systematically (sis tuh **mat** ik lee) In a systematic or planned way
bat mitzvah (bot **mits** vuh) In Hebrew, the words mean "Daughter of the Commandment." It's a Jewish ceremony in which a 13-year-old girl assumes responsibility as an adult by learning Hebrew and leading a religious service. The ceremony for boys is called a bar mitzvah.
synagogue (**sin** uh gog) Place of Jewish worship   **tragedies** (**traj** uh deez) Very sad events   **oral historian** A historian who talks to people to research their stories

Bringing Texas North to Wisconsin

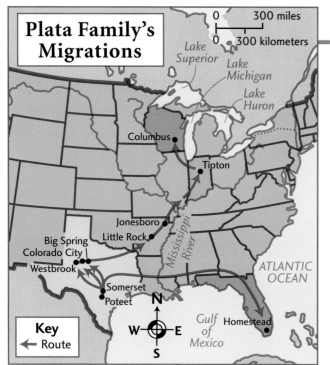

Plata Family's Migrations

Key
← Route

The map shows where the family drove from their home near Poteet, Texas, to places where they harvested crops in different parts of the United States at different seasons.

What brought the Plata family to Wisconsin each spring?

Cris **Plata** is a Mexican American singer-songwriter and musician. He lives with his wife, Ann, on their small farm in Columbia County. Although Cris considered Wisconsin his home once he was a young adult, he spent much of his childhood **migrating** back and forth between Wisconsin and Texas.

Cris was born on a ranch near Poteet, Texas, on November 26, 1954. He is the youngest of three sons. His mother was from the nearby city of San Antonio. Cris's family lived in the basement in the same house with his aunt and her family. The two families managed the **livestock** and took care of the ranch for the owners.

Cris's father was a skilled mechanic who was born in Mexico. He gave his children a choice between going to school or helping the family. When Cris got old enough to see how hard his parents and older brothers worked in the fields, he decided to go to school. Cris said that before he started first grade in western Texas, "My brothers taught me the ABC's, and how to say my name, and the year and month that I was born, and that was all the English I knew." Cris learned easily because he wanted to speak like the other children in his class. But it was hard changing schools so many times during the year.

For most of Cris's childhood, he and his family were **migrant workers**. Cris's family began migrating to Wisconsin when he was 11. His dad found work driving a pea **combine** in Astico, near Columbus. Every year they arrived in April and left in October. Cris found education better in Columbus, so he would get ahead in Wisconsin, then stay ahead when he went back to school in Texas the following October.

Plata (plah tuh)   **migrating** Moving from one region of the country to another   **livestock** Farm animals
migrant workers People who move from place to place to help harvest crops   **combine** (kom bIn) A machine on a farm, driven by a person, to harvest crops

This cover of Cris's 2003 CD, *Life Is Hard*, shows him at age six with his BB gun in western Texas where the Platas spent the winter months. They were part of a large number of Mexican Americans who migrated there to pick cotton at the height of the harvest. Cris's nickname was **Chato**, which means "chubby cheeks" in Spanish. Can you tell why?

Cris and his band performed at **Fiesta Hispana** in Madison in the early 1990s.

Why did Cris make Wisconsin home?

Music was always important to the Plata family. Cris's father and brothers all played guitar, mandolin, and accordion. His mother was a singer who taught everyone else to sing. The radio up north had no Spanish stations, so migrant workers made music themselves in the evenings. Tex-Mex music making was like bringing "a little piece of home with you," Cris said.

After he graduated from high school in Somerset, Texas, Cris went to St. Edward's College in Austin. The city was then a growing center for folk and country music. He felt more drawn to photography and the music written and performed by local musicians than to his studies. He began writing songs and playing music with groups of musician friends. Cris wanted his music to capture the same feelings for Texas that he tried to capture in photographs. For the next few years, he worked, studied photography, and developed his skills as a singer-songwriter in Austin and Dallas.

In 1976, Cris returned to Wisconsin and met his future wife, Ann. Ann grew up on her family's century-old German American farm near Columbus. It was not far from where Cris's family was doing migrant work. They married the next year and moved to Minneapolis for Ann to attend **veterinary** school.

Cris began to play music full-time. But he got tired of being on the road. It was too much like being a migrant worker. In 1980, Ann graduated and began working in Minnesota. Then, she found a job working with a **veterinarian** she knew in the Madison area. The Platas happily moved back. They bought a small house and an acre and a half of land of her family's farm. They bought horses and grew vegetables. Cris's own songs now included Mexican American stories, first in English and then in Spanish as well.

Cris found work that allowed him time to balance music and the life he and Ann enjoyed in the country. His parking and security job in Madison allows him to have enough time to stay connected to the land. Because he had constantly traveled as a child and young man, he loves living on the farm. The Platas make their own **salsa** from their own peppers, onions, and tomatoes. In caring for his horses and land, in his food, and in his music, Cris enjoys working "to bring Texas to Wisconsin."

Chato (**chah** to)　**Fiesta Hispana** (fee **es** tah ees **pah** nah)　**veterinary** (**vet** ur uh nair ee) Having to do with animal medicine or surgery
veterinarian (**vet** ur uh nair ee uhn) A doctor who treats animals　**salsa** (**sahl** sah)

Mai Ya's Long Journey from Thailand to Wisconsin

Mai Ya is wearing a traditional Hmong dress and turban at a Hmong New Year celebration in Madison, Wisconsin.

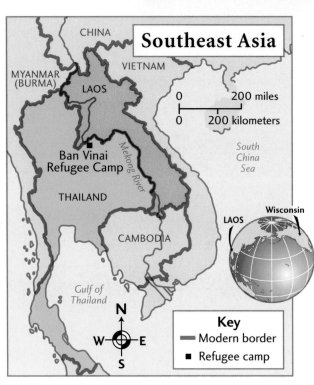

Like many Hmong people, Mai Ya's parents lived in a quiet mountain village in **Laos** before the Vietnam War became a turning point in their lives.

Why did Mai Ya and her family live in a refugee camp in Thailand?

Mai Ya Xiong and her family are Hmong. In 1979, her mother and her father had escaped from their home in **Laos**. They made their way to Thailand on foot. Mai Ya was born there the following year in a refugee camp called **Ban Vinai**. Most of the people in the refugee camp were also Hmong. They had also escaped from their villages in Laos. Life had become too dangerous to keep living there.

In the 1960s, the United States had entered into a war to help the people of South Vietnam. The government asked and then trained young Hmong men to form a secret army. Mai Ya's father was part of that army. But the United States was unsuccessful. In 1973, U.S. troops left Vietnam. Two years later, North Vietnam won the war. Then, Hmong families were in danger from enemy troops. Many of the Hmong families, like Mai Ya's, had to hide in the forests and jungles. They had to move every few days so the soldiers would not catch them. Finally, they crossed the Mekong River to Thailand. They found safety at Ban Vinai.

Mai Ya Xiong (mI yah shong)   **Laos** (lah ohs)   **Thailand** (tI land)
refugee camp A safe place for people forced to leave their homes by war or disaster   **Ban Vinai** (ban vin I)

When Mai Ya came to Wisconsin, she had two younger brothers and two younger sisters. They were all born in the refugee camp in Thailand.

To move to the United States, Hmong people needed a **sponsor**. Mai Ya's uncle was her family's sponsor.

CHILD SPONSORSHIP CARD
I.D. No. 23637
Name MAI YA XIONG   F
Birthdate MAY 22, 1980
Age 4   House No. 7,3,12,4
Came from Laos
Camp Ban Vinai (Loei)
Remarks: Hmong hill tribe from Laos.
Date MAR 1984
INTERNATIONAL CHRISTIAN AID THAILAND

What was life like for Mai Ya in Wisconsin?

In 1987, Mai Ya was seven years old. That's when her family finally was allowed to leave the refugee camp. They came to live in Madison. They traveled in a large airplane. At first the family of seven shared their uncle's apartment. For the first time, they had their own running water, a stove, and a refrigerator. It was very different from the mountain village in Laos or the crowded space they shared in the refugee camp. The weather in Wisconsin was also different from the weather in Thailand. Mai Ya and her brothers and sisters had never seen snow before!

Mai Ya and her parents didn't know how to read or write English when they arrived. Mai Ya started second grade. She took English as a Second Language class to help her understand what her teachers and classmates were saying. By the time she was in seventh grade, she was comfortable speaking in class and with her friends. Yet at home, she and her family spoke only in Hmong. Sometimes it was hard for Mai Ya to go back and forth between the English-speaking and Hmong worlds.

In 1998, 11 years after arriving in Madison, Mai Ya graduated from high school. Then in 2004, she graduated from the University of Wisconsin–Milwaukee. There she studied business and marketing. But she also taught young Hmong-American girls the traditional Hmong dances. She has learned how to build a new life in a new country. Yet she still holds on to her Hmong language and to some of her Hmong customs that she loves. You can read more details about her life and family in *Mai Ya's Long Journey* by Sheila Cohen.

Mai Ya's youngest brother, Andrew, was born in Madison. She helped him learn the English language. She also told him about growing up in Thailand. Part of her Hmong heritage means being connected to her family.

As a university student, Mai Ya said, "I am proud to be Hmong. And what would be lost if we don't preserve some of our traditions? We will eventually lose who we are. That would be a big loss."

sponsor A person, people, or organization that agrees to help refugees who enter the country

Looking Back at Immigration and Settlement in Wisconsin

→ PUSH FACTORS	PULL FACTORS ↗
Too many people living in one place to make a decent living	Good, affordable farmland to support a family
Not enough jobs or not enough food	Better-paying jobs and plenty of food
Other relatives and friends have already left and found some success elsewhere	Letters from family and friends who have moved
People must follow only certain religious faiths	People can follow any religious faith
Not all people are treated fairly	People are treated equally
War	Peace
Natural disaster	Better place to start over

This chart shows some of the reasons that people feel pushed from their homelands and pulled to new opportunities in another country.

This photo shows Cris Plata's father, Crístobal Sr., as a young man. He is standing next to his mother, Luisa. They are at the entrance to their home made of stones and soil in the mountains of the state of **Jalisco** in central Mexico.

What have you learned about why people immigrated and migrated to Wisconsin?

In this chapter, you have read seven different immigration and migration stories of families who came to live in Wisconsin. They each traveled from different places and at different times in history. And they each settled in different parts of Wisconsin. Their journey stories span 138 years—between 1842 and 1987. That's a very long time. Many things in Wisconsin and in the world changed during those years. But people's desires to make their lives, and the lives of their families, better have not changed.

Some of the people in these stories journeyed to Wisconsin as adults alone. Some were married. Some brought their entire families. Others came as children. Although they came at different times, for different reasons, all faced challenges and struggles. In what ways are their stories similar? How are they different? What have you learned about the push and pull **factors** of immigration and migration from these stories? Do you have new questions about your own family's story? Or are you someone who has made the journey to Wisconsin yourself?

Jalisco (hah **lees** ko)   **factors** Any one of the causes that helps bring about a result

How do people make a new life in a new place?

When you go on a trip, do you take something along that reminds you of home? Perhaps you pack one of your favorite books, games, or stuffed animals to keep you from feeling homesick. When immigrants and migrants leave their homelands to move to a new place, they often take things along. These belongings remind them who they are and where they've come from. These things include china, photographs, tools, and religious objects that hold special meaning for them.

Newcomers also bring along things like traditions and ideas that they can't pack in a suitcase. All the people in the stories in this chapter found ways to keep some of their own traditions as they built new lives. For example, when Friedrich Koepsell came to Kirchhayn from Pomerania, he built his family a new house in a new land. But he built this house the way the houses were built back home in Pomerania. He did this to help his family feel at home in a strange place, and to help remind them of their homeland.

What are some other ways people keep traditions they value? What stories does your family tell to remind you of where you came from? What holidays do you celebrate? What special foods do you eat to honor your traditions?

These are the **Stoughton** High School Norwegian Dancers. They celebrate their Norwegian American heritage by dancing traditional folk dances and wearing traditional dance clothing.

Stoughton (stoh tuhn)

Some Places to Visit

- Chippewa Valley Museum in Eau Claire
- Jewish Museum in Milwaukee
- Neville Public Museum in Green Bay
- Old World Wisconsin Historic Site in Eagle
- Pendarvis Historic Site in Mineral Point
- Wisconsin Black Historical Society in Milwaukee
- Wisconsin Historical Museum in Madison

Some Things to Read

- *Casper Jaggi: Master Swiss Cheese Maker* by Jerry Apps
- *Caroline Quarlls and the Underground Railroad* by Julia Pferdehirt
- *Mai Ya's Long Journey* by Sheila Cohen
- *Native People of Wisconsin* by Patty Loew Chapters 5–8
- *A Recipe for Success: Lizzie Kander and Her Cookbook* by Bob Kann
- *They Came to Wisconsin* by Julia Pferdehirt

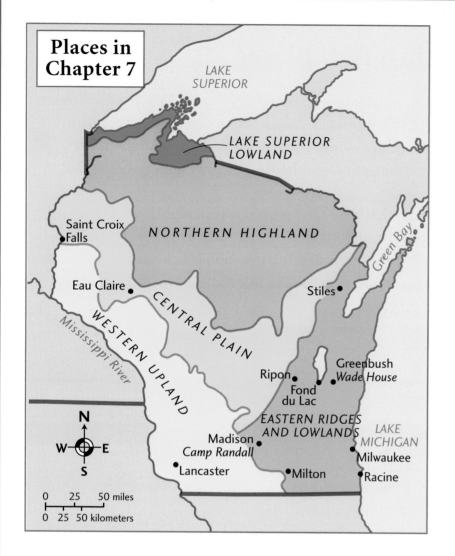

Places in Chapter 7

LAKE SUPERIOR

LAKE SUPERIOR LOWLAND

Saint Croix Falls

NORTHERN HIGHLAND

Green Bay

Eau Claire

CENTRAL PLAIN

Stiles

WESTERN UPLAND

Mississippi River

Ripon

Greenbush
Wade House

Fond du Lac

EASTERN RIDGES AND LOWLANDS

LAKE MICHIGAN

Madison
Camp Randall

Lancaster

Milton

Milwaukee

Racine

N W E S

0 25 50 miles
0 25 50 kilometers

1840

1845

1850

▲
1844
Milton House built

▲
1848
Wisconsin statehood

▲
1850 Fugitive Slave Act

Key Words

- abolitionists
- brigade
- Civil War
- Confederacy
- fugitive slave
- orphans
- recruiting
- secede
- Underground Railroad
- Union

Thinking Like a Historian

 How did many people living in Wisconsin in the mid-1800s view slavery and the South?

 What effect did Joshua Glover and the Fugitive Slave Act have on Wisconsin?

 How did the Civil War affect those who stayed in Wisconsin?

 What was life like for a Wisconsin soldier in the Civil War?

How did the outcome of the Civil War affect Wisconsin and the United States?

Timeline

1855

1860

1865

1854
Joshua Glover escapes to Canada
Republican Party formed at Ripon

1861
Civil War begins

Camp Randall acreage donated and first used to train Union soldiers

1862
Governor Harvey dies

1863
Iron Brigade fights at Gettysburg

Harvey Hospital built in Madison

1865
Civil War ends

Lucius Fairchild first elected Wisconsin governor

1866 Harvey Hospital becomes Wisconsin Soldiers Orphans Home

Free States, Slave States, and Fugitive Slaves

In this chapter, you'll find out more about slavery and freedom and how and why Wisconsin got involved in the Civil War. You'll have a chance to think about the way that war changed the lives of those who left Wisconsin to fight in battles and those who stayed in Wisconsin to help on the home front.

From this map you can see that the Free States are in the North or West and the slave states are in the South. Remember John Greene in Chapter 6? He and his family escaped slavery in Missouri to make their new home at Pleasant Ridge, Wisconsin.

How did slavery divide the North and the South in the mid 1800s?

In 1848 when Wisconsin became a state, it entered the United States as one of the Free States. Look at the map on this page. In the mid-1800s, the United States was a nation divided over the question of slavery. In 1850, California was ready to enter the Union as a Free State.

California would be the first Free State outside of the North. Many people in the North were glad to see another Free State. Most Southerners were not.

Geography explains some of this difference. All of the Slave States were in the South. The South has a longer growing season than the North, so Southerners could cultivate cotton—the South's biggest crop. Many of those who worked cotton fields were African American slaves, who were not paid for their work. Most slave owners believed that they couldn't make money without slave labor.

As the farming of cotton spread across the South, more and more slaves were needed to work in the fields. Southerners wanted to make sure that both slavery and cotton could move west as the country expanded. That's why the South was worried about California entering the nation as a Free State.

Some people in Wisconsin and other states in the North felt that slavery was wrong. They believed that all people should be free to work and live as they wished. In addition, cotton was not grown in the North, and fewer African Americans lived in the region. The question of slavery was pushing the North and the South further apart.

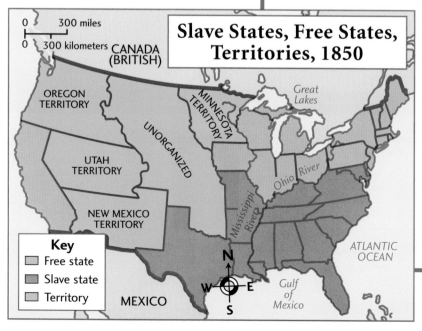

Slave States, Free States, Territories, 1850

0 — 300 miles
0 — 300 kilometers

CANADA (BRITISH)
OREGON TERRITORY
MINNESOTA TERRITORY
Great Lakes
UTAH TERRITORY
UNORGANIZED
NEW MEXICO TERRITORY
Ohio River
Mississippi River
ATLANTIC OCEAN
Gulf of Mexico
MEXICO

Key
- Free state
- Slave state
- Territory

N W E S

Civil War The war between the North and South of the United States, which took place between 1861 and 1865; **civil war** is a war between two groups of people in the same country   **labor** Work

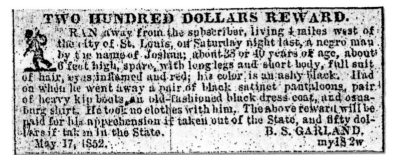

TWO HUNDRED DOLLARS REWARD.

RAN away from the subscriber, living 4 miles west of the city of St. Louis, on Saturday night last, a negro man by the name of Joshua; about 35 or 40 years of age, about 6 feet high, spare, with long legs and short body, full suit of hair, eyes inflamed and red; his color is an ashy black. Had on when he went away a pair of black satinet pantaloons, pair of heavy kip boots, an old-fashioned black dress coat, and osnaburg shirt. He took no clothes with him. The above reward will be paid for his apprehension if taken out of the State, and fifty dollars if taken in the State.   B. S. GARLAND.

May 17, 1852.   my18 2w

This is a copy of a reward notice for the return of Joshua Glover, **fugitive slave**. The notice ran in a Missouri newspaper for two weeks in 1852 after Joshua Glover escaped from his owner, Benammi Garland. Glover made his way secretly to Wisconsin, but he was not safe anywhere in the North. When you read about the Fugitive Slave Act, you'll find out why.

This drawing is the only known image of Joshua Glover. He was about 38 years old when he escaped slavery and made his way north as a fugitive slave.

How did the Fugitive Slave Act affect Wisconsin?

Slavery went against one of the best ideas on which the United States was founded: freedom for all people. Some slaves risked their lives to escape slavery because they really wanted to be free. They ran away from their Southern owners and escaped to the Northern states. These **fugitive slaves** often had help from people who gave them food and shelter on their flights to freedom and new lives.

Lawmakers in a democracy must **compromise** to create laws that all people will follow. Congress created the **Compromise of 1850** to meet the needs of both Northerners and Southerners on the issue of slavery.

The part of this law that caused real trouble and served as a turning point in U.S. and Wisconsin history was the **Fugitive Slave Act.** It required all citizens—North and South—to help return fugitive slaves to their owners. This law made many people in Wisconsin and other free states furious. The country became even more bitterly divided.

Many Southerners thought of slaves only as property that could be bought and sold. When slaves escaped to freedom in the North, Southerners wanted their property back. The Fugitive Slave Act made it a crime for any citizen to help or to hide a slave. This law caused many people who were against the idea of slavery to become **abolitionists**—people ready to fight to **abolish** slavery. Many people in Wisconsin did not became abolitionists. But you'll read about famous Wisconsin abolitionist Sherman Booth and learn more about Joshua Glover on the next page.

fugitive (fyoo juh tiv) **slave** Person escaping from slavery to gain freedom
compromise (kom pruh mIze) To agree to accept a solution to a disagreement that is not exactly what any side wanted
Compromise of 1850 The law passed by Congess that had several parts: First, California could enter the Union as a Free State. Second, New Mexico, Arizona, Nevada, and Utah became territories—neither slave nor free. Third, slaves could no longer be bought and sold in Washington, D.C., the nation's capital. Finally, the Fugitive Slave Act was passed.
Fugitive Slave Act A federal law passed in 1850 that required that all citizens to help return fugitive slaves to their owners
abolitionists (ab uh **lish** uh nists) People working to end slavery before the Civil War   **abolish** (uh **bol** ish) To put an end to something officially or legally

Abolitionists in Wisconsin

How did abolitionists and the Underground Railroad help Joshua Glover?

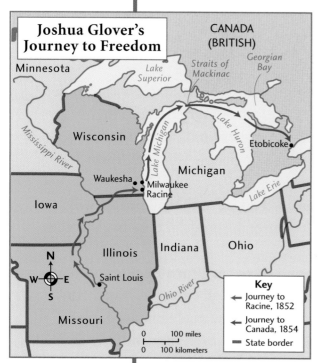

Joshua Glover's Journey to Freedom

Key
← Journey to Racine, 1852
← Journey to Canada, 1854
— State border

Joshua Glover traveled many miles by land and water, and from south to north, to reach freedom.

On page 125 you saw the notice that Joshua Glover's owner, Benammi Garland, placed in a newspaper. In May 1852, slave Joshua Glover managed to escape from Garland's Missouri farm. Most likely he got help from people along the **Underground Railroad (UGRR)**. The UGRR was not a railroad at all but a network of abolitionists—both black and white people—who helped fugitive slaves escape to freedom. Kind UGRR workers would have helped Joshua Glover find his way north to Racine, Wisconsin, which was more than 350 miles from Missouri. Folks from the UGRR would have known that Racine had many abolitionists who also could help fugitive slaves begin a new life.

Joshua Glover lived and worked in Racine as a free man for nearly two years. But the Fugitive Slave Act meant that he could still be returned to his owner—if his owner could find him. One night in early March 1854, Garland and two other men entered Glover's home and captured him. They knew that many citizens in Racine would be angry if Glover were jailed there. Instead, they took him by wagon to a jail in Milwaukee. Garland wanted to keep Glover locked up until the trip back to Missouri could be planned.

News of Glover's capture traveled fast. Abolitionists made plans to free Glover. Sherman Booth gave a powerful speech to a crowd of abolitionists, including many from Racine who joined those in Milwaukee. They surrounded the jail, broke down its doors, and rescued Glover.

For many weeks, abolitionists secretly moved Glover around southeastern Wisconsin to keep him safe. Finally, they returned him to Racine. Once there, they successfully placed him on a Lake Michigan steamboat headed to Canada. Joshua Glover lived the rest of his life in Etobicoke, Canada, as a free man.

Underground Railroad (UGRR) Not a railroad at all but a network of abolitionists who helped fugitive slaves find their way to free states or to Canada before the Civil War

How was the Republican Party formed in Ripon?

Joshua Glover's escape to freedom wasn't the only news in Wisconsin in March 1854. That very month abolitionists and others in Wisconsin opposed to slavery decided to form a new **political party**. These men felt that no political party in the United States was taking a strong enough stand against slavery. In 1854, a group of Ripon citizens gathered in a little schoolhouse to organize what they called the "Republican" political party. That's how Ripon became the birthplace of the Republican Party.

Meanwhile, similar groups of **anti**slavery people met elsewhere and declared themselves to be Republicans. Two years later, the Republicans supported their first candidate for president, but he lost. In 1860, the Republicans nominated Abraham Lincoln for president, and he won. But Lincoln won only in the Free States. Very few voters in the Slave States voted for Lincoln. His election showed that the country was in deep trouble. The Civil War was about to begin.

EASTERN RIDGES AND LOWLANDS

• Ripon

BIRTHPLACE
-:- OF THE -:-
REPUBLICAN PARTY
In this School House March 20th 1854 was held the first Mass Meeting in this country that definitely and positively cut loose from old parties and advocated a new party under the name Republican.

Today we celebrate the importance of the Ripon schoolhouse with this historical marker.

You can still visit the little schoolhouse in Ripon where the Republican Party was formed in 1854.

This letter from Wisconsin Republican Horace Rublee to Abraham Lincoln invited Lincoln to attend the state Republican convention of 1860. This was the year that Lincoln was first elected president.

Madison (Wis) Feb. 13. '60

Hon. Abram Lincoln
*Dear Sirs - The Wiscon-
sin Republican State Convention
to choose delegates to Chicago, meets
in this city on Wednesday the 29th
inst., & I have been instructed,
by the Central Committee, to invite
you to be present, & some time
during your stay, to address
the People upon political
matters.*
I sincerely trust that

political party A group of people organized to win elections and to gain politcal power
anti Against

The Civil War Comes to Wisconsin

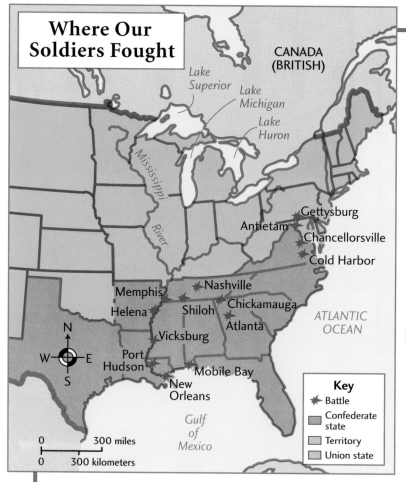

Where Our Soldiers Fought

CANADA (BRITISH)

Lake Superior
Lake Michigan
Lake Huron

Mississippi River

Gettysburg
Antietam
Chancellorsville
Cold Harbor
Nashville
Memphis
Helena
Shiloh
Chickamauga
Atlanta
Vicksburg
Port Hudson
New Orleans
Mobile Bay

ATLANTIC OCEAN

Gulf of Mexico

N
W E
S

0   300 miles
0   300 kilometers

Key
★ Battle
▪ Confederate state
▪ Territory
▪ Union state

How did the Civil War begin?

Abraham Lincoln's election as president of the United States in the fall of 1860 greatly upset Southerners. They knew that he was against slavery expanding to the western territories. They worried about the future of slavery. They worried about keeping their way of life. Beginning with South Carolina, some Southern states decided that they should **secede** from the federal government, often called the Union. These Southern states felt that they had a right to withdraw from the **Union** and form their own government. They called their government the **Confederacy**.

Lincoln and most Northerners disagreed with the South. Slavery had divided the country. But the president and those who supported him believed that, to be strong and survive as a nation, the United States could not be divided. Wisconsin's governor, Alexander Randall, stated, "A state cannot come in the Union as it pleases and go out when it pleases." So, the Civil War actually began over the question of **secession**. Did any states have the right to leave the United States of America and form their own government?

Lincoln's term as president began in March 1861. The very next month, the first shots were fired between the North and the South. The Civil War had begun. More Southern states joined the Confederacy, but four border Slave States decided to remain in the Union. These were Missouri, Kentucky, Maryland, and Delaware.

The North had more states, more people, and more industry than the South. The Union expected a quick victory. But the Civil War lasted four years, and it was long, bloody, and terrible for everyone—those who fought and those who remained at home in Wisconsin and elsewhere.

secede (si **seed**) To withdraw or leave one organization, often to form another   **Union** The United States of America
Confederacy (kun **fed** ur uh see) The government of the 11 Southern states that fought the Northern states in the American Civil War
secession (si **sesh** uhn) Withdrawal from or leaving from one organization, often to form another

In this drawing by artist Louis Kurz, Civil War soldiers are marching at Camp Randall in Madison along what is now University Avenue. More than 70,000 troops were trained and got ready to fight at Camp Randall during the Civil War.

Soldier John Cronk with the 16th Wisconsin **Regiment** wrote this letter. He described details of life at Camp Randall. He told his friend that they ate "bread, beef, pork, potatoes, rice, sugar, beans, syrup and butter four or five times a week . . . We have plenty of food here some times and not much at others."

How did Wisconsin get ready for war?

President Lincoln called for **troops** from all the Union states. Each state already had organized militia companies. But very few of these companies had any experience with actual fighting. Governor Randall asked the state legislature for funds to buy weapons and other equipment that these soldiers would need. He immediately called for other men to volunteer to fight. Many men volunteered.

Governor Randall understood that, in order to fight, men needed to be trained. He said, "The men sent to war should be soldiers when they go, or there will be few of them living soldiers when it is time for them to return." Then the state government created the largest training area in the state for soldiers at Camp Randall. The land lay just west of Madison. About 70,000 men trained where the University of Wisconsin–Madison football stadium stands today. Other soldiers trained at Fond du Lac, Milwaukee, and Racine.

Soldiers were organized into companies. There are 10 companies of 100 men in a **regiment.** Much of the time, they had to **drill** for seven hours a day. Although it was often boring to learn to follow orders and to practice marching or firing a rifle, it was important. Soldiers needed to know how to instantly obey orders if they were to survive in battle. More than 80,000 Wisconsin soldiers served, but more than 12,000 did not return. Some died in battle, and others died from disease or wounds.

Regiment (**rej** uh muhnt) Part of the army (1000 soldiers) under the command of a **colonel** (**kur** nuhl)
troops Soldiers
drill To teach by having the learner practice something by doing it over and over again; to learn by doing something over and over again

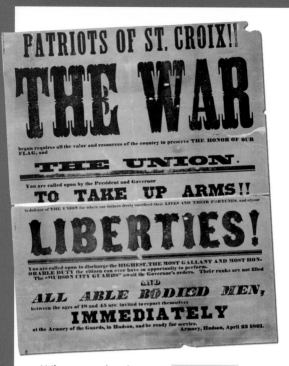

When war broke out, **recruiting** posters like this one went up all over Wisconsin. This poster calls for the patriots of St. Croix to take up arms, that is, to join the army and serve in the war.

When African American men were finally accepted as soldiers, many from Wisconsin served in the 29th Regiment. African Americans had to serve in **segregated** "colored" troops such as **Company** "F."

COMPANY "F," TWENTY-NINTH REGT. U. S. COLORED TROOPS.

NAME.	RESIDENCE.	DATE.	REMARKS.
Adams, John	Sun Prairie	May 9, '64	
Allen, Charles	Carlton	Apr. 22, '64	
Allen, Judson	Milwaukee	Feb. 11, '64	
Allen, Jefferson	Milwaukee	Feb. 11, '64	
Briggs, John	Wheeling, Ill	Mar. 28, '64	
Brown, Felix	Milwaukee	Dec. 21, '63	
Bryon, Lloyd T	Mequon	Mar. 31, '64	Sergt.
Calder, Benjamin			

Those from Wisconsin Who Fought

Who were the soldiers?

When war broke out, both Northerners and Southerners were full of enthusiasm and patriotism. Many men volunteered to fight, even more than President Lincoln at first requested. Men ages 18 to 40 could serve. Farmers, miners, workers, and students from communities throughout the state **enlisted.** Most soldiers were about 20 years old and came from **rural** areas. Often regiments were organized from particular communities, as you can see on the poster recruiting men from St. Croix on your left. The members of one regiment from northern Wisconsin were all lumbermen. When they arrived at Camp Randall, they looked like they were ready to chop down trees. No one then would have guessed that they'd become first-rate soldiers.

When the Civil War broke out, African American and American Indian men in the North volunteered to fight. At the time, however, the federal government accepted only white men as soldiers. But as the war dragged on, and thousands were wounded and killed, fewer volunteered to go. That's when real recruitment began. And finally, the federal government agreed to enlist African Americans and Indians.

These men from Wisconsin Indian nations enlisted as Union soldiers.

recruiting (ree **kroo** ting) Getting people to join the military
segregated (**seg** ruh gay tuhd) Separated or kept apart from the main group
company (**kuhm** puh nee) Group of soldiers
enlisted (en **lis** tuhd) Joined the military
rural (**rur** uhl) Having to do with the countryside or farming

Why is there a statue of Colonel Hans Christian Heg at the state capitol?

You learned in Chapter 6 that many Europeans had immigrated to Wisconsin in the decades before the Civil War. Governor Randall thought it would be good if different immigrant groups formed their own regiments. He called for the 9th Wisconsin Regiment to be recruited from German men and the 17th from Irish men. He appointed Hans Christian Heg as a **colonel** and asked him to recruit Norwegian and other **Scandinavian** men to form the 15th Wisconsin Regiment. Colonel Heg was born in Norway and immigrated with his family when he was 11. The Hegs lived in rural Racine County where many other Norwegian families had made their homes.

Colonel Heg was a strong abolitionist and a member of the Republican Party. He recruited men through the Norwegian-language newspaper. He appealed to the immigrants' love of freedom and explained that enlisting to fight would create "proud memories for the future."

The 15th Regiment that he led became known as the "Fighting 15th." The Fighting 15th trained 16 days at Camp Randall before going off to battles in Missouri, Kentucky, Tennessee, Mississippi, Alabama, and Georgia. Colonel Heg proved to be a great leader. The men of the Fighting 15th were fierce fighters, but they lost many members. War wounds and disease killed one-third of the regiment.

The Battle of Chickamauga in northern Georgia was one of the bloodiest battles of the war. The Fighting 15th had hundreds of men when the battle began, and only 75 when it was over. Colonel Heg himself died. He is buried in the Norway Lutheran Church Cemetery in Norway, Racine County.

You'll see this statue of Colonel Hans Christian Heg when you visit the state capitol in Madison. The statue honors him as a brave military leader.

Peter Thomas was an escaped slave. He served with the Fighting 15th. Then he joined the 18th U.S. Colored Infantry. After the war, he moved to Wisconsin and lived in Beloit and Racine County.

colonel (**kur** nuhl) An officer in the military, just below a general
Scandinavian (skan dih **nay** vee uhn) Someone born in one of the following Northern European countries: Sweden, Norway, Denmark, or Finland

Wisconsin Goes to War: Two Stories

After the Civil War, Old Abe was still quite a show-off. He loved being the center of attention in crowds. When people cheered, he would spread his wings as he is doing here.

Old Abe traveled as a mascot of the 8th Wisconsin Regiment. The regiment fought in battles in the western part of the South. On the map, you can see the states where these battles took place.

Old Abe's Travels

Madison

Chicago

Saint Louis

Ohio River

Frederickston

Cairo

Memphis

Pittsburg Landing

Corinth

Vicksburg

Mississippi River

N
W — E
S

Gulf of Mexico

| 0 | 300 miles |
| 0 | 300 kilometers |

Key
* Battle
■ Confederate state
■ Territory
■ Union state

What made Old Abe the War Eagle so famous?

In 1861, an **eaglet** was captured by Chief Sky, a member of the Ojibwe Nation. Dan and Margaret McCann traded some corn to Chief Sky and got the eaglet as part of the exchange. The McCanns treated the eaglet like a pet.

When the Civil War began later that year, Dan McCann thought that the eaglet would make a good **mascot** for soldiers forming into companies in northwestern Wisconsin not far from the McCann home on the Chippewa River. He found a willing group, Company C, in Eau Claire. Somewhere between Eau Claire and Camp Randall, the company named themselves the Eau Claire Eagles. The company's captain named the eaglet Old Abe, and he became the most famous Civil War mascot.

Old Abe and Company C marched into Camp Randall to the tune of "Yankee Doodle." When they passed in front of Governor Randall, Old Abe grabbed the company's flag with his beak. He flapped his wings and became the center of attention. People immediately thought of Old Abe as a symbol of good luck.

After Company C trained and became part of the 8th Wisconsin or the Eagle Regiment, Old Abe stayed with the soldiers as the regiment fought in 37 battles. Neither Old Abe nor any of the soldiers who carried the **standard** on which he traveled was injured in battle. Such good fortune added to Old Abe's being a symbol of the Union for which they were fighting.

When the Civil War ended, the State of Wisconsin took over the care of Old Abe. He lived in a two-room apartment in the basement of the state capitol and was fed fresh rabbits. He had many visitors and loved to perform and stretch his wings for them.

eaglet A baby eagle
mascot Something that is supposed to bring good luck, especially an animal kept by a military group or sports team
standard The banner, symbol, or flag of a military group or nation

Rufus Andrews was a family man. He missed his wife and children greatly when he was serving in the Union army.

What makes Rufus Andrews's story so different from that of Colonel Heg or Old Abe?

Rufus Andrews was not a famous military leader like Colonel Heg or a symbol of the Union like Old Abe. But his story is typical of many men who served in the Civil War. We know about his life in the army from the diary he kept and from the loving letters he wrote home.

When the Civil War began, Rufus Andrews was 33 years old. He lived in Stiles in Oconto County with his wife, Agnes, and their children: Florence, Almira, and John. Rufus Andrews was a farmer and lumberman in business with his wife's father. He did not volunteer to join the army.

When Agnes' brother decided to volunteer in the Union army, her father became very upset. He worried that his son would be injured or killed in battle. Rufus Andrews then offered to go in place of his wife's brother. He joined the 4th Wisconsin Volunteers in October 1861, because he loved his family. He did not want his wife's father to be unhappy.

Rufus Andrews served in Maryland and Virginia. He spent time in the hospital in Baltimore and in Alexandria because he got sick. Medicine was not very advanced at the time, and many soldiers died from diseases. Rufus Andrews recovered and traveled to Louisiana. There he fought and died in June 1863. While Colonel Heg was a leader whose statue stands at the state capitol, most soldiers who died were remembered only by their families and their communities.

EASTERN RIDGES AND LOWLANDS

Stiles

[handwritten letter:] to get this off ... time to write much: but I will write again in two or three days. Kiss each other for me. My love to you all. Hoping this will find you all well I remain your loving Husband. Continue to write often. Good Bye my Dear for this time

Rufus

What details in this letter home tell how much Rufus Andrews missed his family?

Wisconsin Goes to War: Lives Changed

In this photograph of Cordelia Harvey, you see a woman who worked hard to solve problems facing wounded soldiers and **orphans**.

Thanks to Cordelia Harvey's work, this mansion in Madison became the Harvey United States Army General Hospital during the Civil War. When this photograph was taken after the war, the hospital had become the Soldiers Orphans Home. Once again, Cordelia Harvey had acted to help the sick and the homeless.

Why was Cordelia Harvey known as the "Wisconsin Angel?"

When the Civil War began, Alexander Randall was governor. **Cordelia Perrine** Harvey was the wife of Wisconsin's next governor Louis P. Harvey. In the spring of 1862, Governor Harvey went to the South to see that sick and wounded Wisconsin soldiers were getting the care they needed. While he was stepping from one steamboat to another at Pittsburg Landing, Tennessee, his foot slipped, and he drowned in the Tennessee River. Cordelia Harvey was suddenly a young **widow**.

Cordelia Harvey decided to carry on her husband's work. She visited Southern hospitals for soldiers in cities along the Mississippi River. She was very upset about the lack of good care for soldiers. She felt that Wisconsin soldiers would recover more quickly in hospitals closer to their homes.

Cordelia Harvey collected 8,000 signatures from Wisconsin citizens who supported her idea. She took her **petition** to Washington, D.C. There she met with President Abraham Lincoln and convinced him to set up such hospitals. The Harvey United States Army General Hospital was the first hospital, and it opened in Madison in 1863. It was named in memory of Governor Louis P. Harvey. Two other hospitals opened in Wisconsin—in Prairie du Chien and Milwaukee.

After the war, Cordelia Harvey returned to Madison from the South with six war orphans. She worked to turn the hospital into the Soldiers Orphans Home for children whose fathers had been soldiers killed during the war. At one time, 300 children lived there. You can see why people remember Cordelia Harvey as "Wisconsin Angel."

This wooden peg leg in the collection of the Wisconsin Veterans Museum belonged to a Civil War soldier who lost a leg in battle.

orphans (**or** fuhnz) Children whose parents are dead
Cordelia Perrine (kor **deel** yuh puh **reen**)
widow A woman whose husband has died   **petition** (puh **tish** uhn) A letter that many people sign to express their feelings about an issue or to ask those in power to change something

How did the Civil War change the life of Lucius Fairchild?

Lucius Fairchild was a 30-year-old lawyer in Madison when the Civil War began. He volunteered to fight and became a member of the 2nd Wisconsin Regiment. His Regiment, along with the 6th and 7th Wisconsin, the 19th Indiana, and later, the 24th Michigan, became known as the Iron **Brigade**. This brigade had 5000 officers and men, and all came from what were then Western states: Wisconsin, Michigan, Indiana, and Iowa. They were known as tough fighters, perhaps the toughest of all the Civil War brigades. Like Hans Christian Heg, Lucius Fairchild showed skills that earned him the rank of colonel in the army.

Because the members of the Iron Brigade were such hard fighters, they also suffered more losses than any other brigade. At the battle of Gettysburg, Colonel Fairchild commanded the 2nd Wisconsin. His left arm was so severely wounded that it had to be **amputated** below the elbow. From then on, his shirts and jackets had an empty sleeve, once filled by his left arm.

But Lucius Fairchild's injury did not stop him from being a leader. People immediately saw his empty sleeve as the sign of a brave Union **veteran** who had served his country well. Returning to Wisconsin, Fairchild was first elected as Secretary of State and then, in 1865, he was elected governor. He served three terms in a row, working hard to help veterans. Lucius Fairchild also served as the national leader of the Grand Army of the Republic, an organization that helped the nation's Union veterans. The Civil War truly shaped the leader he became.

This photograph of Fairchild was taken before the Battle of Gettysburg.

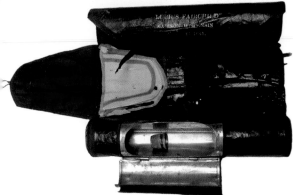

This comfort-bag or "housewife" belonged to Lucius Fairchild. Each housewife held small items—such as needles, pins, thread, and buttons—that soldiers needed to repair their uniforms. Women often made them for family members or other soldiers.

This vest was part of the uniform that Colonel Lucius Fairchild was wearing when his left arm was shattered during the bloody battle of Gettysburg.

Lucius (loo shuhs)   **Brigade** (bri **gayd**) A large military unit, made up of several regiments
amputated (**am** pyuh tay tuhd) Cut off all or part of a finger, arm, or leg, usually because of disease or injury
veteran Someone who has served in the armed forces, especially during a war

Places to Remember the War

How was the Civil War a turning point in our country's history?

You've learned about abolitionists in Wisconsin who helped on the Underground Railroad and in founding the Republican Party. The Civil War marked a major turning point in the history of our country. Even before the North won the war, Abraham Lincoln had issued the **Emancipation Proclamation** that declared slaves free in the Confederate States, but not in border states. Slavery wasn't completely **eliminated** until the 13th **Amendment** to the Constitution went into effect after the war was won. But African American people have had to struggle much longer to be treated equally under the laws of the nation and states. Learning more about abolitionists and the Underground Railroad in Wisconsin is a good way to understand this important part of our history.

This **monument,** built in 1867 on the northeast corner of the courthouse square in Lancaster, was the first such Civil War monument built in Wisconsin.

The Milton House was a stagecoach inn in Milton. Its owner, Joseph Goodrich, was an abolitionist. The inn served as an Underground Railroad "station," or place where fugitive slaves could find temporary shelter. Many fugitive slaves were hidden at the Milton House on their way to Canada. Today the Milton House in Rock County is a historical museum you can visit.

monument (**mon** yuh muhnt) Something set up to honor and keep alive the memory of a person or event. A monument can take many forms: a fountain, statue, building, or stone, for example.
Emancipation Proclamation (i man suh **pay** shuhn prok luh **may** shuhn) An official announcement made by Abraham Lincoln on January 1, 1863, declaring that all slaves in Confederate states were emancipated or freed
eliminated (i **lim** uh nay tuhd) Removed   **Amendment** (uh **mend** muhnt) Official change

How is the Civil War remembered in Wisconsin?

Because about 80,000 Wisconsin men served as soldiers during the Civil War, you can find information about them in communities all over the state. In some places, you can find a monument at a county courthouse or in a public park. Many communities have some kind of memorial or cemetery where Civil War soldiers are buried. Your local or county historical society can help you find one near you. Some local historical societies or libraries have Civil War diaries or letters. You can find large collections at the Wisconsin Historical Society and see many kinds of Civil War artifacts at the Wisconsin Veterans Museum.

Some Places to Visit

- Camp Randall in Madison
- Civil War Museum in Kenosha Public Museum
- Civil War weekend at Wade House Historic Site in Greenbush
- Graves of Cordelia Harvey, Lucius Fairchild, and other Civil War soldiers at Forest Hill Cemetery in Madison
- Little White Schoolhouse, birthplace of the Republican Party, in Ripon
- Milton House in Milton
- Wisconsin Veterans Museum in Madison

Some Things to Read

- *Caroline Quarlls and the Underground Railroad* by Julia Pferdehirt
- *Freedom Train North* by Julia Pferdehirt

This beautiful portrait of Lucius Fairchild at the Wisconsin Historical Society was painted by John Singer Sargent, one of the country's leading painters of the time. You see Fairchild's many medals. But the dark color of his suit makes it difficult to see his empty left sleeve.

These men are firing a canon at the Annual Civil War Weekend at Wade House Historic Site in Greenbush. Going to this event is a great way to learn about the Civil War.

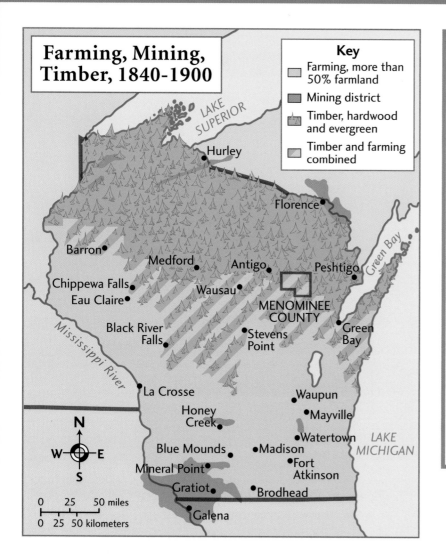

Farming, Mining, Timber, 1840-1900

Key
- Farming, more than 50% farmland
- Mining district
- Timber, hardwood and evergreen
- Timber and farming combined

LAKE SUPERIOR

Hurley

Florence

Barron

Medford · Antigo · Peshtigo

Chippewa Falls · Wausau

Eau Claire

MENOMINEE COUNTY

Black River Falls · Stevens Point · Green Bay

Green Bay

Mississippi River

La Crosse

Waupun

Honey Creek · Mayville

Watertown

LAKE MICHIGAN

Blue Mounds · Madison

Mineral Point · Fort Atkinson

Gratiot · Brodhead

Galena

N W E S

0   25   50 miles
0   25   50 kilometers

Chapter 8:
Lead, Soil, and Sawdust, 1820–1914

- Wisconsin: A Land Rich in Natural Resources
- Getting the Minerals Out
- Farming to Feed the Family
- From One Crop to Many Crops and Many Animals
- Learning about Farming in the Past
- We Become a Dairy State
- From Milking to Marketing
- Timber!
- From the Woods to the Mills
- Lumber, Pulp, and Paper
- Learning More about Mining, Farming, and Logging

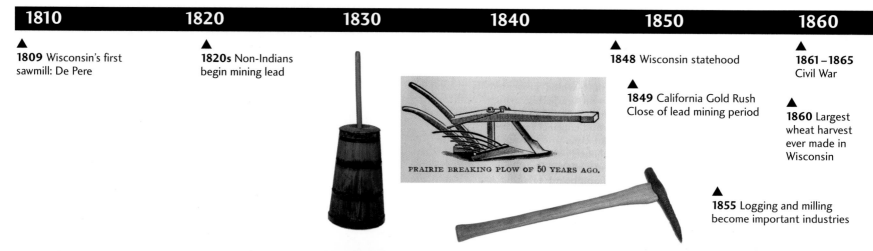

| 1810 | 1820 | 1830 | 1840 | 1850 | 1860 |

1809 Wisconsin's first sawmill: De Pere

1820s Non-Indians begin mining lead

1848 Wisconsin statehood

1861–1865 Civil War

1849 California Gold Rush Close of lead mining period

1860 Largest wheat harvest ever made in Wisconsin

PRAIRIE BREAKING PLOW OF 50 YEARS AGO.

1855 Logging and milling become important industries

Key Words

- agriculture
- census
- dairy cow
- diversified farming
- economy
- invention
- logging
- market
- mineral
- pioneer
- soil
- technology
- transportation

Thinking Like a Historian

How has our use of natural resources in Wisconsin changed over time?

Why did lead mining die out in Wisconsin?

What was life like for a pioneer farm family in Wisconsin?

How can historic photographs and U.S. Federal Census reports help us learn about the past?

How did dairy farming become important to Wisconsin's economy?

What was life like for loggers in Wisconsin?

1870   **1880**   **1890**   **1900**   **1910**

▲ **late 1860s** Chinch bugs damage the wheat harvest

▲ **1869** Wisconsin fourth in national lumber production

▲ **1870–1880** Andreas Dahl photographs farms in Dane and surrounding counties

▲ **1870–1890** A shift from wheat to dairy farming

▲ **1871** The Peshtigo Fire

▲ **1899–1904** Wisconsin leads nation in lumber production

▲ **1914–1918** World War I

Wisconsin: A Land Rich in Natural Resources

This chapter is about people in Wisconsin making a living using three of the state's many natural resources: lead, soil, and trees. You'll read about how some people mined lead ore and others grew farm crops and raised farm animals. You'll also learn about how and why people cut trees from the forests and transported them to sawmills and paper mills. This chapter looks at how people interacted with the environment from the close of the fur trade, about 1820, until the start of World War I, in 1914.

What are natural resources?

Do you like to go camping? Or maybe you like to go hiking? Perhaps you like to go skiing or snowshoeing. These are ways you can **interact** with Wisconsin's natural resources. Natural resources are materials found in nature that are useful to people. When you are active outdoors, you are using Wisconsin's land and air to exercise and have fun.

Throughout time, people have also used natural resources to make a living. Chapter 3 showed how Wisconsin's First People interacted with rocks, trees, soil, and water to make tools, housing, and pottery. They gathered and hunted food from the woods and waters. In Chapter 4, you learned about non-Indians who came here to trap beavers and other small fur-bearing animals. They also interacted with the environment to get furs. They made a living trading or selling natural resources—animal furs.

Our people once owned the lead mines in Southwestern Wisconsin. I have seen Winnebagoes [Ho-Chunks] working in them, long before the Black Hawk War [1832]. There were a good many at work in this way, nearly all the time in summer. Some dug lead for their own use, but most of them got it out to trade off to other Indians for supplies of all sorts. They made lead-mining their regular work. Every fall and spring hunters would go down to the mines and get a stock of lead for bullets, sometimes giving goods for it and sometimes furs. (Ho-Chunk Chief Spoon Decorah, about 80 years old in 1887 when he spoke these words; quoted in Collections of the Historical Society of Wisconsin 13: 458.)

In May 1827, Gratiot's Grove [was] now our home. From the slope of the hill you could see as far as the eye could reach. Miners' **shanties** and **windlasses** in activity. The store was furnishing tools and supplies to hundreds of miners. Three four-horse teams making regular trips to town every other day could hardly supply the demand or transport the lead, **smelted** night and day. (Adele Gratiot, about 70 years old in 1873 when she wrote these words; quoted in Collections of the Historical Society of Wisconsin 10: 261–225.)

soil The top layer of the earth, dirt   **ore** Rock that is mined because it contains valuable metal   **transported** Moved from one place to another
sawmills Places where people use machines to saw logs into lumber   **paper mills** Places where people use machines to turn wood into paper
interacted Took action or engaged with something or someone   **shanties** Small, simple, and temporary buildings   **windlasses** Tools with two handles and a long rope used to lift heavy things like a bucket of lead ore   **smelted** Melted so that the metal can be removed from ore

How has our use of natural resources changed over the years?

Wisconsin's many rich natural resources have always been important to the area's **economy**. From the earliest times until the start of the fur trade, Native people used natural resources to provide the tools, shelter, clothing, and food that they needed. Most of their time went toward gathering and **processing** natural materials by hand. Some Indians also traded natural resources to get things they needed.

Beginning in the 1700s, non-Indian people from other places brought different ideas about using natural resources here. They began using natural resources to make money. As this practice grew, people began inventing and making more and better tools to process more natural resources. Better and faster tools meant more money.

Over the years, the **technology** of work has continued to change. Technology has also changed how far and how quickly we can **transport** products made in Wisconsin to faraway places. Working with our natural resources has become easier, but in some ways more complicated. And it has affected the quality of our land, water, and air.

For centuries, Indians harvested cranberries by hand, without machines of any kind. The annual harvests were a time for visiting as well as for working. Here Ho-Chunk Indians are picking cranberries near Black River Falls about 1905.

From the late 1880s through the early 1950s, people used these hand-held rakes to pick cranberries. While using the rakes meant they could harvest more berries, they had to stop and clear the rakes of weeds and vines.

To increase the number of cranberries harvested, people built engine-powered beaters and rakes. That's what these Northland Cranberry Company workers are doing in this photo taken in 1997 in Warrens in the Central Plain. Now to pick the cranberries, it takes fuel and lots of water, as well as people to run the machines.

economy (ee **kon** uh mee) The goods, services, and money that are made and used by a group of people
processing Preparing or changing something by following a series of steps
technology (tek **nol** oh jee) The use of science and engineering to do practical things, such as make businesses and factories work better   **transport** Bring

Getting the Minerals Out

Miners would transport their raw lead in wagons to furnaces like this one in Galena, Illinois. They would be paid for the number of pounds of lead that they delivered. The furnaces were heated with wood to melt the lead. The hot, liquid lead was poured into molds called pigs.

This map was made in 1829 to publicize the lead-mining area of Wisconsin and Illinois, called the Lead Mining Region of the Upper Mississippi River Valley.

How did miners get the lead out of the ground?

In Chapter 5, you read about Indians mining the natural resource called lead, or galena, in southwestern Wisconsin. They dug shafts about 40 feet deep to gather lead that they traded with non-Indians. As word spread about the lead, non-Indians from Illinois and Missouri moved into the area to mine in the 1820s. Deeper shafts and tunnels became more common when experienced miners from Cornwall, England, arrived in the 1830s.

First, Cornish miners used shovels to dig down about seven feet. Next, they built a platform and a windlass over the hole. The miners used the windlass to pull up heavy buckets of dirt and gravel as they were digging. Three men could dig down about 18 feet per day. As they dug out the **veins** of lead ore, they ran into layers of stone. They pounded a steel drill into the stone to make a hole. Into the hole they placed blasting powder with a "shooting-needle" to make room for a **fuse.** After lighting the fuse, the flame traveled to the blasting powder and "KA-BOOM!" The explosion broke the rock away from the lead. Then miners used the windlass to pull up the lead and the rock to the surface.

Working so far underground was both good and bad for the miners. Because the temperature down below stayed about 52 degrees year-round, it was warmer there than it was on the surface during the winter. However, problems with air supply, cave-ins, and explosions made the work very dangerous.

This is a lead ingot or pig. It weighs about 70 pounds. Lead furnaces produced thousands of these every day.

Miners used picks like this to separate the lead from the stone.

veins (vaynz) Cracks or layers in a rock filled with a mineral   **fuse** (fyooz) A long, slow-burning cord that is lit to set off a blast

Much of the **zinc** mined in southwestern Wisconsin was transported to the Mineral Point–New Jersey Zinc Works in Mineral Point. This image shows what the plant looked like in about 1905. It was the largest employer in the city, until it closed in the 1920s.

These men worked in John E. Burton's iron mine near Hurley. They are standing in the camp in about 1886.

Railroads transported **iron** mined around Hurley to the ore docks at Ashland on Lake Superior. This photo shows the Milwaukee, Lake Shore, and Western Railroad's ore dock in 1885. Can you see the docked ships in the background?

What was mined besides lead?

Workers found small amounts of **copper** ore when they were working the lead mines between the 1820 and 1840s. But when gold was discovered in California in 1848, lead and copper mining in southwestern Wisconsin decreased. Miners left for California and for the Lake Superior copper mines. The lead and copper didn't run out, they just weren't as valuable once gold was found. Many lead miners left Wisconsin for California. In 1850 more than 60 wagons and 200 people left Mineral Point for the gold fields. Those who stayed turned to farming.

A few years later, in 1855, people were mining **iron** in Dodge County at a place called Mayville on the Iron Ridge, in Sauk County on the Baraboo Range, and in Florence County on the Menominee Range. After the Civil War, more iron mining developed in Iron County around Hurley on the **Gogebic** Range. Furnaces for **smelting** the iron sprang up near Mayville and Milwaukee. The Milwaukee Iron Company continued working with iron until the 1920s. Factories used the iron to build tools and machines.

After the Civil War, the **mineral** called **zinc** became valuable. There was a lot of it in the old lead and copper mines in southwestern Wisconsin. Miners hauled up two kinds of zinc: dry bone, found closer to the surface and black jack, found in deeper levels. Zinc mining and smelting continued until the 1920s.

zinc (zingk) A blue-white metal that is used with other metals and for coating metals so that they will not rust
iron A strong, hard metal used to make things like gates and railings   **copper** A reddish-brown metal that conducts heat and electricity well; a mineral
Gogebic (go **gee** bik)   **smelting** Melting ore so that the mineral can be separated from elements that are not useful, such as sulfur
mineral A substance found in nature that is not an animal or a plant. Lead, copper, gold, iron, and zinc are all minerals.

Farming to Feed the Family

How did pioneers build their farms in Wisconsin?

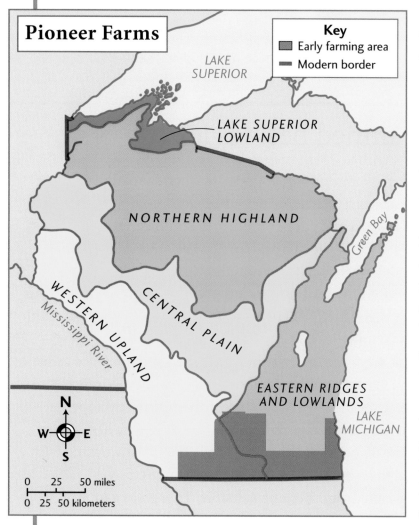

Pioneer Farms

Key
- ■ Early farming area
- ▬ Modern border

LAKE SUPERIOR

LAKE SUPERIOR LOWLAND

NORTHERN HIGHLAND

Green Bay

WESTERN UPLAND

Mississippi River

CENTRAL PLAIN

EASTERN RIDGES AND LOWLANDS

LAKE MICHIGAN

N
W E
S

0   25   50 miles
0   25   50 kilometers

We know from reading Chapter 3 that Indian people were the first farmers in Wisconsin. They interacted with the area's soil, rainfall, and sunshine—all valuable natural resources. They had been farming corn, beans, squash, and pumpkins for hundreds of years when the first non-Indian people began arriving to explore, trade furs, and mine lead. **Pioneer** farmers in Wisconsin were the first non-Indian people to grow plants and raise animals to feed their families.

Pioneers came from the eastern United States and from Europe to buy land in Wisconsin for farming. Some had been fur traders and lead miners. Beginning in the 1830s, they bought land in southeastern and southcentral Wisconsin for $1.25 per **acre.** The land they bought was very **fertile.** That's because it had been covered with **prairie sod** for hundreds of years. They, too, worked with the area's natural resources.

When a pioneer farmer bought 40 acres of prairie with some oak trees growing here and there, one of his first tasks was to cut down and clear the land of trees so he could plant **wheat.** He used the trees to build a small house for his family, and then a small barn for his horse and milk cow. At the same time, he began breaking the prairie, which meant digging down to break up the prairie sod. Then the family could plant and grow wheat and potatoes. Once crops were planted, pioneer farm families in Wisconsin built wooden fences to protect their fields and crops from being destroyed by animals. All family members helped.

Pioneer (pI oh **neer**) One of the first people to work in a new and unknown area   **acre** (**ay** kuhr) Measurement of area equal to 43,560 square feet, almost the size of a football field   **fertile** Good for growing lots of crops and plants   **prairie** (**prair** ree) A large area of flat or rolling grassland with few or no trees
sod The top layer of soil and the grasses and their roots attached to it   **wheat** A plant with a grain that can be made into flour to make bread and other foods

What was life like on a pioneer Wisconsin farm?

If you like to work from the time the sun comes up in the morning until it goes down in the evening, you would like living on a pioneer farm! Being a pioneer farmer was like having two full-time jobs. One job involved taking care of the farm: feeding your farm animals and planting, weeding, and **harvesting** your garden and wheat crops. The second job involved building the farm: clearing trees and prairie sod and building farm buildings to protect your animals, feed crops, and tools. Farmers also helped their neighbors with these tasks. This was part of living in and building communities.

At the same time that the farmer and his wife were building their farm, they were raising their family. The more children in the family, the more workers on the farm! And everyone had chores. Children your age fed and watered the animals and gardens, picked stones from the fields, helped with the harvest, and took care of their younger sisters and brothers.

Each farm family worked to grow and raise most of what they needed to live—right on the farm. This is called **subsistence** farming. They used up everything that the farm produced. Some families stayed in Wisconsin and continued building their farms. Others left the state and moved west of the Mississippi to begin the pioneer experience all over again on the prairies in Iowa, Minnesota, or South Dakota.

Knut Fossebrekke built his pioneer farm, and this log house, in Rock County. Besides growing wheat and potatoes, he trapped and sold furs to make some cash. You can visit his farm because it has been moved to the Old World Wisconsin Museum near Eagle.

This drawing shows a pioneer farm in Lafayette County, in the Western Upland Region, in 1834. How many buildings do you see?

harvesting Gathering in the crops that are ripe   **subsistence** What is needed to survive   **Knut Fossebrekke** (ku **noot fos** uh brek uh)

Farmers used **reapers** like the one in this photo about 1873 in Dane County. Reapers pulled by horses could harvest much more wheat than the cradle the man on the right is holding.

From One Crop to Many Crops and Many Animals

After wheat was harvested, it needed to be **threshed**. This photo shows men using a steam-powered tractor to run a threshing machine near Black River Falls in Jackson County about 1897.

Why didn't wheat farming last?

The pioneer farmers who stayed in Wisconsin continued to build their farms. As they cleared and planted more acres of wheat, they had more wheat than they needed to feed their families. Wheat grew easily in the soil that farmers had recently cleared of trees and prairie sod. It could be grown with little effort between planting and harvesting, and it stored well. Farmers sold the extra wheat for money that they used to continue building their farms. By the 1860s, wheat had become an important **cash crop** in southern Wisconsin.

In 1860, the amount of wheat that Wisconsin farmers harvested was the largest ever grown in the state. The state became well known for its wheat crops. But wheat farming didn't last. Why? Remember the fertile prairie soil that the pioneer farmers worked with? Growing only wheat year after year decreased the richness of the soil. Even though farmers were planting more and more acres of wheat, when it was time to harvest, there was less wheat to cut. The less fertile soil couldn't grow as much wheat as the rich soil. Small black and white insects with red legs, called **chinch** bugs, found their way to Wisconsin about this time. They killed a lot of the wheat plants before they could be harvested. Farmers have continued to grow wheat, even today, but wheat crops are no longer as large or as important as they were in Wisconsin before and after the Civil War.

threshed Separated the grain from the parts of the plant that can't be eaten
reapers Machines that people use to cut and gather grain when it is ripe   **cash crop** A crop grown to be sold off the farm rather than used on the farm   **chinch** (chinch)

What other crops did Wisconsin farmers begin to grow in place of wheat?

As the growing of wheat became less successful, farmers began to grow a variety of other crops. In place of wheat, they began growing oats, hay, and corn to feed their animals. Some farmers in the Central Plain region began growing cranberries, while others in the region grew potatoes. Both were cash crops. Farmers in parts of southern Wisconsin grew **tobacco.** In Sauk County, many farmers grew hops. They sold their dried hops to factories called **breweries** where workers used the hops to brew beer.

At the same time that farmers expanded the kinds of crops they grew, they also began raising a variety of farm animals. They raised sheep, milk cows, and chickens. The farmers made money by selling wool from the sheep, milk from the cows, and eggs from the chickens. Some farmers also raised hogs and beef cattle for meat.

The practice of raising a variety of different crops and animals is called **diversified farming.** This is a kind of **agriculture.** Diversified farming helped soil stay fertile and gave farmers more chances to earn money. As new people continued to come to Wisconsin in the late 1800s, they found the good farmland in southern Wisconsin was already taken. So they bought land farther north where the soil wasn't as good and the growing season was shorter. Growing a variety of crops and animals helped them make the best use of their land. But some land was so poor that even diversified farming was not enough to maintain the farm.

Martin **Luetscher** II built this farmstead in Honey Creek Township, in Sauk County. Artist Paul **Seifert** painted this watercolor of the farm around 1875. How many different types of crops and farm animals can you find?

Luetscher (**lit** shur)　Seifert (**see** furt)　**tobacco** (tuh **bak** oh) A plant with large leaves. The leaves are chopped and dried to be used for smoking or chewing. **breweries** (**broo** ur ees)　**diversified** (di **vur** suh fId) **farming** Growing and raising a variety of crops and animals rather than focusing on one crop or one type of animal **agriculture** (**ag** ruh kul chur) Another word for farming

Learning about Farming in the Past

How do we read photographs?

Andreas Larsen Dahl came from Norway to Wisconsin in 1869. He worked as a photographer between 1870 and 1880, traveling around southcentral Wisconsin. He took all of the photos you see on this page. They are part of a large collection of his photos that now belong to the Wisconsin Historical Society. You can see the collection by visiting the Wisconsin Historical Society's **Archives**. Many of his photos can be seen online on the Society's website. Ask your teacher or parent to help you find them.

People in farm families didn't have much spare time to write about their lives as farmers, especially when they were first building their farms. One of the ways we can learn about farming in the past is by learning how to read old photographs. Yes, you can read photos even when they don't include any words! Think of each photograph as a mystery waiting to be solved. Your job is to search the photo for clues just like a good detective. Study each photo on this page and read its caption carefully. The captions will help you find some clues. By trying to answer the questions in the captions, you'll be on your way to becoming a photo detective!

This **stereopticon card** tells you the name of the photographer and where he was working. That helps us date this photo. We know that Dahl took pictures between 1870 and 1880. What else does this image tell you? Were the people working when Dahl took this picture, or were they posing for the camera?

This view of a farmhouse and its farmyard date to about 1870. Based on the number of buildings and the amount of fencing, how old might this farm be?

Archives A safe place for storing historical records and photographs
stereopticon (stair ee **op** tuh kon) **card** A pair of photographs mounted side by side on either glass or cardboard, and also called stereo views. When people look at the card through a stereopticon viewer, the photo looks three dimensional.

What can we learn from census reports?

Another way we can learn about farming in the past is by learning how to read **census** reports. Every 10 years, our government takes a count of all people living in the United States. Census takers record the names, ages, and jobs of everyone living at each address.

At the Wisconsin Historical Society Library, you can read the U.S. Federal Census reports for 1850, 1860, 1870, and 1880 to find out who lived on farms in your area. The reports include "Agricultural Schedules" that record how many acres each farmer owned, and what kinds of animals and crops were raised. Take a look at the sample on this page.

403

SCHEDULE 4.—Productions of Agriculture in the Town of Rosendale. Dis. Mg **in the** enumerated by me, on the 22 d **day of** October **1850.**

Name of Owner, Agent, or Manager of the Farm.	Improved	Unimproved	Cash value of Farm.	Value of farming Implements and Machinery.	Horses.	Asses and Mules.	Milch Cows.	Working Oxen.	Other Cattle.	Sheep.	Swine.	Value of Live Stock.	Wheat, bushels of.	Rye, bushels of.	Indian Corn, bushels of.	Oats, bushels of.	Rice, lbs. of.	Tobacco, lbs. of.
Clinton Anderson	90	390	5000	100	3		4		8		5	350	500		200	80		
Fredrich Jeret	50	150	3000	50			2	2			4	100	110		70	100		
Johnthan Dodd	100	162	2500	100	2		5		10		16	423	2000		200	1000		
Moses Biggers	50	130	2500		1		4	2			4	200	150		73	100		
Isac Moodringf	16	61	500				4	2				120	150		100			
Henry Hatstew	60	100	2500	50	2		8	4				200	150		200			
Lenood Minyas	100	120	3000				4	4				200	400		50			
Robert Minyas	80		1000				4	2				190	300		50			
Henry Anderson	40	80	2000		2		8	2			4	250	200		50			
Constant Souler	40	100	1300				1	4		1		150	200		70			
John Akeson	25	35	600	10			3	2		5	13	130	150		40			
George F Curtis	50	190	2500	100			16	4	8	17	17	475	450		200	40		
Henry W Walcot	63	179	2500	200	2		2	2	5		7	275	430		200	200		
Almon Bencow	100	240	3600	50	2		4		8	28	10	300	400		150	200		
John Crofsman	100	220	3000	100	2		5	2	7	20	7	375	200		200	250		
Charles Lyman	40	200	2000	25				2			7	70	500			25		
Abel Kelly	12	88	800	85			2	2	5		4	140	80		50			
Osaw Cook	40	120	1300	75	2		4	1	2		7	280	125		50	100		

Look at line 17 of this Agricultural Schedule from the 1850 **census**, from the town of Rosendale near Fond du Lac. What is the farmer's name? How many acres of improved land does he have? What kind of animals does he raise? What kind of crops does he grow?

census (sen suhs) An official count of all the people living in a country or district

We Become a Dairy State

How did Wisconsin become a dairy state?

Most pioneer farmers had one **dairy cow** if they were lucky. Farm families used the milk from their cows for drinking, cooking, and making butter—to feed themselves. By the 1870s, some farmers in Wisconsin began raising more than one dairy cow.

Raising dairy cows was a lot of work compared to growing wheat or raising other kinds of animals. During the summer, dairy cows ate **pasture** grasses. During the winter, they ate **silage** and hay. In the early days, silage was dried pasture grasses. Dairy cows needed milking each morning and each evening, seven days a week. They needed shelter during Wisconsin's cold winters.

Some farmers who had been raising dairy cows in New York moved to Wisconsin and began dairy farming here. The soil was better and there was more land to farm here. These farmers brought their knowledge of dairy farming and shared it with others. Some became leaders of the dairy industry in Wisconsin. They worked with other farmers, scientists, and the state government to help farmers change from diversified farming to dairy farming. Wisconsin became a leading dairy state in the United States.

This is a **silo** being built about 1900 near Black River Falls in Jackson County. At the time, silos became popular as a place to store cow feed for over-winter feeding. So Wisconsin dairy farmers built silos near their barns.

These are **Jersey** cows being lined up for judges at the State Fair near Milwaukee around 1900. The Jersey cow gives the richest milk. Its milk has the most **butterfat**. **Guernsey** cows are brown and tan. **Holstein** cows are black and white. Some farmers also raised Brown Swiss cows for milk.

silo (**sI** loh) A tower used to store food for farm animals   **Jersey** (**jur** zee) A breed of cattle that is raised for milk
butterfat The fatty part of milk. Milk is usually sold according to the amount of butterfat it has.   **Guernsey** (**gurn** zee) A breed of cattle that is raised for milk
Holstein (**hohl** steen) A breed of cattle that is raised for milk   **dairy** (**dair** ee) **cow** Cow that makes milk   **pasture** (**pas** chur) Grazing land for animals
silage (**sI** ludj) Grain, grass, or corn that is cut, chopped, then packed into a silo

How did William Hoard help dairy farming?

William **Hoard** moved from New York to Wisconsin as a young man, in 1857, when farmers here were growing wheat. A few years later when problems began with the state's wheat crops, Mr. Hoard wanted to help. He remembered how farmers in New York had changed from wheat farming to dairy farming.

One thing Mr. Hoard did to help Wisconsin farmers raise dairy cows was to found the Wisconsin Dairymen's **Association,** in 1872. A few years later he began writing newspaper articles about good dairy farming practices. Then he started publishing a magazine called *Hoard's Dairyman*, full of information to help dairy farmers. Next he started his own dairy farm near Fort Atkinson. He wanted to be sure that his ideas about dairy farming were good ideas. So he tried out his ideas on his own farm before writing about them in his magazine. He died in 1918.

William **Hoard** was one of several men at an important meeting in Watertown in Jefferson County in 1872. At this meeting these men created a plan to expand Wisconsin's dairy industry. They founded the Wisconsin Dairymen's **Association**. Hoard also was governor of Wisconsin from 1889 to 1891.

Hoard's Dairyman has been providing information for dairy farmers for over 120 years—since 1885!

Hoard (hord)   **Association** (uh soh see **ay** shuhn) A group of people joined together for a common reason

From Milking to Marketing

What did farmers do with all the milk their cows produced?

Feeding, milking, and **breeding** dairy cows were all important tasks on dairy farms. But finding a **market** for all of the milk that a barn full of cows could produce every day was important, too. Milk is **perishable**. It is likely to spoil quickly. So dairy farming before the days of **refrigerators** meant that most of the milk had to be made into butter or cheese before the milk spoiled.

Some farmers in Wisconsin who had come from New York, Germany, and Switzerland made cheese at home, soon after they milked their cows. But most Wisconsin farmers didn't know how to make their own cheese. Or they didn't have the time and equipment to make it on their farms.

So it was important for the farmers to get their fresh milk to nearby **creameries** or cheese **factories** as quickly as possible. They needed wagons, horses, and good roads to travel between their farms and creameries and factories. They also needed dealers who would buy the butter and cheese and transport it to cities and sell it to stores.

Again, the members of the Wisconsin Dairymen's Association helped dairy farmers. They also helped the owners of the creameries and cheese factories. They helped develop markets for butter and cheese, and later for ice cream. They worked with scientists and the state government to help dairy farmers succeed and dairy farming grow in Wisconsin.

Farmers hauled milk cans full of milk using horse-drawn wagons. They took the milk to **creameries** like this one. Some creameries in Wisconsin were also called **co-ops**. A creamery co-op was owned and run by a group of people who were also dairy farmers. Other co-ops for cheese were called cheese factory co-ops.

creameries (kreem ur ees) Factories that turns cow milk into butter and cream
co-ops (koh ops) Stores or buildings in which members own shares of the business. Short for **cooperative** (koh **op** ur uh tiv).
breeding Mating and having young   **market** A demand for something, such as milk   **perishable (pair** ish uh buhl) Likely to spoil or decay quickly
refrigerators (ri **frij** uh ray turz)   **factories** Buildings where products, such as lumber or paper, are made in large amounts, often using machines

Most Wisconsin farm families owned a butter **churn** like this one. They used it to turn cream into butter for use on the farm. You can see butter churns like this at the Stonefield Historic Site in Cassville.

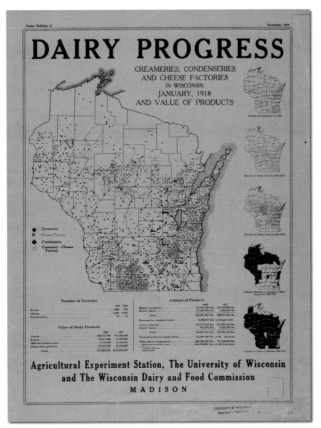

Dr. Stephen Babcock worked for the College of Agriculture at the University of Wisconsin–Madison. In 1890, he invented one of the most important tools for the dairy industry. His **invention** helped farmers measure how much butterfat was in each cow's milk. Did you know that ice cream has at least 10% butterfat?

Workers at the Barron Co-op Creamery in Barron, in Barron County, about 1900 stand near the very large butter churns. The churns are full of butter that the workers would have packed into the smaller barrels next to the churns.

This map shows creameries and cheese factories in Wisconsin as of January 1918. Leaders at the University of Wisconsin and in state government worked together to make this map. The map helped **promote** Wisconsin as the dairy state.

Dr. Babcock's tool for testing butterfat in cow's milk. It was called a butterfat tester.

Did you know it takes 10 pounds of milk to make one pound of cheese? Casper **Jaggi** began making cheese as a boy in Switzerland. As a teenager, he joined his brothers in the Swiss community of New Glarus, in Green County. Later, he opened his own Swiss cheese factory in Brodhead.

You can see this rake for cutting cheese curd on exhibit at the Wisconsin Historical Museum in Madison.

churn A machine in which cream is made into butter   **promote** To help with the growth and development of something.
Jaggi (**yah** gee)   **invention** (in **ven** shun) A new, important thing that someone makes or thinks of

Timber!

What was work like in the woods?

It took two **buckers** using a two-handled saw to cut large trees like this into lengths that could be hauled out of the woods. These men are working near Florence, close to the Wisconsin-Michigan border, about 1880.

A few pages back, you read about miners and pioneer farmers who worked with the area's rich deposits of lead and fertile soil. Lumberjacks also worked with the state's natural resources. Lumberjacks were men who worked in Wisconsin's northwoods, far from the lead mines and early farms. Their job was cutting down pine trees that had grown so large that some stood 200 feet tall! These trees were valuable to the state's **timber** industry.

Logging began as lead mining was ending, in the 1840s. Over the next 50 years, loggers cut down most of the white pine growing near waterways. Pine logs were floated down these waterways to sawmills. When railroads arrived in northern Wisconsin, it became easier to ship pine that did not grow near waterways. Also, hardwoods like oak and maple—which do not float—could now be shipped. This wood was used to build homes, farms, and stores both here and all across the country.

When the timber industry began, lumberjacks used axes to chop down the trees. After the 1880s, they began using crosscut saws. Either way, it was hard and dangerous work. After cutting down a tree, the men trimmed the branches from the tree trunk. Then they cut each tree into logs that were 12 to 16 feet in length so they could be moved out of the forest.

This is the **logging** crew at D. Sullivan's Logging Camp near **Antigo** in Langlade County in 1886. Logging, or cutting down trees and cutting them into logs, was winter work. The frozen and snow-covered ground made it easier to move the logs out of the woods.

buckers People who saw logs into lengths   **logging** Harvesting trees to be made into wood for building   **Antigo** (an ti goh)
timber Trees that were cut to be made into wood for building

This is the bunkhouse at a lumber camp near Chippewa Falls in 1900. What does this photo tell you about camp life? How did they heat their bunkhouse? How did they dry their clothes? How did they spend their time when they weren't cutting down trees?

The men of Rice Lake Lumbering Camp #6, in Barron County, are washing their clothes during the winter of 1913. Sunday was always wash day.

What was a logging camp?

Because loggers worked deep in the forest away from settlements, during the winter, it made sense for them to live in the woods near their work. They built a camp out of logs. One building served as their bunkhouse where they slept. Another building was the cook shanty where they ate. The cook and his helper prepared big meals to give the loggers energy to do their hard and heavy work in the woods.

Logging camps were not fancy. They were work camps. The main camp activity was cutting down trees and preparing them to leave the forest. Lumberjacks worked six days of every week. They tried to cut down as many pine trees as they could before spring, when the water was high. There were many different jobs in a logging camp, but the cook was the most important. Lumberjacks would even find work at another camp if the cook was bad!

In the evenings and on Sundays, they made music with fiddles they had brought from home, and they carved toys and puzzles from small, leftover pieces of wood. Some loggers told stories to amuse each other. Over the long winter, the loggers became a small community of friends working for the same goals.

Some of the loggers had come to the Wisconsin woods from logging camps in the northeastern United States and from Canada. They had experience taking down trees. They taught their logging skills to other loggers who worked as farmers during the spring, summer, and fall. The farmers left their farms and families at home during the winter when they worked as lumberjacks in northern Wisconsin.

Most logging camps included a building where loggers could eat inside. But loggers also ate in the woods near where they were working. This photo shows loggers eating in the forest north of Glen Flora in Rusk County about 1900.

From the Woods to the Mills

Most of the time loggers used oxen—great work animals—to drag logs out of swamps. Horses were faster for moving logs. The teamster, driving the sleigh, drove the logs to the nearest river. The river would take over the job of moving the logs. The oxen and the horses headed back into the forest to haul more logs out of the woods and to the river.

Once the logs were cut and trimmed, loggers loaded them onto sleighs like this. The man on top is the "skybird"—one of the most dangerous jobs in camp. The other men were known as "hookers." They hooked chains around the logs to pull them up on the sleigh. The loggers in this photo, taken near Black River Falls in 1900, used horses to pull the load out of the woods.

These are rafts of sawn lumber used to transport lumber.

This Chippewa Lumber & Boom Company crew is driving logs on the Chippewa River during the spring of 1905. Making a river drive was very dangerous work. Log drivers had to jump from log to log while in the water. **Peaveys**, which these men are holding, were used to move these slippery logs. Rivers, like the Chippewa and the Wolf, were important to the state's timber industry. The river's moving waters provided **transportation** that carried the logs to the sawmills. Some of these same rivers were the water-highways during the fur trade.

Loggers used log-mark hammers like this one to pound their logging camp's mark on the cut ends of their logs. This was an important task. Every logging camp along a logging river hauled their logs and stacked them along the river's bank. The logs often got mixed in with other camps' logs. Men sorted logs by finding the log mark, and the logging company was paid for the logs with its marks.

One of the worst things that could happen during a log drive was a logjam, like this one on the Chippewa River in 1903. Most jams occurred when a few logs caught on a rock or another obstacle, and other logs piled up behind. Loggers built dams to increase the water flow to push the logs from stream to river to larger river.

Because it took several weeks to drive logs on the rivers, the cooks came along to make food for the lumberjacks. This photo shows a cook's tent that floated on a log raft on the Wisconsin River in 1913.

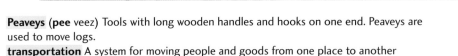

Peaveys (**pee** veez) Tools with long wooden handles and hooks on one end. Peaveys are used to move logs.
transportation A system for moving people and goods from one place to another

Lumber, Pulp, and Paper

This is the pulp mill near Waupun, in Dodge County, around 1874. Some of the smaller pieces of wood that didn't make good lumber made good pulp. Machines at a pulp mill turned these pieces of wood into pulp that was used in making paper. Compare the size of the man with the wheelbarrow to the stacks of cut wood.

How did Wisconsin's lumber industry develop and change over time?

Cutting down trees and driving logs down the rivers to the mills was hard work. But there was plenty more hard work to do turning logs into lumber at factories called sawmills. Rivers like the Wisconsin, Black, and Chippewa transported logs to the sawmills; they also supplied waterpower for these early sawmills.

Important places on Wisconsin's large rivers became sawmills. Cities like Oshkosh, Stevens Point, Wausau, Eau Claire, and La Crosse grew up as lumber towns. Once the sawmills had turned the logs into lumber, the major rivers and Great Lakes ports were used to transport the lumber. Between 1860 and 1910, sawmills were very busy places. They were important to the state's economy.

The river's water was used to power the sawmills. In the early years the **current**, or movement of water, turned a large outdoor wheel. This large wheel could then turn smaller indoor wheels. The smaller wheels powered the saws that cut the logs into boards of lumber. After the 1850s, sawmill workers burned wood to heat river water into steam. This steam powered the sawmill's machines. With this new technology, steam-powered saws worked faster than water-powered saws. More logs could be turned into boards.

Two groups of people made their living from lumber. Most worked as loggers or in the sawmills. A few built Wisconsin's lumber industry. As a group, these men had money, land, and business experience. Some of these businessmen became wealthy.

Pulp mills and paper mills sprang up along Wisconsin's logging rivers. Pulp mills turned parts of trees into pulp, an ingredient used in making paper. Both pulp mills and paper mills needed river water to make pulp and paper, and to power their machines. Many Wisconsin communities once active as lumber towns now became paper centers.

current (kur uhnt)

By the 1880s, most of the fertile farmland in southern Wisconsin was already settled. Some people tried farming in northern Wisconsin on land that had been cleared of trees by the timber industry. People called this area the Cutover because tree stumps were all that was left of the forests. These men on the Christopher **Paustenbach** farm, near Medford in Taylor County, are clearing tree stumps using a stump-pulling machine in 1895.

Illustration of the Peshtigo River on fire from *Harper's Weekly*, November 25, 1871.

BIRD'S EYE VIEW OF
PESHTIGO
WISCONSIN SEPT 1871.
Destroyed by Fire Night of October 8th 1871.

When trees are logged, the branches left behind are burned to remove them. This **slash** was often burned to clear the land for farming. During the months leading up to the Peshtigo Fire in 1871, slash on a great deal of land near **Peshtigo** in Marinette County was being burned. Drought and high winds led to a firestorm that burned the entire town to the ground. The fire also burned more than a million acres of forest. More than 1200 people lost their lives. This bird's-eye view of Peshtigo was drawn a month before the fire.

slash The branches and parts of a tree too small to saw during logging   **Peshtigo** (**pesh** ti goh)   **Paustenbach** (**paw** stuhn bok)

Learning More about Mining, Farming, and Logging

Wisconsin's natural resources: then and now

In this chapter, you read about how people have used Wisconsin's minerals, soil, and forests—all natural resources—to make their livings underground, in the fields, and in the woods. You've also read about how technology changed the way that people worked between the early 1800s and the early 1900s. Technology changed the ways people transported natural resources and the kinds of products that were made.

You can learn more about mining, farming, and logging in Wisconsin by looking around you. You can even visit places where people used to work—in mines, on farms, in cheese factories, and at logging camps, sawmills, and paper mills. Keep your eyes open! Learning about how people have used Wisconsin's natural resources in the past will help you understand the choices people make today in the world of work, and how you may make choices in the future.

This is a photo of a logging camp in the woods in Jackson County taken more than 100 years ago. The loggers, their camp, and many of the old trees are gone. This site is now part of the Black River State Forest. You can hike and enjoy nature in the woods where loggers once worked. Thanks to hard work and management, this land today continues to provide trees for lumber and a place for **recreation**.

recreation (rek ree **ay** shun) An activity meant to be enjoyed, like sports or games

Some Places to Visit

About Mining
- Iron County Historical Museum in Hurley
- Tower Hill State Park near Spring Green
- Pendarvis Historic Site in Mineral Point

About Farming
- Chippewa Valley Museum in Eau Claire
- Hoard Dairy Shrine and Historical Museum in Fort Atkinson
- Stonefield Historic Site in Cassville
- Old World Wisconsin Historic Site near Eagle
- University of Wisconsin Dairy Barn in Madison

About Logging and Lumbering
- Lumberjack Steam Train/Wisconsin Forestry Museum in Laona
- Cathedral of the Pines in the Nicolet National Forest near Lakewood
- Herling Sawmill at Wade House Historic Site in Greenbush
- Menominee Logging Camp Museum in Keshena
- Paul Bunyan Logging Camp in Eau Claire
- Peshtigo Fire Museum in Peshtigo

Today, forest harvest methods encourage regrowth of the forest.

Some Things to Read

About Mining
- *Learning from the Land: Wisconsin Land Use* by Bobbie Malone, Chapter 4

About Agriculture
- *Casper Jaggi: Master Swiss Cheese Maker* by Jerry Apps
- *Learning from the Land: Wisconsin Land Use* by Bobbie Malone, Chapter 7

About Logging and Lumbering
- *Learning from the Land: Wisconsin Land Use* by Bobbie Malone, Chapter 6
- *Wisconsin Forest Tales* by Julia Pferdehirt
- *Working with Water: Wisconsin's Waterways* by Bobbie Malone and Jefferson J. Gray, Chapter 7

Chapter 9 Places

LAKE SUPERIOR

Superior

Ashland

LAKE SUPERIOR LOWLAND

Cumberland

NORTHERN HIGHLAND

Chippewa Falls

Marinette

Green Bay

Eau Claire

WESTERN

CENTRAL PLAIN

Mississippi River

Cochrane

La Crosse

Oshkosh

Green Bay

LAKE MICHIGAN

UPLAND

Kohler
Sheboygan

EASTERN RIDGES AND LOWLANDS

Madison

Milwaukee

West Allis

Mineral Point

Racine
Kenosha

Janesville

N
W—E
S

0   25   50 miles

0   25   50 kilometers

Chapter 9: Transportation and Industry Change Wisconsin

- Wisconsin's Changing Landscape
- Shipping by Water: From Schooners to Steamers
- Shipping by Land: Railroads
- Big Industry Leads to Bigger Cities
- The Growth of Milwaukee
- Engineers and Entrepreneurs
- Comparing and Contrasting Wisconsin's Top Industries
- A New World for Workers
- Progressives and Positive Change
- Turning Points in Transportation and Industry

1825	1835	1845	1855	1865

▲
1825
Erie Canal built

▲
1851
First Wisconsin railroad line built

▲
1855
The Soo Locks in Sault Ste. Marie opens

▲
1861
First steamboat built at Manitowoc

▲
1867
Christopher Latham Sholes invents the typewriter

▲
1857
First railroad lines completely cross the state from east to west

▲
1865
First railroad bridge across the Upper Mississippi River

▲
1861
Edward P. Allis forms the Edward P. Allis Company

Key Words

- entrepreneurs
- industrialization
- industry
- labor
- labor unions
- manufacturing
- Progressives
- reformers
- rural
- urban
- wages

Thinking Like a Historian

 How did shipping and railroads build cities?

How did industry change cities?

 How did industrialization change work on farms and in cities?

 What skills did industrial entrepreneurs need to succeed?

In what ways were the lives of workers in the late 1800s and early 1900s different from the lives of workers today? In what ways were they similar?

What kinds of things did Progressives want to change?

The First **CASE** Gas Tractor Built in 1892.

1875	1885	1895	1905	1915

1883
John Michael Kohler begins to manufacture enameled cast-iron plumbing fixtures in Sheboygan

William Horlick invents malted milk in Racine

1890
Stephen Babcock invents tester for measuring butterfat in milk in Madison

Whaleback steamers begin being built in Superior

1892
J.I. Case Company in Racine produces the first gas-powered tractor

1907
Harley-Davidson becomes an official company

1916
Peak year for railroad construction in Wisconsin

Largest Cities, 1890

Key
- • Population less than 50,000
- ○ Population more than 250,000
- ▬ Modern border

LAKE SUPERIOR

Superior

LAKE SUPERIOR LOWLAND

NORTHERN HIGHLAND

Green Bay

Eau Claire

CENTRAL PLAIN

Marinette

Mississippi River

WESTERN UPLAND

Green Bay

Oshkosh

LAKE MICHIGAN

La Crosse

Sheboygan

EASTERN RIDGES AND LOWLANDS

N W E S

Madison

Milwaukee

Racine

0 25 50 miles
0 25 50 kilometers

Wisconsin's Changing Landscape

This chapter is about how Wisconsin changed from being mostly **rural** to a state with more than one large city. You'll read about how transportation by land and water grew and changed. Railroads and steamboats brought more resources in and took more products out of the state. As businesses grew in cities, new jobs changed where and how businesses and workers worked. As always, changes brought new problems and new ideas about how to solve them. There's lots to learn in this chapter that moves us closer to the way we live today.

How did Wisconsin's growing cities change the landscape?

In the last chapter you saw many photographs of people working on farms and in forests. Those photos are full of information about what most of Wisconsin looked like between 1865 and 1900. Most of the state's landscape at that time was **rural.** Open prairie or thick forests remained where people weren't farming or logging. More people in the state lived in rural areas than in cities.

By 1900, however, more and more people stopped working on farms and moved to cities to work in factories. Many places became **urban,** the opposite of rural. Cities such as Milwaukee, Racine, Oshkosh, and La Crosse grew as people moved to town to work in new factories or businesses. Other cities were just beginning to develop. At the same time that cities were getting larger, many farms in the state were staying the same size.

Cities were proud of such growth. They showed their pride by hiring artists who traveled around the state drawing **aerial** maps for cities that hired them. These artists worked on top of a hill or a tall building overlooking a city while they made their maps. For this reason, we call these maps "bird's-eye views." When you look at the bird's-eye-view maps on the next page, you are seeing the city as if you were a bird looking down while flying over the urban landscape.

rural (rur uhl) To do with the countryside or farming   **urban** (ur buhn) To do with or living in a city   **aerial** (air ee uhl) In the air

This photo of the village of **Cochrane**, in Buffalo County in the Western Upland region, was taken around 1910. You can see the group of houses and the road, but you can also see the countryside, the rural landscape. Compare this photo with the bird's-eye view of Ashland below. See how many differences you can find between a village and a city.

An artist drew this map of the city of Ashland, in the Lake Superior Lowland region, in 1890. Ashland's location on Lake Superior helped it grow into an important shipping city. Notice the many docks along the shoreline where ships stopped to load and unload. The city's population nearly doubled between 1880 and 1890.

BIRDS EYE VIEW LOOKING SOUTH, COCHRANE, WIS. #1.—'10.

ASHLAND, LAKE SUPERIOR, WIS.

1890. INCREASE IN TEN YEARS, 11,000.

POPULATION 16,000.

PUBLISHED BY THE ASHLAND DAILY PRESS.

MARK A. RICHARDS ENGRAVING CO., MILWAUKEE.

Cochrane (kahk ruhn)

Shipping by Water: From Schooners to Steamers

This painting shows Milwaukee's harbor on Lake Michigan about 1858. The harbor expanded because of the growth in lake traffic after the Erie Canal was built in the 1820s.

How did shipping develop on the Great Lakes?

The first large **vessels** in the 1800s on the Great Lakes were sailboats called **schooners**, which needed wind to move. Until the 1860s, shipbuilders in Manitowoc and Milwaukee built wooden schooners with lumber from Wisconsin's logging **industry**. Gradually, wooden **steamboats** came to replace schooners; within the steamboat engine, coal burned and heated water. Powered by steam created in this way, steamboats could move even on windless days. They could also carry more **cargo** and more passengers than sailing vessels.

By the 1880s, large amounts of iron ore, lumber, and wheat were shipped east and south from Wisconsin. And large amounts of coal and steel were shipped back to the state. This cargo was too heavy for wooden schooners and steamboats.

So shipbuilders in Manitowoc, Milwaukee, and Superior began building large steam-powered steel vessels known as steamers. Schooners and steamboats were recycled into **barges** used to haul lumber, coal, and other resources. By 1900, Superior's shipyards were building many of the new steel cargo vessels on the Great Lakes!

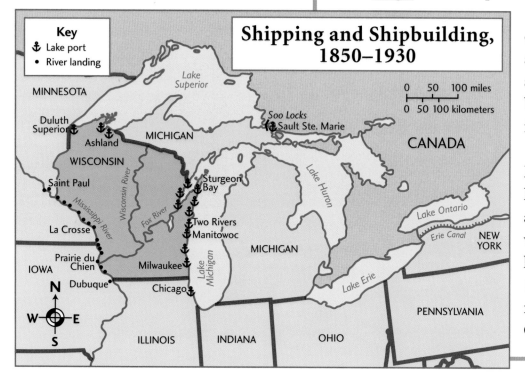

Shipping and Shipbuilding, 1850–1930

Key
⚓ Lake port
• River landing

0 50 100 miles
0 50 100 kilometers

---

vessels (**ves** uhlz) Ships or large boats   **schooners** (**skoo** nurz) Sailing vessels with masts or tall poles that stick up through the boat's deck and sails that run lengthwise
industry A type of business   **steamboats** Large wooden boats powered by steam created in a coal-fired engine. Because of this power, steamboats could easily carry people and goods upriver. Unlike schooners, steamboats could travel on windless days.   **cargo** Goods carried by ship or other kinds of transportation
barges (**bar** jehz) Long, flat-bottomed boats

What shipping took place on the Mississippi River?

The Mississippi River is part of Wisconsin's western border. It is also the most important river in the United States. Do you remember how the fur traders traveled down the Mississippi with their furs? During the Lead Rush, steamboats brought settlers and supplies up the river from St. Louis to the Lead Region. Then they carried lead south to St. Louis and to New Orleans. Landings at Prairie du Chien and La Crosse were made larger to take care of the extra shipping and river traffic.

Steamboats were the main river vessels. When north-south railroads were built, people began traveling on trains instead of steamboats. Even today, the Mississippi River remains important for cargo shipping.

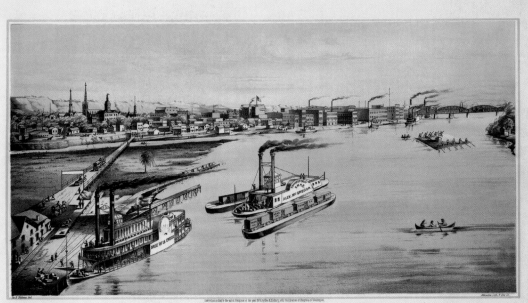

La Crosse, Wis. 1873

Steamboats, like those in this postcard above, carried cargo and people up and down the Mississippi River in the mid- and late 1800s. La Crosse was the center of steamboat travel on the Upper Mississippi River during this time.

Schooners, like this one, were popular on the Great Lakes in the early and mid-1800s.

Shipping by Land: Railroads

How did railroads connect Wisconsin's cities and waterways?

At the same time that people were developing harbors on the Great Lakes and the Mississippi River, people began **promoting** and building railroads. The first railroad in Wisconsin was built in 1851. By 1857, a railroad line crossed the state between Lake Michigan and the Mississippi River. Over the next ten years, 33 new railroads came into being. This meant that natural resources and finished products could now travel by train from the port of Milwaukee all the way to Prairie du Chien or La Crosse. From there they could be loaded onto steamboats going north or south on the Mississippi River.

As railroads grew across the state, cities worked hard to get the railroad companies to build rail lines to and from them. In fact, some cities sprang up just in hopes of becoming a railroad city because the railroad would bring people and factories. Even the names of the railroad companies give you hints about the way railroads grew. For example, one such early railroad was the Milwaukee, Lake Shore, and Western Railroad Company. The name mentions only one city and tells you which direction the railroad is growing. By 1893, it was joined by the Chicago, St. Paul, Minneapolis, and Omaha Railway Company. This company wanted to let people know that it connected Wisconsin cities with cities in other states.

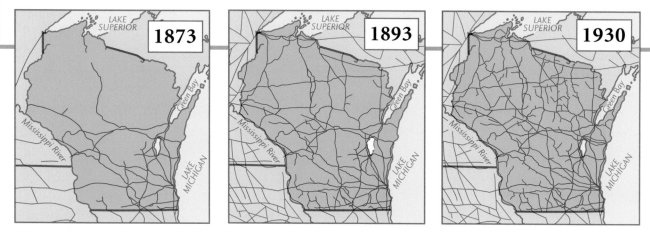

The red lines on these maps are railroads. Notice how the number of railroads increased between 1873 and 1930.

promoting Helping with the growth or development of something and making the public aware

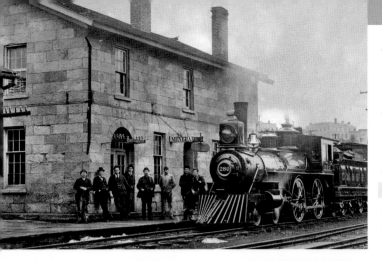

This is the train depot in Mineral Point around 1890. It was built in 1857 and is the oldest depot in Wisconsin still standing. Today it is a railroad museum that you can visit during the summer. **Locomotive** No. 280 of the Chicago, Milwaukee and St. Paul Railroad sits nearby.

This aerial view of Milwaukee's rail yards about 1940 shows how important rail transportation was to the city's economy. How did it smell and sound at ground level?

Railroad companies hired workers to build the railroad lines that cross the state. They also hired workers like these to work at each railroad station. Some workers sold tickets and served passengers. Others loaded goods on and off the trains. Some repaired the trains and the rails. These men worked for the Wisconsin & Michigan Railroad at Peshtigo in 1907.

This is the harbor at Green Bay around 1900. Railroad bridges cross the harbor so that goods can travel by rail to and from ships in the harbor.

Locomotive (loh kuh **moh** tiv) An engine used to push or pull railroad cars

Big Industry Leads to Bigger Cities

How did Wisconsin industries help cities grow?

In Chapter 8, you learned about how many people made a living in Wisconsin in the mid- and late 1800s. They used the natural resources in different regions of Wisconsin to develop different ways of making a living: mining, farming, and turning forests into lumber and paper. About this same time, large numbers of immigrants were arriving in Wisconsin. More workers, improvements in transportation, and changes in technology created all kinds of new jobs. Some forward-thinking people were coming up with new ways to get work done faster and more **efficiently**. Sometimes this meant inventing new kinds of tools and equipment to make work easier. As a result, life was changing for people in cities and on farms. We call this period the rise of industries or **industrialization**.

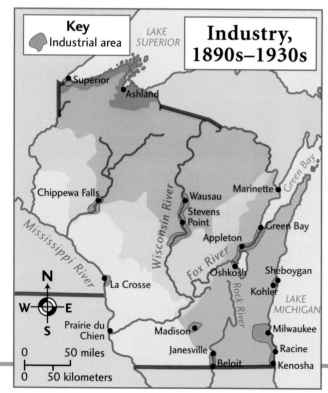

Key
Industrial area

Industry, 1890s–1930s

Industries like lumbering, commercial fishing, ice harvesting, **tanning**, brewing, and meatpacking **processed** natural resources. That is, factory workers took raw materials found in nature and turned them into products people would buy. Wisconsin **manufacturers** also created new products from materials that came from beyond our borders. In different parts of the state, factories known as canneries processed green beans, corn, and other vegetables. Some factories **manufactured** wooden products such as doors or furniture. Others manufactured clothing, shoes, tractors, large equipment, bicycles, boats, **overalls**, and outboard motors. That's why being able to ship things to and from the state was so important. Shipping and industries of all kinds brought workers from farms to town. Towns and cities grew and grew.

---

efficiently (i **fish** uhnt lee) Working without wasting time
industrialization (in dus tree uh luh **zay** shuhn) The development of large industries in an area   **tanning** Making leather from animal hides
processed (**prah** sest) Prepared or changed by a series of steps, such as wheat being processed into flour, or animal hides being processed into leather
manufacturers (man yuh **fak** chur urz) People whose factories produce large quantities of goods, often using machines
manufactured (man yuh **fak** churd) Something made, often by machines, in a factory operated by many people doing different kinds of work
overalls Loose pants with shoulder straps and a panel covering the chest

These men are working at Lehigh Coal and Iron Company in Superior. Jobs in shipping, shipbuilding, and industrial work brought immigrants and other newcomers to town. Superior grew from the ninth-largest city in the state in 1890 to the second-largest in 1910.

These men are butchering hogs at the Oscar Mayer Company in Madison in 1931. Butchers are some of the skilled workers in meatpacking factories.

This is a box of Horlick's malted milk manufactured in Racine. William and James Horlick were brothers who immigrated from England to Racine. In 1883, they created a healthy food supplement. They **patented** their invention years later as "malted milk." People liked it just for the taste. If you enjoy malted milk balls or like to drink malts, then you have the Horlick brothers to thank.

John Michael **Kohler** and his family emigrated from Austria. In 1873 he bought a **foundry** in Sheboygan that made farm equipment. In 1883, he made an **enameled cast iron** horse **trough**. When four short legs were added to it, it could be used as a bathtub. He then began **manufacturing** other plumbing **fixtures**. He was the first such manufacturer in the country. The Kohler Company, just west of Sheboygan, still manufactures plumbing fixtures today.

patented Received a legal document that gives the inventor all the rights to manufacture or sell the invention   **Kohler** (**koh** lur)
foundry A factory for melting and shaping metal   **enameled** Made of a glasslike material melted and then cooled to make a smooth, hard surface
cast iron Iron that has been shaped by being poured or casted into a mold   **trough** (trawf) A long narrow container from which animals can eat or drink
manufacturing (man yuh **fak** chur ing) Making something, often by machines, in a factory operated by many people doing different kinds of work
fixtures Things fixed firmly in place like a sink or a bathtub

Guido Pfister and Frederick Vogel were German men who immigrated to Milwaukee. They became partners in Pfister & Vogel Leather Company. Their business, shown here, became the largest tanning company in the city.

The Growth of Milwaukee

How did Milwaukee become Wisconsin's center of industry?

Milwaukee had the main ingredients for becoming Wisconsin's industrial giant. First, its location where three rivers feed into Lake Michigan was ideal for shipping. Second, it was also the railroad center of the state. Third, Milwaukee had the state's largest population. In the late 1800s, many people living there were immigrants from Germany. They had already learned manufacturing skills in Germany, especially in brewing, milling, tanning, and meatpacking. Those with skills and money became **entrepreneurs** who built factories in Milwaukee. They were able to provide jobs for those immigrants with skills but no money to build factories of their own. Factories also provided other jobs for those who wanted to work but had fewer skills. All of these men and women became the workers.

Processing industries developed first in the city. These industries used the natural resources from farms, forests, and the earth that were shipped to Milwaukee. Flour milling, tanning, brewing, meatpacking, ice harvesting, and iron milling were the first major industries that made the city the state's industrial center. One industry often helped another grow. For example, brewing and meatpacking work depended on ice harvesting in the days before electrical refrigeration. In winter, Milwaukee's rivers provided that ice. What other natural resources made processing industries grow?

Tanning was a smelly business, but this Pfister & Vogel worker was probably glad for the work. The leather he and others produced in the tannery supplied boot, shoe, and glove manufacturers all over the country.

Guido Pfister (**gwee** doh **fis** tur)   **entrepreneurs** (ahn truh pruh **nurz**) People who start new businesses and are good at finding new ways to make money

This photograph from 1920 shows the Allis-Chalmers Manufacturing Company in Milwaukee. At the time, the company was one of the world's largest manufacturers of **turbine** engines, electrical machinery, and machinery for flour mills and mining.

How did Milwaukee become the Machine Shop of the World?

As Milwaukee grew, another kind of industry developed in Milwaukee: manufacturing metal products. These industries manufactured all kinds of machinery and **equipment:** everything from milk pails and gears to tractors, motorcycles, cranes, and machines to build other metal products. They did not depend on nearby natural resources. Instead, they depended on human ideas and skills.

These industries needed **engineers** as well as forward-thinking entrepreneurs. Milwaukee was a city with many creative and well-trained individuals. The making of machinery and equipment employed many more workers. More jobs brought more immigrants from Europe and those migrating from other parts of the United States. Milwaukee became a leading manufacturing center in both processing industries and metal-based manufacturing. Milwaukee became known as the Machine Shop of the World. Other industries in the city, such as printing, also grew successfully.

Notice how small the men are in comparison to the steel casing they are putting together at Allis-Chalmers. It is designed to cover a **hydraulic** turbine engine. What details in the photograph can help you figure out when it was taken?

turbine (**tur** buhn or **tur** bIn) An engine driven by water, steam, or gas passing through the blades of a wheel that makes it turn. Turbines are often used with other machinery to produce electrical power.
hydraulic (hI **draw** lik) Liquid-powered. Hydraulic machines work on power created by liquid being forced under pressure through pipes.
equipment (ee **kwip** muhnt) Tools and machines needed or used for a particular purpose
engineers (en juh **nirz**) People trained to design and build bridges, railroads, roads, machines, and other equipment

Engineers and Entrepreneurs

Why does industrial growth depend on both entrepreneurs and engineers?

You've learned that the world of work is constantly changing. People have always needed to adapt to changes that affect how to make a living. Some people adapt more quickly than others. In the industrial world of the late 1800s and early 1900s, entrepreneurs took the lead. Even when successful, they were always looking for new ways to make money. Entrepreneurs were the "idea" people. They needed engineers to invent new ways to turn those big ideas into real products.

Edward P. Allis is typical of such entrepreneurs. When he came to Milwaukee as a young man, he was in the tanning business. Then he decided he wanted to be a manufacturer. He bought a **bankrupt** machine shop, the Reliance Works. He hired engineers and workers to build flour-milling equipment, small steam engines, and other equipment. Allis believed that his workers could build any equipment—even if they'd never manufactured anything like it before! He just hired the experts he needed to design products that people wanted. Soon his expert engineers and workers produced all kinds of machinery. The equipment that the Edward P. Allis Company manufactured in Milwaukee was shipped all over the world.

In 1861, Milwaukee entrepreneur Edward P. Allis started his own manufacturing business, the Edward P. Allis Company. By 1901, the company had merged with other companies and became known as Allis-Chalmers. Allis-Chalmers went on to become one of the world's largest manufacturers of heavy machinery. Look at the photo of Allis-Chalmers again on page 173. The city of West Allis grew up around the factory.

bankrupt Without enough money to pay what a company or person owes

How did the Davidson brothers and Bill Harley develop their first motorcycle?

As Milwaukee 10-year-olds in 1891, Arthur Davidson and Bill Harley were best friends. They thought how nice it would be if their bicycles had motors to make going uphill and other places faster and easier. They dreamed about building a motorcycle engine. They were **persistent** enough to see that dream come true.

Arthur's dad and two older brothers worked in railroad shops. They built parts to keep the trains in top condition. When Arthur and Bill visited, they learned a lot just by watching the men as they worked.

In 1901, Bill and Arthur worked in a bicycle shop. They worked after hours at the Davidsons' home. It took the boys two years to build a motorcycle that actually worked. And that was only after Arthur's brother Walter joined them. Walter was a skilled **machinist.** They sold their first motorcycle the same year, and it lasted 100,000 miles!

In 1907, Arthur's other brother, William, became part of the team. That year, the four young men formed the Harley-Davidson **Corporation.** They were not the first to build a working motorcycle. Arthur, Bill, Walter, and William just kept improving their motorcycles to make them safe and long-lasting. Their drive for quality made Harley-Davidson motorcycles popular around the world.

This woodshed in the Davidsons' backyard became the boys' "factory" where they built their first motorcycle.

One of the first Harley-Davidson motorcycles

Harley-Davidson Milwaukee factory in 1919

persistent (pur **sis** tuhnt) Refusing to stop or give up   **machinist** (muh **shee** nist) A worker who shapes metal by using machines and tools
Corporation (kor puh **ray** shuhn) A large business company

Comparing and Contrasting Wisconsin's Top Industries

In Milwaukee, Christopher Latham Sholes invented the first typewriter in 1867. Typewriters made writing any kind of document easier. How did this change the way many people worked?

Wisconsin's 20 Leading Industries, 1880

1. Flour and grain products
2. Lumber and timber products
3. Tanned and finished leather
4. Liquors and beer
5. Iron and steel manufacturing
6. Meatpacking
7. Clothing manufacturing
8. Carriages, wagons, and materials
9. Molded metal and machine shop products
10. Agricultural equipment
11. Wooden boxes, doors, etc.
12. Cigars and cigarettes
13. Furniture manufacturing
14. Boots and shoes
15. Barrel making
16. Butter and cheese
17. Woolen material manufacturing
18. Paper and wood pulp
19. Printing and publishing
20. Saddles and harnesses

Wisconsin's 20 Leading Industries, 1920

1. Butter, cheese, and condensed milk
2. Molded metal and machine shop products
3. Cars, trucks, tractors, etc. (excluding motorcycles)
4. Meatpacking
5. Tanned and finished leather
6. Engines and waterwheels
7. Lumber and timber products
8. Paper and wood pulp
9. Flour and grain products
10. Knit material manufacturing
11. Boots and shoes
12. Ship and boatbuilding
13. Agricultural equipment
14. Furniture and refrigerators
15. Automobile-related industries
16. Copper, tin, and sheet metal products
17. Iron and steel manufacturing
18. Printing and publishing
19. Candy manufacturing
20. Electrical machinery manufacturing

How did the top industries in Wisconsin change from 1880 to 1920?

The two charts at left show many changes in the state's leading industries between 1880 and 1920. These changes caused a large shift in the types of products that Wisconsin industries produced during this time.

- What industries helped the state move from wheat to dairy farming?
- What do the charts tell you about the lumber industry?
- What do the charts tell you about changes in transportation?
- What industries created new jobs between 1880 and 1920?
- What changes in industries caused jobs to disappear between 1880 and 1920?
- What evidence can you find of the way new inventions changed the way people lived?
- What other conclusions can you draw from studying this information?

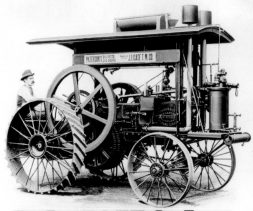

The First **CASE** Gas Tractor Built in 1892.

In 1892, the J.I. Case Company in Racine produced the first gas-powered farm tractor. How did this invention change life on Wisconsin farms?

This photograph was taken in 1914 at the Plymouth Cheese Factory west of Sheboygan. In it you see cheese makers "hooping," or putting the curd into a cheese mold. This is just one step in making cheddar cheese.

The Thomas B. Jeffery Company of Kenosha built this Jeffery car in 1915. Kenosha was already becoming a major car-building city. How does the Leading Industries chart reflect this information?

In 1919, the Boone Tire Factory in Chippewa Falls, Wisconsin, **employed** all the workers you see here at the factory.

employed Paid someone for working at the business, organization, farm, etc.

A New World for Workers

When this photograph was taken in 1914, these workers at International Harvester's Milwaukee Works were pouring melted metal into small containers. Think how hot that metal must have been! Spilling it on your hands would have been both painful and dangerous.

What was work like for factory workers in early Wisconsin industries?

Take a close look back at the photographs of the factories and workers on pages 169 through 177. Many workers had only recently moved from farms into towns and cities. Many of the places where people worked in industries were much different from anything they had ever known before. The industrial workplace was much more complicated than the workplaces of the past. Many factories were large, often with hundreds of workers. Often the conditions under which they worked were difficult.

Many factories had equipment that had been only recently created. Workers had to be trained to use such equipment. Some equipment could be dangerous if not used properly. Workers often worked long hours for low **wages**. Few laws protected them. If they were injured on the job, they had no one to help them or their families. They may never have met or even seen the factory owner who made money from their **labor.**

One worker could do very little alone to make things fairer. So factory workers got together to organize into **labor unions**. These organizations wanted to make the world of work better for workers. Labor unions worked to demand things like safer workplaces, shorter hours of work, and higher wages.

This photograph shows workers at the Parker Pen factory in Janesville in 1925. How do you think this factory sounded?

wages Money paid for work done, especially work done by the hour　**labor** Hard work
labor unions Organizations of wage workers formed to help them deal with issues such as the amount of wages paid for work and safer working conditions.

Newsboys in Milwaukee organized their own labor organization, the Newsboys' Republic.

Between 1915 and 1932, Milwaukee newsboys also published their own newspaper, *Newsboys World*. They filled its pages with delivery tips, ideas for community projects, and even jokes.

Why did some children work for wages in the late 1800s and early 1900s?

Children have always worked around the house or on farms helping their families. Today, many teenagers work at after-school jobs. In the late 1800s and early 1900s, however, many children on farms and in cities had to work for wages, just like adults. Their families needed their wages in order to live. Some children had to work instead of going to school.

Some working children were as young as eight years old. They worked full days for very little pay. Many grew up without time to play and without learning to read. Most of these children worked in factories, such as bicycle shops or breweries. Some sold newspapers, matches, gum, or flowers on the streets of cities. Some children in rural areas were hired to help harvest crops, such as sugar beets or cranberries.

In the late 1800s, young boys worked alongside older workers at the **Meiselbach** Bicycle Factory in North Milwaukee. What problems might such **child labor** cause?

Newsboys Boys from ages 8 to 17 who sold daily newspapers in the late 1800s and early 1900s
child labor Children working for wages in factories, in mines, or on farms

Meiselbach (mī zel bock)

Progressives and Positive Change

This button was once worn by a supporter of Robert M. "Fighting Bob" **La Follette** during one of La Follette's **campaigns** for governor. He was elected as governor of Wisconsin in 1900. Then he became a U.S. Senator in 1906. He is Wisconsin's most famous **politician**.

Who were the Progressives?

Progressives were people in the late 1800s and early 1900s who believed in progress. In fact, sometimes this period of time is known as the Progressive era. You may already know the term "progress." It means to move forward or improve. Progressives believed that all **social** problems *could* be solved, and so they supported positive changes in science and government.

As you've been reading, new inventions and technologies were quickly changing the world of work. First the railroad and then the invention of the bicycle and the automobile seemed to speed life up in many ways. Progressives were **reformers** who thought that state government should take the lead in solving problems that arose from such changes.

"Fighting Bob" **La Follette** and his wife, Belle Case La Follette, were the most famous Progressives of them all.

"Fighting Bob" La Follette speaks to a crowd at a county fair from the back of a wagon during his 1896 campaign for governor. He had to run three times before he won in 1900.

La Follette (luh **fah** luht)   **campaigns** (kam **paynz**) An organized series of actions and activities carried out in order to win something, like an election
politician (pol uh **tish** uhn) Someone who runs for or holds a government office
Progressives People in the late 1800s and early 1900s who worked for positive change in government, education, and other areas
social (**soh** shuhl) Having to do with the way people behave in groups and live together as communities   **reformers** People who want to change things for the better

MR. LA FOLLETTE'S STRONGEST CARD.

WISCONSIN

BEFORE AND AFTER THE RAIL ROADS

MODEL STATE GOOD LAWS

LAFOLLETTE REFORMS

"EXHIBIT A"

"Fighting Bob" La Follette campaigned for governor in 1900 on a special train. His energetic speaking style helped him win over voters. What does the difference between these two campaign photographs tell you about changes in Wisconsin at this time?

This cartoon shows Bob La Follette taking credit for one of the reforms he fought for. The railroad is shown as a powerful octopus strangling a young girl. The young girl stands for the people of the state who had to pay whatever prices the railroad set for shipping. La Follette wanted to protect the people of Wisconsin by limiting the powers of the railroad industry.

What made "Fighting Bob" La Follette so famous?

The Progressive movement in Wisconsin began in the 1890s when "Fighting Bob" La Follette fought for **political** changes in the state. As a reformer, he wanted to make government answer to all the people, not just those with power and money. That's why he fought to **regulate** railroads and other industries. As governor, he also worked to pass laws to limit child labor and to help workers.

Like most Progressives, La Follette believed that democracy is based upon knowledge. He and other Progressives worked to make the University of Wisconsin more than a place to educate college students. La Follette believed that the state university should develop programs and research to serve the needs of all the citizens of Wisconsin. This partnership became

known as the "Wisconsin Idea." Many other states and the federal government followed this model that Wisconsin Progressives introduced.

Belle La Follette spoke with great feeling when she was fighting for women's **suffrage** in 1915. But suffrage was still several years away.

suffrage (**suf** rudj) The right to vote   **political** (puh **lit** uh kuhl) Having to do with politics, or the way a city, county, state, or nation governs itself
regulate (**reg** yoo layt) To control or manage

Turning Points in Transportation and Industry

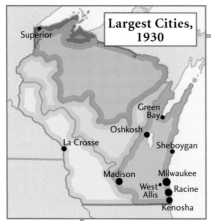

Largest Cities, 1930

What were some of the turning points in transportation and industry?

From the late 1800s to the early 1900s, Wisconsin began to enter the modern world. Think back over the turning points you read about in this chapter. Great Lakes shipping moved from schooners to steamboats to steamers. Railroads became the main way to ship across land. Gas-powered farm equipment changed work on farms across the state. Many small businesses became large industries. At the beginning of this period, many more people lived on farms. By 1930, half of the people in Wisconsin had moved to cities and towns. Work changed for nearly everyone. And by the end of this period, the state had passed laws to make workplaces safer and workers' jobs safer. The road maps on the next page let you know that the automobile was beginning to change life even more!

Milwaukee Farmer's Market, 1875

View of Wisconsin Avenue in downtown Milwaukee, 1930. Compare these two photographs and list as many differences as you can.

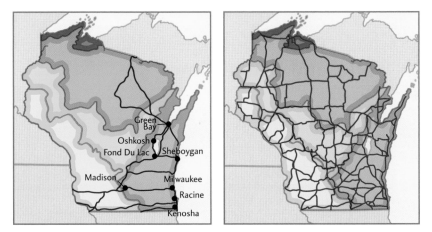

Just as railroads began to crisscross Wisconsin in the late 1800s, road building began to take off in the early 1900s. Why?

THE HARBOR, SUPERIOR, WIS.

This aerial view shows Superior's harbor on Lake Superior around 1915. Shipping on Lake Superior grew when the **Soo Locks** at **Sault Ste. Marie** opened in 1855. You can see the location on the map on page 166 in this chapter. The Soo Locks linked Lake Superior to the other Great Lakes. And Superior became an important harbor and shipbuilding center.

ERIE STEAMSHIP CO.

The S.S. *Meteor* is a whaleback boat, designed and built in Superior in 1896. Captain Alexander McDougall's efficient design allowed the boat to carry a heavy cargo. The S.S. *Meteor* is the last surviving whaleback. It is now a museum you can visit in Superior.

Soo Locks The part of the canal built at Sault Ste. Marie that can raise and lower the water level, so that boats can be raised or lowered to get to and from Lake Superior
Sault Ste. Marie (soo saynt muh ree)

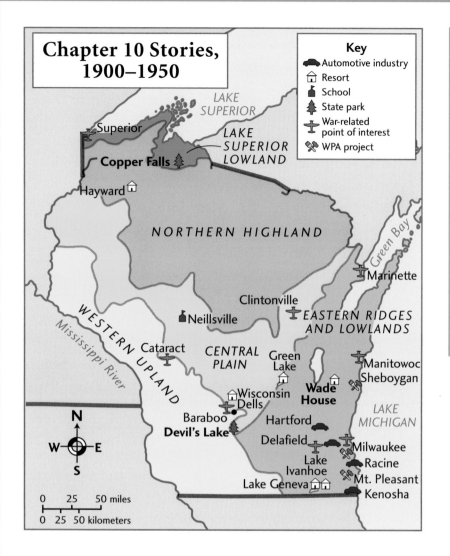

Chapter 10 Stories, 1900–1950

Key
- 🚗 Automotive industry
- ⌂ Resort
- 🏫 School
- 🌲 State park
- ✈ War-related point of interest
- ⚒ WPA project

LAKE SUPERIOR

Superior

LAKE SUPERIOR LOWLAND

Copper Falls 🌲

Hayward ⌂

NORTHERN HIGHLAND

Green Bay

Marinette ✈

Clintonville

Neillsville 🏫

EASTERN RIDGES AND LOWLANDS

Mississippi River

WESTERN UPLAND

Cataract

CENTRAL PLAIN

Green Lake ⌂

Wade House

Manitowoc ✈
Sheboygan

Wisconsin Dells ⌂

Baraboo
Devil's Lake 🌲

Hartford 🚗

Delafield

Lake Ivanhoe

Lake Geneva ⌂⌂

Milwaukee ✈⚒
Racine ⚒
Mt. Pleasant
Kenosha 🚗

LAKE MICHIGAN

N W E S

0   25   50 miles
0   25   50 kilometers

Chapter 10: Good Times, Hard Times, and Better Times

- Changes in Ways of Living
- New Century, New Roads
- Vacations for Some
- Wisconsin Goes to War: World War I
- The Great Depression: Looking for Work and Making Do
- Wisconsin Goes to War: World War II
- People Return to Peace and Work

1895   **1900**   **1905**   **1910**   **1915**   **1920**

▲ **1895**
Wisconsin League for Good Roads is founded in Milwaukee

▲ **1902**
Jeffery Automobile Company manufacturers Rambler in Kenosha

▲ **1906**
Harley-Davidson begins manufacturing motorcycles in Milwaukee

▲ **1908**
Otto Zachow and William Besserdich invent 4-wheel-drive automobile in Clintonville

▲ **1912**
Arthur P. Warner invents speedometer in Beloit

▲ **1914**
War breaks out in Europe

▲ **1917**
United States enters World War I

▲ **1919**
Peace Settlement of World War I

Key Words

- Great Depression
- neutral
- New Deal
- tourism

Thinking Like a Historian

 Wisconsin is the country's most German state. How did World War I affect this group and others?

 How did the automobile affect the building of state roads and the development of tourism in Wisconsin?

 In what ways did the Good Roads Movement affect Wisconsin today?

 How did government programs help people during the Great Depression?

How did World War I and World War II affect Wisconsin industries? How did Wisconsin industries help the war effort?

How did life change in Wisconsin after World War II?

What made events between 1900 and 1950 good times, hard times, and better times for those who lived through them?

| 1925 | 1930 | 1935 | 1940 | 1945 |

1929
Great Depression begins

1932
Franklin D. Roosevelt is elected President

1941
United States enters World War II

1945
World War II ends

Changes in Ways of Living

In this chapter, you'll find out about two different kinds of changes in Wisconsin that took place between 1900 and 1950. Some changes, like the invention of the automobile, changed the way people worked, traveled, and played. Other changes—like the Great Depression and World War II—were turning points for everyone in the world, not just Wisconsin. At the close of these 50 years, both kinds of changes gave people many more choices about where to live and how to make a living.

How do people react to changes in ways of living?

In the last chapter you learned about many changes that affected the way people lived and worked. The years between 1900 and 1950 brought more improvements that created still more changes for people in Wisconsin and across the United States.

For example, the invention and production of automobiles made travel easier and faster. Cars allowed people to work farther from home and to travel more easily to places that railroads didn't reach. Visiting new places gave people new ideas. New ideas, in turn, brought new changes in the way people lived.

The invention and growing use of electricity and the radio also changed life during this time period. Electricity changed work in factories and businesses and changed the way people lived in their homes in the cities. Over time, electricity also reached and changed life in rural areas.

The radio brought people together, even when they couldn't travel to share ideas and learn from others. People all over the country could listen to programs from faraway places.

This car passed under a railroad track near **Bonduel** in **Shawano** County around 1910. How would your life today be different without a car or a truck?

These programs also brought new ideas that, in time, affected the way people lived. Where do you get new ideas for how to dress, what music to listen to, or how to find out what's going on in your community?

In 1934, the Connor Radio Store in Madison sold radios to people in both urban and rural areas of the state. The radio brought news from around the state and the country much more quickly than the newspaper.

Bonduel (bon doo el)   Shawano (shah noh)

How did schools change between 1900 and 1950?

What year was your school built and how many classrooms does it have? How many teachers? Did you know that in the 1930s, there were about 6000 rural one-room schools in Wisconsin? What is a one-room school? It is a building with only one teacher in one classroom teaching students in several grades all at the same time. Why were there so many one-room schools in the state in the 1930s?

In the last chapter you read about how more and more people in Wisconsin were moving from rural areas to urban areas. It took a while for schools to catch up with this shift in where people were living. State lawmakers passed laws in 1917 and 1919 that provided school buses to transport rural students to urban schools. But some changes take time! By the 1950s many one-room schools were no longer being used as schools because more students were traveling to nearby urban areas to attend large schools with many teachers and many classrooms.

School buses, like this one in Rock County in 1950, delivered rural students to larger **consolidated** districts.

Teacher Mrs. Orvilla Zillic and her 17 students took a break from their schoolwork when this photograph was taken in 1948 at the Reed School. For 36 years between 1915 and 1965, students in first through eighth grades attended this one-room rural school!

Today, you can visit the one-room Reed School with your classmates or with your family. It is located near Neillsville in Clark County. Reed School is now one of the Wisconsin Historical Society's Historic Sites. When you visit, you'll be able to compare and contrast the way your school looks and works today.

consolidated (kuhn **sol** uh day tuhd) Joined together

New Century, New Roads

In the mid-1800s, Sylvanus Wade built Wade House as a stagecoach stop along the **plank road** between Sheboygan and Fond du Lac in the village of Greenbush. Today it is a Wisconsin Historical Society Historic Site. When you visit, you will learn much about travel with horse-drawn vehicles. You'll be able to compare and contrast travel then and now.

Why did Wisconsin people need better roads in the early 1900s?

The first roads in Wisconsin followed Indian paths. In the 1830s, soldiers widened some of these older paths when they built the Military Road between forts in Green Bay and Prairie du Chien. Wooden, or plank, roads followed. Still, wagon and stagecoach travel on such roads was slow and often dangerous. Then, railroads replaced roads as the main overland routes.

By the late 1800s and early 1900s, however, people were beginning to demand better roads to travel by bicycle, automobile, and motorcycle. In 1895, some Milwaukee bicyclists formed the Wisconsin League for Good Roads. A few years later, the county built bike paths along public roads. This success was part of the **Good Roads Movement,** another Progressive push to improve life in Wisconsin.

Better roads allowed farmers and businesses to get their products to markets more quickly. But people needed to know which roads to travel. In 1918, Wisconsin became the first state to come up with a system for numbering its highways to help people find their way. Odd numbers went north-south. Even numbers went east-west. And county roads were named by alphabetical letters. Between 1920 and 1930, the number of miles of state highways in Wisconsin increased from about 5000 to over 30,000 miles and has just kept on growing!

Look what a problem drivers faced when State Highway 80, south of Elroy in Juneau County, was being built!

plank roads Roads typically built of wood planks two inches thick and eight feet long, which were nailed to four-inch squares of wood
Good Roads Movement People working together to have the state improve road conditions and build highways

What made southeastern Wisconsin an early center for car manufacturing?

Early Motor Vehicle Industry

Key

Industry
- Automobile
- Motorcycle
- Tractor
- Truck
- Invention

Motorcycle makers Bill Harley and the Davidson brothers weren't the only people in southeastern Wisconsin interested in gasoline-powered vehicles. In the early 1900s, engineers and entrepreneurs formed companies to build automobile factories in port cities like Milwaukee, Racine, and Kenosha. Lake Michigan made shipping easy, and many skilled workers already lived in the area.

More than 80 different kinds of cars have been made in Wisconsin in the last 100 years. And three important automobile features still used in cars and trucks today were also invented in Wisconsin: four-wheel drive, the speedometer, and the steel frame. Look at the map and chart below to learn more about manufacturing of motor vehicles around Wisconsin!

Sites and Firsts of Wisconsin's Motor Vehicle Industry

	Appleton	1917–1927	Reliance Truck Company makes military and civilian vehicles
	Beloit	1912	Arthur P. Warner invents the speedometer
	Clintonville	1908	Otto Zachow and William Besserdich invent four-wheel-drive car
	Eau Claire	1917–1940	Gillette Safety Tire Company makes tires
	Hartford	1905–1930	Kissel Kar Company makes civilian and military vehicles
	Janesville	1918	General Motors Company begins making tractors
		1923	General Motors Company begins making Chevrolets
	Kenosha	1902–1916	Jeffery Company makes Ramblers
		1916–1927	Winter Trucks makes military vehicles
	La Crosse	1900	F.J. Wiggert builds early motorbike but never patents it
	Milwaukee	1906–1942	Harley-Davidson's original owners make motorcycles for civilians and military
		1904	Arthur Oliver Smith invents steel auto frame
	Oshkosh	1917–1945	Oshkosh Truck Corporation makes heavy-duty vehicles for civilians and military
	Racine	1903–1925	City's largest employer, Mitchell-Lewis Motor Company, builds cars

OSHKOSH 4-Wheel-Drive Motor Trucks
Power On All Four
Goes Anywhere The Wheels Can Touch The Ground

Vacations for Some

How did Wisconsin's highways help tourism?

Travel Anywhere on "Lucky 13" Without Detours This Year

Ross's Teal Lake Lodge is a **resort** near Hayward that has been run by the same family for over 80 years.

You just learned about Wisconsin's Good Roads Movement and automakers. That combination—plus our natural resources—helped build a new state industry: **tourism**. Families who owned automobiles began driving these new roads for summer vacations. Many left crowded cities like Chicago and Milwaukee to enjoy the green forests and cool lakes in Wisconsin. They believed that being active outdoors was good for the mind and the body, so they fished, hiked, camped, swam, and canoed.

Many families drove on newly built Highway 13. It ran from Beloit on the Illinois border north to Bayfield on Lake Superior. **Resort** owners along the highway called it "Lucky 13." Those traveling Highway 13 were lucky because they drove past Wisconsin's capital city, Madison, and the Wisconsin Dells as they headed north. Small towns along the way were also lucky. They welcomed **tourists** to their restaurants, gas stations, and shops.

Once they arrived in northern Wisconsin, some families stayed in **rustic** cottages and did their own cooking and cleaning. Others stayed in larger **lodges** where they had their meals cooked and their rooms cleaned. Not all of the logging camps you already read about disappeared! People turned some of them into such resorts.

This **brochure** shows the route that Lucky 13 followed in the 1920s—plus attractions along it like the state capitol, the Wisconsin Dells, cheese factories, and state parks.

resort (ri **zort**) A place where people go to rest and relax
brochure (broh **shur**) A booklet, usually with pictures, with information about a product or service, such as a vacation brochure
tourism (**tur** iz uhm) Traveling and visiting places for pleasure   **tourists** (**tur** ists) People who travel and visit places for pleasure
rustic Having to do with the country   **lodges** Cabins used for a short stay

In the late 1800s and early 1900s, H. H. Bennett took photographs of lumbermen, Ho-Chunk Indians, vacationers, and rock **formations** in the Wisconsin Dells. These photographs made people want to visit. Today *you* can visit the H.H. Bennett Historic Site in Wisconsin Dells, where you can see his photographs and cameras.

Where else did families vacation in Wisconsin?

Wealthy families might vacation for weeks at a time, or even for the whole summer, in northern Wisconsin. They also stayed at resorts in Lake Geneva, Green Lake, or Door County. But most families did not have as much time or money. Still, they loved to go fishing, swimming, canoeing, and hiking. They might have camped at one of the campgrounds created in Wisconsin's state parks or forests during 1920s or 1930s. Or, they might have visited Wisconsin Dells in the Central Plain. It's been a favorite place for day trips and weekend visits for more than 100 years!

This family is camping in Devil's Lake State Park in 1919. Where do you think they slept? Where do you think they cooked their meals? How do you think they cleaned their clothes? Devil's Lake State Park is one of Wisconsin's first state parks. It was established in 1911—and you can still visit it today.

Many resorts were not open to all people. This brochure has **"Restricted Clientele"** printed on it. That is another way of saying that Jewish and African American families were not welcome. In the 1920s, some African American families from Chicago created their own resort near Lake Geneva called Lake Ivanhoe. Also nearby was Nippersink, a resort created by Jewish families around this same time.

formations (for **may** shuhnz) Shapes of something
restricted (ri **strik** tuhd) Kept within limits   **clientele** (klI uhn **tel**) Customers

Wisconsin Goes to War: World War I

World War I Europe, 1914–1918

Key
- Allies
- Central Powers
- Neutral country

EUROPE

North Sea
GREAT BRITAIN
GERMANY
BELGIUM
RUSSIA
FRANCE
AUSTRIA-HUNGARY
ROMANIA
Black Sea
SERBIA
BULGARIA
ITALY
TURKEY
PORTUGAL
GREECE
ATLANTIC OCEAN
Mediterranean Sea

0 — 300 miles
0 — 300 kilometers

The **Allies** and the **Central Powers** fought against each other in World War I. Many people in the United States wanted to remain **neutral** and stay out of what they felt was "Europe's war."

How did World War I affect Wisconsin?

In 1914, war broke out in Europe. Two groups of nations—the Allies and the Central Powers—fought each other, as you can see on the map on this page. Robert La Follette and nine of Wisconsin's 11 congressmen voted against the war. But finally, in 1917, our country entered on the side of the Allies.

The war immediately affected Wisconsin citizens, just as it did those in other states. Some, like La Follette and Milwaukee congressman Victor Berger, remained against the war. But many young men became soldiers and went to fight in Europe.

Many women went to work in factories in Wisconsin cities, making equipment for the military. The women also made other materials that men had made before they left to fight. The government wanted everyone to keep "wheatless" Wednesdays and "meatless" Fridays, so that more food could be shipped to our soldiers. And everyone hoped that the war would end soon.

These four women at the Four Wheel Drive Company in Clintonville were building trucks for the American and British armies during World War I. Employees helped the company to manufacture more than 20,000 trucks during the war years.

Allies (al eyes) People or countries that support one another. In World War I, the Allies were Great Britain, France, Russia, Italy, and later, the United States.
Central Powers In World War I, Germany, Austria-Hungary, and Turkey fought together against the Allies **neutral (noo** truhl) In a war, describing a person or country that does not support either side

World War I pilot Rodney Williams of Delafield was wearing his U.S. Air Service uniform in 1918 when this photograph was made. Williams was the only Wisconsin pilot known as an "ace," for shooting down five enemy aircraft.

What happened to the German Americans in Wisconsin during World War I?

This **sedition** map appeared in the *New York Sun* in 1918. The shaded areas show regions of German American settlement in Wisconsin. The mapmaker **suspected** that people in these areas did not support our soldiers fighting in World War I.

In 1918, nearly half (45%) of those living in Wisconsin were German immigrants or had German ancestors. Now that the United States was fighting against Germany, many people questioned the German Americans' loyalty to this country. Some people attacked German Americans as being "un-American." Some thought Wisconsin itself would not do its part to help win the war.

But in fact, many German Americans also fought as soldiers. Like their neighbors, German Americans bought U.S. "liberty bonds" to raise money to support the troops. Some German people changed their names to "Americanize" them so others wouldn't know they had German heritage. People started calling frankfurters "hot dogs" and sauerkraut "liberty cabbage." German Americans suffered during this time. Wisconsin worked hard to prove that *all* its citizens wanted a quick victory that would return soldiers and sailors home.

The Central Powers agreed to stop fighting and negotiate peace on November 11, 1918. That became known as **Armistice** Day, in honor and in memory of those who fought. We celebrate November 11th as Veterans Day today.

German immigrants Paul and Matilda Wegner designed and built this cement and glass gold star at their farm near Cataract, Wisconsin. They built the star as a memorial to soldiers who died fighting in World War I.

sedition (si **dish** uhn) Moving others to take action against a government
Armistice (**ahr** muh stis) An agreement to stop fighting

suspected (suhs **pek** tuhd) Believed to be bad without proof

The Great Depression: Looking for Work and Making Do

Why are the 1930s known as the time of the Great Depression?

For many people, the 1920s offered good factory jobs making farm equipment, cars, and other goods. Farmers, however, were having a hard time. They had increased their crops during World War I to feed soldiers and people in Europe who needed food. After the war, no one needed as much food, and prices of crops fell.

Other workers who were doing well believed that the economy of the country was getting better and better. Many people borrowed money from banks to buy cars, homes, and other goods. But then, banks lent too much money. Prices fell. Banks failed. Factories closed.

The year 1929 marked the beginning of the **Great Depression**. Between 1930 and 1933, nearly half the factory workers in Wisconsin lost their jobs. Many families lost their homes. Men known as **hoboes** traveled on railroad boxcars looking for work. People all over the country suffered. They wanted the government to do something to help make their lives easier.

In November 1933, these men were out of work and standing in line for jobs at the Public **Employment** Office in Madison.

During the early years of the Great Depression, homeless people lived in shacks and tents along the Milwaukee River in Lincoln Park on the city's north side. People in cities across the country lived in tents, too. These areas of tents and shacks were known as **Hoovervilles**, because President Herbert Hoover was the president of the United States when the Great Depression began, and some people blamed President Hoover for the hard times.

Employment A person's regular work or job   **Hoovervilles** (**hoo** vur vils)
Great Depression An event during the 1930s, when many people lost their jobs and homes and people all over the United States and other countries suffered
hoboes (**hoh** bohz) People who are poor and homeless, and often ride freight trains looking for work

How did the government help people survive?

In 1932, the American people elected a new president of the United States, Franklin D. **Roosevelt**. He promised that he would help to end the Great Depression. He and the federal government created many programs to help people provide their families with food, shelter, and clothing. These programs were known as the **New Deal.** Some programs, like the **Works Progress Administration** or **WPA**, created jobs for people who were out of work. People working for the WPA built roads, parks, bridges, schools, and other projects that made life better for Americans all over the country. Some of the things that WPA workers built still stand today in cities and parks around Wisconsin. Sometimes you'll find signs telling you that workers in the WPA, or in another New Deal program, built them.

Other New Deal programs helped protect workers. Some protected farmers. All the programs helped people in many ways, but none really ended the Great Depression.

These workers are clearing brush in Mt. Pleasant, in Racine County, as part of the **Works Progress Administration (WPA)** program, a government program that hired people who needed work.

WPA workers built this rustic bridge at Copper Falls State Park, near Mellen in Ashland County.

These children in Sheboygan are posing on the steps of a WPA-built cabin at Sheboygan's Kiddie Camp. The camp was created in the 1920s to provide the city's needy children with plenty of fun outdoor activities and healthy food. The WPA added more buildings in 1935 and 1937.

Works Progress Administration (WPA) A Federal New Deal program started in the Great Depression that gave people jobs building parks, roads, and bridges
Administration (ad min ih **stray** shuhn) A group of people in charge of an organization or business   **Roosevelt** (**rose** uh velt)
New Deal President Franklin D. Roosevelt's programs designed to help end the suffering of Americans during the Great Depression

Wisconsin Goes to War: World War II

How did Wisconsin citizens help the United States win World War II?

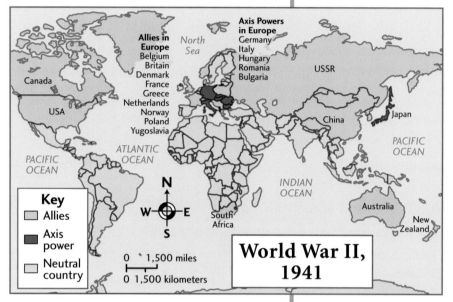

Key
- Allies
- Axis power
- Neutral country

Allies in Europe
Belgium
Britain
Denmark
France
Greece
Netherlands
Norway
Poland
Yugoslavia

Axis Powers in Europe
Germany
Italy
Hungary
Romania
Bulgaria

Canada
USA
North Sea
USSR
China
Japan
ATLANTIC OCEAN
PACIFIC OCEAN
PACIFIC OCEAN
INDIAN OCEAN
South Africa
Australia
New Zealand

0 1,500 miles
0 1,500 kilometers

World War II, 1941

When the United States entered World War II in December 1941, Wisconsin citizens immediately wanted to help their country. Many joined the military. About 320,000 Wisconsin men served as soldiers, sailors, and airmen. About 9000 women also enlisted in the armed forces. But fighting overseas was only a small part of the war effort.

The war made demands on industries and individuals all over the country. Industries made war-related products, including **ammunition**, ships, boats, and submarines. Wisconsin's families also helped the war effort. They collected scrap metal that was recycled to meet the needs of these

World War I was supposed to be "the war to end all wars." But Germany **invaded** **Czechoslovakia** and Poland in 1939, which set off a second and much larger war. World War II divided the world into **Axis** powers (countries that fought on the side of Germany, Italy, and Japan) and **Allies**. The Allies organized to fight against Axis powers. The United States entered only after the Japanese bombed Pearl Harbor in Hawaii at the end of 1941.

industries. People learned how to use less gasoline, sugar, coffee, and meat so that our military forces could have more.

After the hard years of the Great Depression, people were glad to be back working good jobs with good pay. And with so many men on battlefields around the world, women took jobs that had been considered "men's work." They built ships and submarines and made ammunition. With so many people moving to cities to work in war-related industries, World War II permanently changed Wisconsin. Our state became more closely linked to the rest of the world.

invaded In war, sent armed troops into a country to take it over   **Czechoslovakia** (chek oh sloh **vah** kee ah)
Axis Countries who fought on the side of Germany in World War II, including Bulgaria, Hungary, Italy, Japan, and Romania
Allies Countries who fought against the Axis powers in World War II, including Australia, Belgium, Brazil, Britain, Canada, China, Denmark, France, Greece, the Netherlands, New Zealand, Norway, Poland, South Africa, the United States, USSR, and Yugoslavia
ammunition (am yoo **nish** uhn) Things that can be exploded or fired from weapons, such as bullets

These three young girls brought an old iron bed to a scrap drive in Woodville in St. Croix County in 1942. Their small town of only 500 people turned in over 105 tons of scrap metal!

This photograph shows the April 1942 **launching** of the USS *Peto*. This was the first of 28 submarines produced by the Manitowoc Shipbuilding Company. Because the Manitowoc River is so narrow, the submarines built in the city had to be launched sideways, as you see here.

These women were **welders** at the Manitowoc Shipbuilding Company and worked in the submarine-building program. Women also helped build ships in Marinette, Sturgeon Bay, and Superior.

Major Richard I. Bong from Poplar in Douglas County was known as the Ace of Aces in World War II. As a fighter pilot who flew above the Pacific Ocean, he flew in 200 combat missions and destroyed 40 enemy planes.

launching (**lawn** ching) Putting a boat or other vessel into the water
welders People who join pieces of metal or plastic by heating them until they are soft enough to bond or join together

People Return to Peace and Work

Many Wisconsin women worked during World War II in the armed forces or in factories making war equipment. After the war ended in 1945, most women quit their jobs and stayed at home to have children and take care of their families. The mother and daughter in this Milwaukee household are washing dishes together in 1955.

What was life in Wisconsin like after World War II?

After the war ended in 1945, Wisconsin citizens who had been serving in the armed forces returned home. People were all relieved that the Depression and the war were over. They were glad to be back to their lives, however changed. People in the state became busy building even more highways, automobiles, tourist resorts, and new houses. Now more people lived in cities than in rural areas. More one-room country schools disappeared, and more large schools were built in Wisconsin cities. Cities like Green Bay, Eau Claire, Stevens Point, Whitewater, and Wisconsin Rapids grew quickly after the war. The number of farms in Wisconsin continued to shrink, but the farms that remained grew larger and larger. Wisconsinites looked forward to the future, but they also remembered the hard times of war and the Great Depression. They hoped there would be no more hard times.

Not all Wisconsin women left their jobs when the war ended. Isabel Olson made tires for the United Rubber Company in Eau Claire in 1949.

Even though the world wars were over, people in Wisconsin did not forget about them or the people who served their state and country. This photo shows people remembering Veterans Day on November 11, 1952, in Madison. The two women in the center of this photo are members of the **Women's Relief Corps**. The man is a member of the **Veterans of Foreign Wars**.

Some Places to Visit

- Chippewa Valley Museum in Eau Claire
- Devil's Lake State Park in Baraboo (WPA-built)
- Door County Maritime Muesum in Sturgeon Bay
- EAA AirVenture Museum in Oshkosh
- H. H. Bennett Studio Historic Site in Wisconsin Dells
- Hartford Heritage Automobile Museum in Hartford
- Herbster Community Center in Herbster, Bayfield County (WPA building from 1939)
- Milwaukee Public Museum
- Neville Public Museum in Green Bay
- Reed School Historic Site in Neillsville, Clark County
- Wade House Historic Site and Wesley Jung Carriage Museum in Greenbush
- Wisconsin Historical Museum in Madison
- Wisconsin Maritime Museum in Manitowoc
- Wisconsin Veterans Museum in Madison

Things to Read

- *Eyewitness World War I* by Simon Adams
- *Eyewitness World War II* by Simon Adams
- *Harley and the Davidsons: Motorcycle Legends* by Pete Barnes
- *Jennie's War: The Home Front in World War II* by Bonnie Hinman

Women's Relief Corps (kor) A group of women acting together to honor all citizens who have served our country in any war
Veterans of Foreign (for uhn) **Wars** A group of veterans who help each other by serving their community

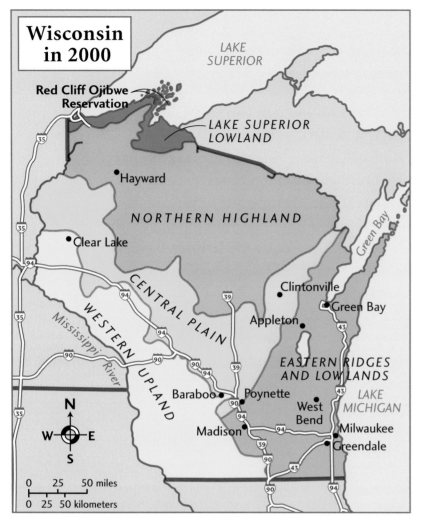

Wisconsin in 2000

LAKE SUPERIOR

Red Cliff Ojibwe Reservation

LAKE SUPERIOR LOWLAND

Hayward

NORTHERN HIGHLAND

Clear Lake

Green Bay

CENTRAL PLAIN

Clintonville

Appleton

Green Bay

WESTERN UPLAND

Mississippi River

EASTERN RIDGES AND LOWLANDS

Baraboo

Poynette

West Bend

LAKE MICHIGAN

Madison

Milwaukee

Greendale

N W E S

0   25   50 miles
0   25   50 kilometers

1945   **1950**   **1955**   **1960**   **1965**   **1970**

1946
The Cold War begins

1948
Wisconsin celebrates 100 years of statehood

1949
Communists take control of China

1950
Senator Joe McCarthy begins to hunt for Communists in the United States
Korean War begins

1952
Wisconsin Historical Society's first historic site opens, Villa Louis in Prairie du Chien

1953
Korean War ends

1956
Interstate 94 begins to be built in Waukesha County

1957
Milwaukee Braves win World Series

1965
Vietnam War begins

1967
Green Bay Packers win the first Super Bo

1968
Milwaukee holds its first Summerfest festival

1970
Earth Day celebration begins

Key Words

- activist
- capitalist economy
- Civil Rights movement
- Cold War
- communist government
- developers
- equal rights
- globalization
- interstate highways
- land use
- protested
- suburbs
- terrorist

Thinking Like a Historian

 How did fear for our nation's security lead us into the Korean War, the conflicts in Vietnam, and the Gulf War?

 How has concern for our natural environment changed in the past 50 years?

In what ways have people in Wisconsin enjoyed our natural resources for recreation?

How were the Equal Rights movements between 1950 and the present turning points for our state and our country?

How did Wisconsin citizens react to 9/11?

| 1975 | 1980 | 1985 | 1990 | 1995 | 2000 |

1975
Vietnam War ends

1976
First time Wisconsin-born speedskater wins Olympic medal

1982
In baseball, Milwaukee Brewers shortstop Robin Yount is American League Most Valuable Player; Brewers win American League championship

Late 1980s
United States recognizes Ojibwe off-reservation hunting and fishing rights; sport fishing groups clash with Native spearfishermen

1999
Ojibwe activist Walt Bresette dies

1998
Wisconsin celebrates 150 years of statehood

2001
9/11 attacks

Wisconsin and the World

In this chapter, you'll learn about what historians call the "recent past," the time between 1950 and the present. Many huge changes have taken place during this time. Larger highways and faster cars made travel easier. Faster air travel and computers changed the way people lived and the kinds of work they did. Jobs in different locations pulled families further apart. Wars and other events both connected our country to other countries and separated us by the things we believed in. Some changes put Wisconsin's environment at risk. As we look to the future, both Wisconsin and the United States face many new choices about how we get along with each other and with the rest of the world.

This photograph shows a Wisconsin family gathered in their living room around a television in 1955. By that time, 20 million households in the United States had TV sets. This meant that families across the country could be watching TV shows such as *Leave It to Beaver* and *I Love Lucy*.

How has Wisconsin become connected to the nation?

By the 1950s and the 1960s, almost everyone in Wisconsin had telephones. After World War II, some soldiers found jobs installing phones in homes and businesses. Many people had had to wait for the war to end before their phones could be installed. Talking on the telephone made it easier and quicker to stay in touch with family and friends living in other cities and in other states.

Television also connected people. Now people across the country could watch the same programs on TV. By the early 1960s, they could also watch the same half-hour news programs. In 1963, President John F. Kennedy was shot in Dallas, Texas. Television news programs allowed people throughout Wisconsin and the country to be **eyewitnesses** to what happened. By watching the same information on television and talking about it on the telephone, people in Wisconsin became and stayed connected to people outside of the state.

This is an aerial view of U.S. Highway 41 and Wisconsin Highway 26 near Oshkosh in 1967. Highway engineers designed this special **intersection** that looks like a half cloverleaf. Drivers could turn onto Highway 41 from Highway 26 without stopping. And other drivers already on Highway 41 didn't need to stop to let new drivers on the road! These new types of highways meant people could travel farther in less time. As travel became quicker and easier, people did more of it.

intersection The point at which two things meet and cross each other   **eyewitnesses** People who have seen something take place and can describe what happened

How has Wisconsin become connected to the world?

Changes in technology have also connected Wisconsin and the United States with the rest of the world. In 1955, engineers began laying telephone cables underneath the Atlantic Ocean. This made it possible for people in North America and in Europe to talk with each other by phone. By the 1990s, the Internet made it possible to share information and ideas quickly with people living in other countries. Improvements in technology have allowed people to do business with people all over the world and to transport raw materials and finished products all over the globe! The word **globalization** didn't even exist before the 1940s. People use the word often these days to describe how the United States has become connected by technology and by business with other countries. Think about this word as you read this chapter. Our connections to others beyond our country continue to grow and change.

Because clean air and water are important to the well-being of everyone in the world, they are **global** issues. When you work to clean up our environment in your community, you connect to all the people in the world who are working on their communities.

After World War II, more people began traveling by air. The building and flying of airplanes and jets increased rapidly. This DC-3 airplane at Green Bay's Straubel Airport in 1966 flew people to and from Milwaukee.

This Wisconsin legislator is working on a computer at his desk in the state capitol in Madison in 2000. Computers make it easier for people to work more efficiently and to communicate quickly with people all over the world.

global Having to do with the earth and everything on the earth
globalization (gloh buhl uh **zay** shuhn) A connection among different countries through business and technology

Wisconsin Goes to War: Fighting Communism and the Korean War

Why did the United States fight Communism?

The Allies won World War II. But soon after the war, old differences between two of those Allies, the Soviet Union and the United States, made us enemies. These countries had the strongest militaries and the most dangerous weapons on earth. Yet they held very different views about government and the economy.

You know that our country has a democratic government in which people elect leaders and have rights and liberties protected by law. We have a **capitalist economy** where people freely choose jobs and make money from their work. People pay taxes to the government, but government does not control what people do. The Soviet Union had a **communist government**. It gave people much less freedom and many fewer rights.

After World War II, both countries wanted to spread their ideas to other countries. Many people in the United States worried about communism. They feared the idea of it "infecting" our country and spreading to others. This era is known as the **Cold War**. That's because the United States and the Soviet Union never fought each other directly in "hot" battles. But the threat of communism spreading *did* bring us into wars elsewhere around the globe.

In 1952, this Wisconsin family built a bomb shelter in the basement of their home. Like so many others, they feared an attack by the Soviet Union and were trying to protect themselves.

Senator Joseph McCarthy from Appleton was a powerful speaker who liked attention. In 1950, he accused many people in the United States of being communists, even though he had no evidence to prove it. McCarthy did more than any other American to create fear that Communism was infecting people in our country. His **accusations** ruined many people's lives in the years before American citizens realized how untrue and damaging his threats had been.

accusations (ak yoo **zay** shuns) Charges that someone has done something wrong   **capitalist** (**kap** uh tuh list) **economy** An economic system in which individuals own their property and their own businesses   **communist** (**kom** yoo nist) **government** A system of government in which businesses and property are controlled by the state, and individuals have fewer rights than in capitalist societies
Cold War The period between the late 1940s and the late 1980s when the United States actively tried to keep communism from spreading around the globe

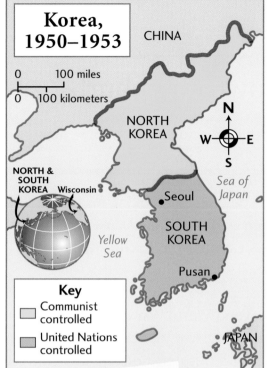

Korea, 1950–1953

CHINA

0   100 miles
0   100 kilometers

NORTH KOREA

N W E S

NORTH & SOUTH KOREA — Wisconsin

Sea of Japan

Seoul

SOUTH KOREA

Yellow Sea

Pusan

Key
Communist controlled
United Nations controlled

JAPAN

What was the Korean War about?

Like the Soviet Union, China fought on the side of the Allies in World War II. Then China had a civil war of its own. In 1949, the communist forces won. That victory caused more fear in our country.

Korea was China's southeastern neighbor. It was an **independent** country that was divided at the end of World War II into two separate countries. North Korea had a communist government. South Korea's government was friendly to the United States. When North Korea invaded South Korea in 1950, the United States sent troops to help the South Koreans. The United States wanted to protect South Korea from becoming a communist country.

About 132,000 Wisconsin citizens served in the military in Korea. The Korean War is sometimes called America's "forgotten war." But it was part of the Cold War struggle to contain communism. At the end of the fighting in 1953, North Korea was still separated along the same border from South Korea. The country remains divided the same way today.

The American soldier in uniform in this photograph is Sergeant Landon **Risteen**. He left his home in Baraboo and went to South Korea to **serve** as a nurse in a war hospital near the city of Pusan. He helped care for the many North Korean and Chinese prisoners there. Standing with him is Mr. Kim, the Korean helper in his area.

This elderly Korean man is passing by rice fields or paddies, just like those Sergeant Risteen described in his letter home.

Sergeant Risteen's parents saved all the letters he sent to them from South Korea. He wrote this one not long before he left for home in 1952. Now they are all in the collection of the Wisconsin Historical Society where you can read them.

25 August 1952

Dear folks,

After three solid days of steady rain, the clouds are finally disappearing this morning and the sun is out once more. Brother how it did rain. Seemed kind of good, the because the water for the Koreans in Pusan is way down, b drinking water and waterfor their rice paddies. So, now they will have plenty to last out the summer and are hap again. The only bad feature of so much rain is the mudd mess it creates around the post here. The main road get just like a sea of flowing mud and it's actually hard to walk on it. But a day or two of sunny weather and you even remember that it rained. So the last week of Augu upon us and I hope it hurries by as fast as the rest o month has. Had a swell letter from Jan's father yeste one from Pete in Austria. He's reveling in t ... t he has been able to hear at the Sa ... d he and his wife plan to ... hich will be in O ... and the

Risteen (ris **teen**)   **serve** To do your duty in some form of service
independent Free of the control of other people or things

Suburbs and Interstate Highways

New jobs and new **suburbs** created larger **metropolitan** areas. How did such growth affect the countryside? How did such growth affect the environment?

How did new jobs lead to the growth of suburbs?

When soldiers returned to Wisconsin from World War II, they wanted new homes, new cars, and new jobs. Factories in southeastern Wisconsin had helped produce materials needed for the war. Now the factories were ready to create materials for peacetime, including motors, motorcycles, engines, and automobiles. They were all looking for more workers. Many returning soldiers found jobs at factories such as Harley-Davidson or Allis-Chalmers in Milwaukee and West Allis or American Motors Company in Racine. Many of these returning soldiers and their families settled in southeastern Wisconsin, which was already the largest industrial area in the state.

The Great Depression and World War II had frozen people's ability to buy houses. Now jobs created the need for more housing. And this new housing was built farther away from the factories where people worked. **Developers** bought up large amounts of land and built houses. New neighborhoods required empty land. Beginning in the 1940s, many new **suburbs** were built on land that had been used for agriculture. This growth was especially true for Milwaukee. Of course, suburbs grew up around urban areas throughout Wisconsin. Suburbs continue to grow today.

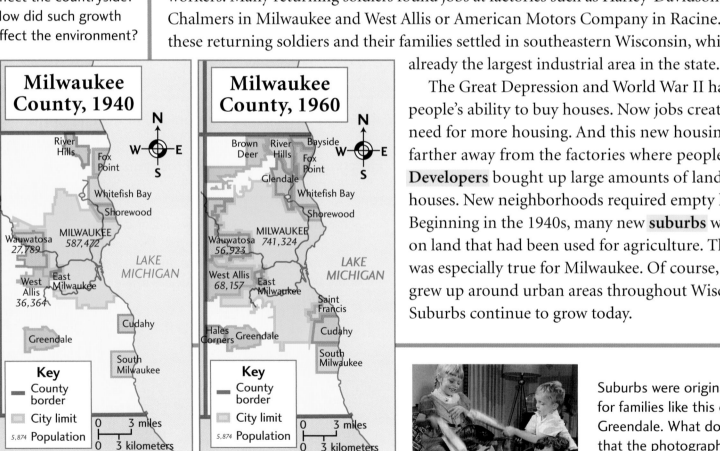

Milwaukee County, 1940

N W E S

River Hills
Fox Point
Whitefish Bay
Shorewood
MILWAUKEE 587,472
Wauwatosa 27,789
LAKE MICHIGAN
West Allis 36,364
East Milwaukee
Cudahy
Greendale
South Milwaukee

Key
— County border
City limit
5,874 Population
0   3 miles
0   3 kilometers

Milwaukee County, 1960

N W E S

Brown Deer
River Hills
Bayside
Fox Point
Glendale
Whitefish Bay
Shorewood
MILWAUKEE 741,324
Wauwatosa 56,923
LAKE MICHIGAN
West Allis 68,157
East Milwaukee
Saint Francis
Hales Corners
Greendale
Cudahy
South Milwaukee

Key
— County border
City limit
5,874 Population
0   3 miles
0   3 kilometers

Suburbs were originally built for families like this one in Greendale. What do you think that the photographer is trying to tell people about this family? What do you think that this photograph is trying to tell you about life in Greendale?

suburbs Homes and shopping centers located beyond the main settled areas
metropolitan (met roh **pol** uh tuhn) Having to do with a large city
Developers People or businesses that build and sell houses and buildings

Better highways only increased the use of car travel! Even with more interstates, traffic jams, like this one, still happen. What are some solutions to this kind of problem?

What land-use choices were made when interstate highways were built in Wisconsin?

During World War II, steel manufactured in Wisconsin and other states was for military uses. People could not buy new cars. They could not travel far because gasoline was **rationed.** After the war, all of this changed. Once again, people could buy new cars made in Wisconsin and elsewhere. And the cars being made were bigger and faster than before. With many better-paying jobs and many people moving to suburbs, people needed new cars as never before.

With all these new cars, Wisconsin citizens wanted more and better roads. The federal government purchased land in the 1940s to construct new four-lane highways. These were later called **interstate highways.** The first stretch of interstate highway in Wisconsin was Interstate 94, or I-94, in Waukesha County in 1956. By the year 2000, there were four different interstate routes running through Wisconsin: I-43 between Milwaukee and Green Bay, I-94 between Milwaukee and Hudson, I-90 between Janesville and La Crosse, and I-39 between Portage and Rhinelander. If you've ever taken a long car trip in Wisconsin, chances are you were on one of Wisconsin's interstate highways.

This is a model for a suburb in Sun Prairie, just east of Madison. What do you think the little white rectangles are supposed to be? What do you think the long white lines might be? What kind of **land use** is this?

This bulldozer is moving boulders during the building of I-94 in Waukesha County. How do you think large highways affect the natural environment? What questions do these large highways raise about land use?

land use Decisions and actions regarding land and the environment   **rationed** Allowed only limited amounts
interstate highways Large paved roads designed to accommodate many cars and high speeds. Interstates have medians separating lanes going in the opposite direction. Interstate highways connect different states or cities within a state.

Protecting Our Environment

How did Aldo Leopold help us think about land use?

Aldo Leopold grew up in eastern Iowa in the late 1800s. He loved to hunt and fish in the woods and waters near the Mississippi River. When he grew up, he traveled and worked as a forest ranger and studied and wrote about nature. This was at the very time that industries and cities were beginning to grow larger. Aldo Leopold realized that this urban growth threatened wild animal populations and their habitats.

Later, Leopold studied and taught **ecology** at the University of Wisconsin in Madison. As a university professor, he taught the idea that humans should respect land and treat it as part of their community.

He and his family put this idea into practice. The Leopolds bought some worn-out farmland near Baraboo in the Central Plain region. Too many trees had been cut down. Few places were left for wild animals to make their homes. To correct this, the family planted prairie grasses, wildflowers, and thousands of pine trees. Birds and animals then began to return!

Aldo Leopold wrote a book called *Sand County Almanac* about his work at the farm. The book was published in 1949, a year after Leopold died. In *Sand County Almanac*, Leopold described many things, like wild Canada geese landing in a cornfield: "They tumble out of the sky like maple leaves . . . toward the shoots of welcome below." It is still one of the most famous nature books in the world!

As a grown-up, Aldo Leopold loved to do many of the same things he did as a boy, especially being out in nature. Here, he is about to head out bird-watching on his farm.

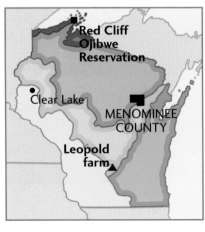

Red Cliff Ojibwe Reservation

Clear Lake

MENOMINEE COUNTY

Leopold farm

The Leopolds turned an old chicken coop at their farm into a weekend cabin, which they called the Shack. You can visit the Shack at the Aldo Leopold Legacy Center near Baraboo.

ecology (ee **kol** uh jee) The study of the environment as a community of living things

How have other people in Wisconsin worked to protect our environment?

In the mid-1800s, Chief Oshkosh and other Menominee Tribal elders worked to protect their Nation's forest.

In the late 1900s, Red Cliff Ojibwe elder Walter Bresette was an **activist** for the environment. He talked about an ancient idea common to many Native people. When they made decisions, they thought about how their actions would affect those who followed—up to seven generations into the future. Walter Bresette wanted people to protect our environment for the next seven generations that will follow us.

E. M. Griffith was Wisconsin's first Chief State Forester from 1903 to 1915. Just as the lumberjacks in Chapter 8 cut down trees to clear the land for agriculture and provide wood for growing cities, foresters today work with loggers and others to sustainably manage Wisconsin's forests—to make sure they remain healthy. Griffith was a leader in managing forests in ways that are good for people, animals, and the trees and land themselves. His ideas continue to influence foresters in Wisconsin—and throughout the world.

Gaylord Nelson—from Clear Lake, Wisconsin—was a U.S. Senator. He won protection for the St. Croix Wild and Scenic Riverway and the Apostle Islands National Lakeshore. In 1970, he founded Earth Day. He wanted April 22 to be a day every year when people would realize that they have to work to protect our air, land, and water.

activist (**ak** ti vist) Someone who actively shows concern for an issue by writing, speaking, carrying signs, or marching in public

Organized Sports and Sports Fans

Where does the "Lambeau" in Lambeau Field come from?

Earl Lambeau grew up in Green Bay in the early 1900s. He earned the nickname "Curly" for his dark wiry hair. Curly loved to play sports in his school and in his neighborhood. When he and his friends didn't have enough money to buy a football, they made one—out of a sack filled with dirt! His love for football kept growing. In 1919, Curly was working for the Indian Meat Packing Company. He convinced the company to sponsor a football team that he would coach—and play on. The team soon became known as "the Packers." Supporters became Packer Backers.

Curly Lambeau was the Packers' star player from 1921 to 1929. He was the Packers' only coach until 1949. He led the Packers to win more than 200 games, including six world championships. Curly was also one of the founders of the National Football **League**, or NFL, in 1922—a big step in professional sports. In 1965, the Green Bay Packers' stadium was named Lambeau Field in honor of the Packers' founder and first coach.

The Green Bay Packers, under Coach Vince Lombardi, won the first two Super Bowls—in 1967 and 1968. Here he signs an autograph for a young fan.

Curly Lambeau was one of the first—and greatest—Green Bay Packers. In 1965, the Packers' stadium was named Lambeau Field in his honor.

The Packers won the Super Bowl again in 1997. Mike Holmgren was the coach. Brett Favre, who wore this jersey, was the quarterback.

League (leeg) An organized group of sports clubs or teams

What professional baseball teams have played in Wisconsin?

When the Braves baseball team moved from Boston to Milwaukee in 1953, the city was ready to play ball. The city of Milwaukee had wanted its own major league baseball team since the 1930s. And Milwaukee's hardworking people wanted a good team to cheer for! Their excitement showed. When the Braves' players came to Milwaukee, 12,000 excited people were there to welcome them at the train station. **Slugger** Hank Aaron and pitcher Warren Spahn were some of the Braves' best players in the 1950s. The Braves got better and better. And in 1957, they won the World Series! But in 1966, they left Milwaukee for Atlanta.

Since 1970, the Brewers—not the Braves—have been Milwaukee's baseball team. The Brewers won the American League championship in 1982, when Robin Yount was chosen as Most Valuable Player. Today, you can see the Brewers play at Miller Park in Milwaukee, which was built in 2001. When it rains, a roof—like the roof of a convertible car—comes over the stadium to keep the fans and players dry.

Baseball has been played for more than 150 years in Wisconsin—and not just by professionals. Workers from companies—such as these men from Deering Works in 1910—as well as town and semiprofessional teams also play baseball.

"Hammerin' Hank" Aaron played for the Braves and Brewers from 1954 to 1976. His nickname comes from hitting lots of home runs. In 1982, he was voted into baseball's Hall of Fame.

Warren Spahn was one of the Braves' best pitchers. He was voted into baseball's Hall of Fame in 1973.

Slugger A baseball player who hits lots of home runs

Hunting and Fishing: Wisconsin Traditions

Many Wisconsin families enjoy deer hunting today.

A fish decoy made by Ojibwe carver John Snow from Lac du Flambeau

A handmade wooden duck decoy from 1939

Spearfishing by the light of torches was a tradition among Eastern Woodland Indian Nations.

Bird hunters and their dogs near Black River Falls in 1895

Why does Wisconsin have such strong outdoor traditions?

Remember Chapter 3 about Wisconsin's First People? We know that for at least 10,000 years, Indians have hunted and fished in Wisconsin. Spear points and fishhooks that archaeologists have found tell us that for much of that time, people hunted and fished in order to survive. Otherwise they would have starved! Today many people in Wisconsin hunt and fish. It is still a very important part of Wisconsin's culture. Although some people now do it only for **recreation,** it remains part of how we see ourselves today. And Wisconsin's many forests, lakes, and rivers have always held lots of fish and game.

Look at the images going around this page. At first—like the spearfishermen in the image on the far left and the deer-hunting family next to them—they may appear very different. Some images are from very long ago; others are from today. The clothes are different. The tools are different. But what do the tools in all of the pictures have in common? How are the activities similar? In what ways does your family—or a family that you know—keep its own outdoor traditions?

recreation (rek ree **ay** shuhn) The games, sports, hobbies, and so forth that people enjoy in their spare time

How has winter recreation changed over time?

Many activities we now call "winter sports" used to be just ways of traveling and surviving during Wisconsin winters. Today snowshoeing, sledding, cross-country skiing, ice-skating, and ice fishing are mostly done for fun in Wisconsin. Still, like hunting and fishing, they are an important part of our state's culture. They are part of who we are.

Other winter sports have developed more recently. They have no impact on our survival. They are ways that Wisconsinites enjoy winter. **Curling**, ice hockey, speed skating, ski jumping, downhill skiing, and snow boarding are some of these. As long as there is snow and ice, Wisconsin people will find ways to enjoy it.

Snowboarding is popular in Wisconsin—and just about everywhere there's snow.

Wisconsinites have **dominated** the sport of speedskating over the last 30 years. Wisconsin speed skater Casey FitzRandolph won a gold medal in the 2002 Winter Olympics in the men's 500-meter race.

This ice fisherman is holding a big northern pike caught on the Black River in the Western Upland region.

dominated (**dom** uh nay tuhd) Controlled something by using strength or power
curling A sport where players push a large stone over the ice into the other team's goal to score points

Struggles and Protests for Equal Rights

What are equal rights?

In the 1950s, some people in Wisconsin and the United States became concerned about **equal rights** for all citizens. They believed that African American people were not treated the same as white people. Even though the Civil War had ended slavery almost 100 years earlier, African Americans still often couldn't live in the same areas as white people. In some places, they couldn't work the same jobs or receive the same services as white people.

This concern about equal rights grew into a movement that historians call the **Civil Rights movement.** The Civil Rights movement began in the 1950s and lasted through the late 1960s. As this movement grew, more people became concerned about equal rights for women, for Indian people, for disabled people, and for others. Concerns about equal rights continue today in Wisconsin and around the world.

This woman and her child in Milwaukee around 1954 were part of the **Civil Rights movement**. They were showing their concern about **segregation** in schools. They didn't want African American children to attend schools that were separate from the schools attended by white children.

People who wore this pin believed that Ojibwe Indian people in Wisconsin did not have the right to fish and hunt off of their reservations using traditional methods such as spearfishing.

People who wore this pin believed that Ojibwe Indian people in Wisconsin had the right to fish and hunt off of their reservations using traditional methods such as spearfishing. Treaties signed in the mid-1800s reserved this right.

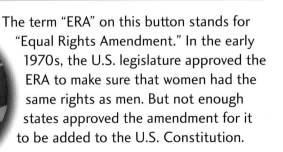

The term "ERA" on this button stands for "Equal Rights Amendment." In the early 1970s, the U.S. legislature approved the ERA to make sure that women had the same rights as men. But not enough states approved the amendment for it to be added to the U.S. Constitution.

Civil Rights The individual rights that all members of a society have to freedom and equal treatment under the law
movement A group of people who have joined together to support a cause, as in the Civil Rights movement
segregation The act or practice of keeping people or groups apart   **equal rights** Equality—the same rights for everyone

How have Wisconsinites protested for equal rights?

Some people showed their concern for equal rights by actively speaking out for their ideas at public meetings. They **protested** against laws and ideas that didn't treat all people equally. Some wore buttons and pins on their jackets or hats. Others took part in **marches** and **demonstrations**. Some carried signs stating their beliefs. Others got elected to public office so that they could work to change laws and ideas that weren't fair. Since the 1950s, more people have more actively protested in different ways for many different reasons. But they have all been exercising their constitutional right to speak freely about their ideas and beliefs.

The man with dark-rimmed glasses in this photo is Father James **Groppi**. He was a Roman Catholic priest and active in the Civil Rights movement in Wisconsin. In the late 1960s, Father Groppi led over 200 **marches** in Milwaukee to draw attention to the need for fair housing for African Americans. In this photo, he is leading a **demonstration** in Milwaukee. The youth pictured here represent the Youth Council of the National Association for the Advancement of Colored People (NAACP), which also believed in fair housing.

The woman in the photo is Vel Phillips. Before she became the first woman judge in Milwaukee County and the first African American to serve as a judge in Wisconsin, she became a lawyer and an activist. She was concerned about equal rights for women and African Americans. In 1967, she joined Father Groppi in marches for fair housing in Milwaukee. In 1978, she was elected as Wisconsin's secretary of state.

Groppi (grop ee) **marches** Large groups of people walking together in order to protest or express their opinion about something
demonstration When people join together to protest something **protested** Objected to something strongly and publicly

Wisconsin Goes to War: Vietnam and Protests

What was the Vietnam War about?

The Vietnam War took place between 1965 and 1975, far from Wisconsin in southeastern Asia. Like the Korean War, this war was a part of the Cold War. Also like Korea, Vietnam was divided into a Communist North Vietnam and a non-Communist South Vietnam. Communist North Vietnam wanted a united country under Communist rule.

The Vietnam War was also a civil war. The Soviet Union and China helped North Vietnam. The United States sent a few troops at first and then large numbers of troops to South Vietnam to help fight against communism.

The fighting lasted much longer than any other war in U. S. history. Richard Nixon was president of the United States in 1973, when he began bringing U.S. troops out of Vietnam and back home to this country. The war ended in 1975 when North Vietnam took over South Vietnam's capital city. Many people in South Vietnam left their country and lived as refugees in other countries, including in the United States.

This photo shows Air Force Captain Lance Sijan. He was born in Milwaukee in 1942, and he died in North Vietnam in 1968. Just before the airplane he was flying exploded, he parachuted into the jungle. Despite attempts by U.S. soldiers to rescue him, he was captured and held as a prisoner of war. He died while he was a prisoner. After his death the United States awarded him the Medal of Honor for his bravery.

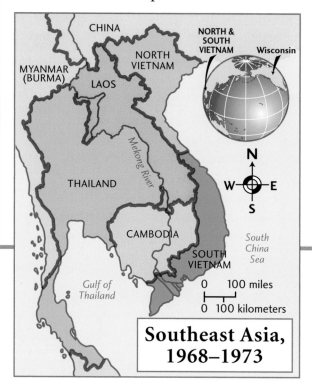

Southeast Asia, 1968–1973

Does part of this map look familiar? You saw it when you read about Mai Ya Xiong in Chapter 6. Her family immigrated to Wisconsin after the war.

These people are marching in Madison near the state capitol building in 1972 to protest the Vietnam War.

This photo shows people in Milwaukee in 1968, carrying signs that show they were in favor of the war in Vietnam.

How did people in Wisconsin react to the Vietnam War?

More than 57,000 people from Wisconsin served in the U.S. armed forces in Vietnam. Back home in Wisconsin, people disagreed about the war. Some people didn't believe that our country should be involved in the war. They protested publicly against the war. Many protesters were university students. Others disagreed with these protests and held their own protests in favor of the war.

Wisconsin Goes to War: The Gulf War and 9/11

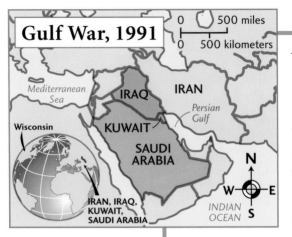

Gulf War, 1991

What was the Gulf War?

In August 1990, Iraq invaded the small neighboring country of Kuwait. This action set the stage for what became the Gulf War. Iraq refused to leave Kuwait. In January 1991, the United States and a group of other nations began Operation Desert Storm to help Kuwait. It was a successful air war that lasted only 42 days. Iraq withdrew its troops from Kuwait. American troops returned home.

What was the war like for one Wisconsin woman soldier?

These photographs show Stacy **Jalowitz** and her unit in the desert in Kuwait.

After Stacy **Jalowitz** graduated from high school in Hayward, she served as a **pharmacy technician** in a medical unit of the Army National Guard. In November 1990, her unit was **activated.** Jalowitz's unit learned how to set up a tent hospital. Then she and her unit were sent to Saudi Arabia in late January 1991. From there, they traveled by helicopter and bus to the Kuwait desert, where they set up their hospital to treat wounded soldiers. She spent 22 days there helping take care of things in the pharmacy. When Jalowitz finally flew back to Wisconsin later that spring, she wrote that she had to have "my friend pinch me to make sure I was not dreaming. It was hard to believe that we were actually home."

Jalowitz (jal o witz)   **pharmacy (far** muh see) A place where medicines and drugs are stored and sold
technician (tek **nish** uhn) Someone trained to work with any specialized equipment   **activated** Called into service in an emergency or war

What does 9/11 mean to Americans?

On the morning of September 11, 2001, the worst **terrorist** attack in the history of our nation occurred. Nineteen terrorists **hijacked** four different airline flights. The first plane crashed into the North Tower of the World Trade Center in New York City. A few minutes later, a second plane crashed into the South Tower. Both buildings collapsed, and the site is now known as the **World Trade Center Site**. A third plane crashed into the **Pentagon** in Arlington, Virginia, near Washington, D.C. The fourth plane crashed in the countryside of Pennsylvania. Its target remains unknown. In all, 3000 people died. The **Al-Qaida terrorist network** claimed responsibility for the attacks. We call these attacks "9/11" because they happened on September 11.

This tragedy shocked the American people and the world. President George W. Bush said that the attacks marked the beginning of the American war on terror. People here in Wisconsin and all over the world expressed their sympathy to all those who lost loved ones. People also actively worked to help those who survived.

The 9/11 attacks marked the beginning of a new century. They also present a challenge to everyone around the world to search for solutions that lead to peace and understanding among all nations.

Wisconsin quilter Lois Jarvis created this quilt. Each block of the quilt includes the face of someone killed in the attack on the World Trade Center. She chose the color gray to capture the smoke, dust, and sadness that people experienced after the attack.

Workers at Seagrave Fire **Apparatus** in Clintonville build fire engines for cities all over the United States, including New York City. After the World Trade Center was attacked, many firefighters died trying to rescue people, and many fire engines were destroyed. Seagrave built 54 new trucks for New York City. Many people donated money to give this special pump truck to the Fire Department of New York, with the beautiful "Never Forget" **mural** painted on it. Why are these symbols on the truck important?

World Trade Center Site The site where the World Trade Center buildings stood before September 11, 2001
apparatus (ap uh **rat** uhs) Equipment or machines made to do a job
mural A painting created directly on a wall   **terrorist** Someone who uses violence to threaten or attack others   **hijacked** Took illegal control of a plane or other vehicle
Pentagon A building with five sides that is the headquarters of the U.S. Department of Defense
Al-Qaida (al **ky** dah) **terrorist network** A very loose organization, originally founded by Osama bin Laden in Afghanistan (af **gan** uh stan) in the late 1980s. Al-Qaida uses violence to try to destroy anything that opposes its own view of Islamic rule.

Bringing People Together

How have people celebrated Wisconsin?

Wisconsin turned 100 years old in 1948 and 150 years old in 1998. As Wisconsin "grew up," some of its citizens thought it was important to save some of the state's early history for future generations. For example, the Wisconsin Historical Society began in 1846 and opened its first historic site a little more than 100 years later. That was in 1952 when Wisconsin Historic Site Villa Louis in Prairie du Chien was created. By 2007, the Society had opened 10 historic sites where people could learn about and celebrate state and local history.

Wisconsinites did more than work to save their history. People also continued to set aside forests for recreation and to protect the environment. People worked hard to protect them from being developed by industries or turned into cities or suburbs. For example, the Wisconsin Department of Natural Resources opened its eighth state forest, Black River State Forest, in 1957. That same year, Wisconsin's state parks had 5 million visitors! In 2000, Wisconsin's first state park, Interstate State Park near St. Croix Falls in northwestern Wisconsin, turned 100 years old!

In 1968 Milwaukee began hosting Summerfest, its annual music festival on the Lake Michigan shoreline. By the 1990s, the festival grounds began hosting other festivals, including the Indian Summer Festival, Polish Fest, and African World Fest. Just imagine how many people have come together over the years at Wisconsin's historic sites, state forests, state parks, and festivals. Special celebrations and special places like historic sites and state parks bring many Wisconsin people together.

This is the front hall of the mansion at Villa Louis Historic Site in Prairie du Chien. After about 50 years of operation by the Wisconsin Historical Society, the staff worked hard to change the way the mansion looked inside to reflect how it looked when the Dousman family called it home in the 1890s. You can celebrate Wisconsin history by visiting Villa Louis.

These kayakers are exploring the Apostle Islands National Lakeshore in the Lake Superior Lowland region. Thanks to Senator Gaylord Nelson, Wisconsinites can celebrate this unique landscape and know that it is protected for future generations.

Circuses are another place where people get together. The Golden Age of Chivalry Wagon is one of more than 200 restored wagons at Circus World Historic Site in Baraboo. Visiting Circus World is lots of fun—and a great way to learn more about the history of circuses.

Some Places to Visit

- Aldo Leopold Legacy Center and the Aldo Leopold Farm and Shack near Baraboo
- Circus World Historic Site in Baraboo
- Green Bay Packers Hall of Fame at Lambeau Field in Green Bay
- Milwaukee County War Memorial Center in Milwaukee
- Villa Louis Historic Site in Prairie du Chien
- Wisconsin Black Historical Society in Milwaukee
- Wisconsin Historical Society's Historic Sites and Museum
- Wisconsin Korean War Veterans Memorial in Plover
- Wisconsin state parks, forests, and recreation areas around Wisconsin
- Wisconsin Veterans Museum in Madison

Some Things to Read

- *Curly Lambeau: Building the Green Bay Packers* by Stuart Stotts
- *Escape from Saigon: How a Vietnam War Orphan Became an American Boy* by Andrea Warren
- *Korea: Veterans Tell Their Stories of the Korean War 1950–1953* by Linda Granfield
- *Learning from the Land: Wisconsin Land Use* by Bobbie Malone, Chapter 8
- *September 11* by Mary Englar, John Mulligan, and Rosemary G. Palmer
- *Working with Water: Wisconsin Waterways* by Bobbie Malone and Jefferson J. Gray, Chapter 8

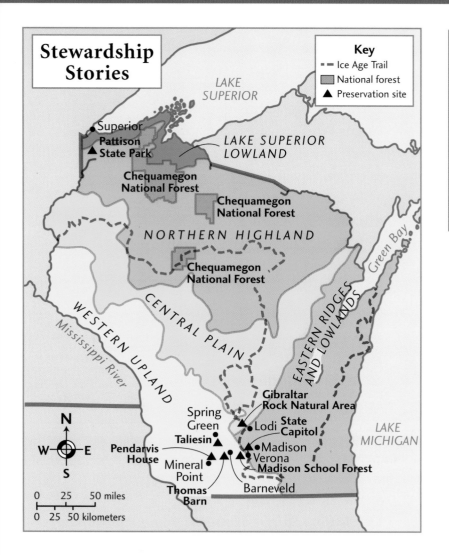

Stewardship Stories

Key
- – – Ice Age Trail
- ▢ National forest
- ▲ Preservation site

LAKE SUPERIOR

LAKE SUPERIOR LOWLAND

Superior

▲ Pattison State Park

Chequamegon National Forest

Chequamegon National Forest

NORTHERN HIGHLAND

Chequamegon National Forest

Green Bay

Mississippi River

WESTERN UPLAND

CENTRAL PLAIN

EASTERN RIDGES AND LOWLANDS

Gibraltar Rock Natural Area

Spring Green

▲ Lodi State Capitol

LAKE MICHIGAN

Taliesin ▲

Pendarvis House ▲

Mineral Point

▲ ▲ ▲ Madison

Verona

Madison School Forest

Thomas Barn

Barneveld

N W E S

0   25   50 miles
0   25   50 kilometers

Chapter 12:
A Place with a Future

- Taking Care of Our State's Story
- Saving Our Places and Our Spaces
- Protecting Wisconsin's Story

1900   **1910**   **1920**   **1930**   **1940**   **1950**

▲
1911
Frank Lloyd Wright begins building Taliesin near Spring Green

▲
1917
Current Wisconsin capitol built

▲
1952
Wisconsin Historical Society opens its first historic site, Villa Louis in Prairie du Chien

Key Words

- Conservancy
- heritage
- historic preservation
- preserve
- restored
- stewardship

Thinking Like a Historian

  Why did people in Wisconsin begin working to preserve historic places?

Why do people in Wisconsin work to protect our environment?

Why is stewardship important to Wisconsin's future?

Can you identify any turning points in this chapter? What makes them turning points?

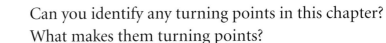

| 1960 | 1970 | 1980 | 1990 | 2000 | 2010 |

▲
1959
Frank Lloyd Wright Foundation takes over Taliesin after Frank Lloyd Wright dies

▲
1980
Ice Age National Scenic Trail established

▲
2001 Restoration of Wisconsin state capitol complete

▲
2005 Driftless Area Land Conservancy helps save the Thomas Barn near Barneveld

▲
Today What will you do to save Wisconsin's story?

Taking Care of Our State's Story

In this chapter, you'll learn how people have been working to protect places and spaces from the past. You'll see how their work has saved much of our state's history. And you'll find out what you can do to save Wisconsin's story.

How do people take care of Wisconsin's history?

Have you visited any of the museums, historic sites, state parks, or state forests mentioned in earlier chapters of this book? If not, perhaps you'll have the chance to do so during your summer break from school. If you have, then you've begun to discover how people are taking care of Wisconsin's history, our state's story.

People across Wisconsin have been working to take care of the state's important buildings and landscapes. These places and spaces are important because they form some very important evidence that documents our history. These special places and spaces each tell a part of Wisconsin's story that would otherwise be forgotten or lost.

Some places and spaces are in urban areas. Others are in rural areas. Some, like museums and parks, are open to the public and can be visited. Others belong to private individuals and are not open to the public. Some historical buildings have been placed on the National **Register** of Historic Places. Some landscapes and historic sites are identified by historical markers telling their story. Why do you think people work to save old buildings and important spaces?

Turn back to Chapter 1 to the photo of the Wisconsin statue being **hoisted** up to the top of the capitol dome in 1914. Now look again at the top of the dome in this photo. This photo was taken in 1990, 76 years after the statue was first **installed**. Workers have built a cage around the statue so they can clean and repair it. They are making it look like it is brand new again. What would happen to the statue if nobody cleaned and repaired it?

hoisted Lifted up   **installed** Put in place   **Register** Official record

How has the Thomas family taken care of its family farm?

This is Harold Thomas cutting hay on his family's farm. Behind him is the Thomas Stone Barn. It is located near Barneveld. The barn was built in 1881 from plans drawn by Harold's grandfather, Walter Thomas. Walter and his wife, Margaret, had come to southwestern Wisconsin from the country of Wales, in the British Isles. They hired three Welsh stonemasons to build their barn.

In 2005, the barn needed a new roof. Harold and his family worked with the Driftless Area Land **Conservancy** to protect the barn *and* their 180 acres of farmland. Not only is the barn an important artifact, but part of their farmland has never been plowed. It is still a prairie, just like pioneer farmers found here in the 1840s. So the Conservancy paid the Thomas family for the right to prevent their farmland from being developed. And the Thomas family used the money to pay for a new roof for the barn! The Thomas family still lives on their farm.

Harold Thomas working on his family's farm

Conservancy (kuhn **sur** vuhn see) A group or organization that works to protect valuable things such as natural resources, forests, and wildlife

Saving Our Places and Our Spaces

This is a photograph of the inside of **Taliesin**, near Spring Green. Frank Lloyd Wright designed Taliesin as both his home and studio. He was an architect who designed many important buildings in Wisconsin and other states and countries. By saving and visiting Taliesin, we can connect with this famous architect and his work.

This photograph of Frank Lloyd Wright was taken in 1930, when he was living at Taliesin. The next year he and his wife created a school of architecture there. The Frank Lloyd Wright School of Architecture is still active today.

How do places connect us to the past?

Buildings—like stone spear points, birchbark canoes, or motorcycles—are artifacts. Because buildings are built and used by people, they provide evidence about how people lived in the past. Buildings show us change and continuity over time. As artifacts, they keep us connected to people and events from the past.

People **restore** buildings to connect with and celebrate their **heritage.** Sometimes a building is worth saving because it is connected with a famous person or because it is one of a kind. Sometimes someone restores a building that represents the special history of a neighborhood, community, or region. Restoring and protecting old buildings is hard and expensive work, but it is an important way to save our state's story.

Taliesin (tal ee **es** ehn) Frank Lloyd Wright named his house Taliesin, which means "shining brow" in the Welsh language.
restore Bring back to original condition   **heritage** (**hair** uh tij) Valuable, important traditions handed down from generation to generation

How do spaces connect us to the past?

Landscapes are also living features of our heritage. They provide us with evidence about how people have interacted with the land over time. People value important spaces because they remind them of their own history. Sometimes spaces need cleaning up to make them last into the future. Other spaces need help staying the way they are. For example, people collect prairie seeds each fall and plant them each spring to help make sure that prairies continue to exist. Remember reading about the Ice Age Trail in Chapter 2? Hiking this trail helps us connect with the last glacier that came through Wisconsin thousands of years ago. Volunteering to help keep the trail in good condition is an example of **stewardship**. And stewardship is a great way to stay connected with special spaces.

These students are writing in their notebooks while on a field trip to Madison School Forest near Verona. Learning about nature is an important first step toward being a good steward!

If you look closely, you'll see people planting little pine trees in the **Chequamegon** National Forest in northern Wisconsin. Remember the tall pine trees that loggers cut down in Chapter 8? The people in this photo are planting trees in the 1930s to bring the forest back to this part of the state.

Here is a forest of hardwoods and pines in Pattison State Park, south of Superior. Careful forest stewardship helps keep this forest healthy.

Chequamegon (shuh **wah** muh guhn)   **stewardship** (**stoo** wurd ship) Personal responsibility for taking care of something that is not one's own

Protecting Wisconsin's Story

What can you do to help protect Wisconsin's story?

The very first step toward saving Wisconsin's story is learning about the state's history. You have already taken that important first step. You have read this book! Reading this book has helped you understand some of the most important parts of Wisconsin's rich history.

Another step you can take is visiting some of the state's museums, historic sites, state parks, and state forests. Get to know the historic places and special spaces in your community. And get to know the people who volunteer or are paid to take care of these places and spaces. Continue reading about Wisconsin.

As your understanding of Wisconsin history grows, you will begin to appreciate the state's heritage. The more you care about Wisconsin's story, the more you will want to help **preserve** it. Perhaps you will volunteer to help at the museum or historic site in your community. Or maybe you'll help gather prairie seeds at the local nature center. Perhaps you'll read your favorite chapter in this book to your younger sister or brother or friend. Take the next step and do something! Through your stewardship and **historic preservation** activities, you will be preserving Wisconsin's story for the future.

This family is looking out from Gibraltar Rock in Columbia County onto a beautiful valley and its farms. Visiting places like this is a great way to appreciate Wisconsin's beauty—and make sure it is preserved for tomorrow.

preserve To protect something so that it stays in its original state
historic preservation (prez ur **vay** shuhn) The act of saving old places and spaces, taking care of what we have rather than tearing it down and building new places

These visitors climbed up Gibraltar Rock in 1912. Today the site is part of the Gibraltar Rock State Natural Area.

Some Places to Visit

- Chequamegon National Forest in the Northern Highland
- Circus World Historic Site in Baraboo
- Gibraltar Rock State Natural Area near Lodi
- Ice Age Trail; trailheads in Potawatomi State Park, Hartman Creek State Park, Interstate State Park and points between
- Madison School Forest near Verona
- Pattison State Park south of Superior
- Pendarvis Historic Site in Mineral Point
- Taliesin (Frank Lloyd Wright's home and studio) near Spring Green

Some Things to Read

- Badger Biographies Series published by the Wisconsin Historical Society Press
- *Learning from the Land: Wisconsin Land Use* by Bobbie Malone
- *Working with Water: Wisconsin Waterways* by Bobbie Malone and Jefferson J. Gray

This is the Wisconsin state capitol today. Restoration on it was completed in 2001. Restoration of spaces and places allows future generations to connect with the past.

Pronunciation Key

as in:

a cat (kat), plaid (plad), half (haf), laugh (laf)

ah father (**fah** THur), heart (hahrt), dark (dahrk), sergeant (**sahr** juhnt)

air dairy (**dair** ee), care (kair), carry (**kair** ee), berry (**bair** ee), bury (bair ee), bear (bair), air (air), prayer (prair), where (whair), their (THair)

aw all (awl), walk (wawk), taught (tawt), law (law), broad (brawd), bought (bawt)

ay say (say), page (payj), break (brayk), aid (ayd), neighbor (**nay** bur), they (THay), vein (vayn), gauge (gayj), gaol (jayl)

e bet (bet), says (sez), deaf (def), friend (frend), many (**men** ee), said (sed), leopard (**lep** urd)

ee bee (bee), team (teem), fear (feer), even, (**ee** vuhn), receive (ri **ceev**), people (**pee** puhl), relieve (ri leev), key (kee), machine (muh **sheen**), phoenix (**fee** niks), Caesar (**see** zur)

i bit (bit), busy, (**biz** ee), been (bin), sieve (siv), women (**wim** uhn), build (bild), hymn (him), England (**ing** gluhnd)

I ice (Is), lie (lI), bye (bI), aye (I), height (hIt), high (hI), eye (I), buy (bI), sky (skI)

o odd (od), hot (hot), watch (wotch), honest (**hon** ist)

oh bureau (**byur** hoh), open (**oh** puhn), oh (oh), sew (soh), boat (boht), toe (toh), low (loh), brooch (brohch), soul (sohl), though (THoh), yeoman (**yoh** muhn)

oi boil (boil), boy (boi)

oo pool (pool), move (moov), shoe (shoo), through (throo), rule (rool), blue (bloo), fruit (froot), threw (throo), croup (kroop), maneuver (muh **noo** vur), adieu (uh **doo**)

or order (**or** dur), more (mor)

ou house (hous), bough (bou), now (nou)

u good (gud), should (shud), full, (ful)

uh cup (kuhp), come (cuhm), does (duhz), flood (fluhd), trouble (**truhb** uhl), motion (**mo** shun), comma (kom uh), magician (mah **jish** uhn), women (**wim** uhn), button (**buht** uhn)

ur burn (burn), pearl (purl), stern (sturn), bird (burd), worker (**wurk** ur), journey (**jur** nee), myrtle (**mur** tuhl), measure (**mezh** ur)

yoo use (yooz), cue (kyoo), you (yoo), few (fyoo), beauty (**byoo** tee), view (vyoo), feud (fyood), queue (kyoo), yule (yool)

b bad (bad), rabbit (**rab** it)

ch child (chIld), watch, (wahch), future (**fyoo** chur), question (**kwes** chuhn), righteous (**rI** chuhs)

d dog (dawg), add (ad), billed (bild)

f fad (fad), effort (**ef** urt), laugh (laf), phone (fohn)

g get (get), egg (eg), ghost (gohst), guest (gest), catalogue (**cat** uh lawg)

h hot (hot), who (hoo)

hw what (hwuht)

j joy (joi), badger (**baj** ur), soldier (sol jur), magic (**maj** ik), exaggerate (eg **zaj** uh rayt)

k kind, (kInd), coat (koht), back (bak), folk (fohk), account (uh kount), acquire (uh kwIr), chemist (kem ist), liquor (lik ur)

l like (lIk), tell (tel)

m me (mee), common (**com** uhn), calm (kahm), climb (klIm), solemn (**sol** uhm), paradigm (**per** uh dim)

n net (net), dinner (din ur), knife (nIf), pneumonia (noo **moh** nyuh), gnaw (naw)

ng long (lawng), ink (ingk), tongue (tuhng)

p cap (kap), happy (hap ee)

r run (ruhn), carry (**ker** ee), wrong (rawng), rhyme (rIm)

s say (say), cent (sent), scent (sent), miss (mis), twice (twIs), psychology (sI **kahl** uh jee), schism (**siz** uhm)

t tell (tel), bottom (**bot** uhm), stepped (stept), caught (kawt), Thomas (**tom** uhs), pterodactyl (ter uh **dak** tuhl)

th thank (thangk)

TH that (THat), breathe (breeTH)

v vain (vayn), of (uhv), Stephen (**stee** vuhn)

w web (web), quick (kwik), choir (kwIr)

y yet (yet), opinion (oh **pin** yuhn), hallelujah (hal uh **loo** yuh)

z zero (**zir** oh), has (haz), buzz (buhz), busy (**biz** ee), scissor (**siz** ur), xylophone (**zI** luh fohn)

zh measure (**mezh** ur), azure (**azh** ur), garage (guh **razh**), division (duh **vizh** uhn)

Glossary

Note: Entry dots match chapter color.

A

- **abolish** (uh **bol** ish) To put an end to something officially or legally
- **abolitionists** (ab uh **lish** uh nists) People working to end slavery before the Civil War
- **abundant** (uh **buhn** duhnt) More than enough
- **accusations** (ak yoo **zay** shuns) Charges that someone has done something wrong
- **acres** Measurements of area equal to 43,560 square feet. An acre is almost the size of a football field.
- **activated** Called into service in an emergency or war
- **activist** (**ak** ti vist) Someone who actively shows concern for an issue by writing, speaking, carrying signs, or marching in public
- **adaptation** (ad ap **tay** shuhn) Act of changing to fit different conditions
- **adapted** (uh **dap** tuhd) Changed or adjusted to fit different conditions
- **administration** (ad min uh **stray** shuhn) A group of people in charge of an organization or business
- **aerial** (**air** ee uhl) In the air
- **agents** (**ay** juhnts) People who have the power to act for others
- **agriculture** (**ag** ruh kul chur) Another word for farming
- **Al-Qaida** (al **ky** dah) **terrorist network** A very loose organization, originally founded by Osama bin Laden in Afghanistan (af **gan** uh stan) in the late 1980s. Al-Qaida uses violence to try to destroy anything that opposes its own view of Islamic rule.
- **Allies** (**al** eyes) People or countries that support one another. In World War I, the Allies were Great Britain, France, Russia, Italy, and later, the United States.
- **Allies** (**al** eyes) Countries who fought against the Axis Powers in World War II, including Australia, Belgium, Brazil, Britain, Canada, China, Denmark, France, Greece, the Netherlands, New Zealand, Norway, Poland, South Africa, the United States, USSR, and Yugoslavia
- **amendment** (uh **mend** muhnt) Official change
- **American Revolution** (rev uh **loo** shuhn) (1775–1783) The war in which the American colonies won their independence from Great Britain
- **ammunition** (am yoo **nish** uhn) Things that can be exploded or fired from weapons, such as bullets
- **amputated** (**am** pyuh tay tuhd) Cut off all or part of a finger, arm, or leg, usually because of disease or injury
- **ancestors** (**an** ses turz) Family members who lived long ago

- **anti** Against
- **apparatus** (ap uh **rat** uhs) Equipment or machines made to do a job
- **apprentice** (uh **pren** tuhs) A person learning a trade or art
- **aquatic** (uh **kwat** ik) Living or growing in water
- **archaeology** (ahr kee **ol** uh jee) The study of past people based on the things they left in the places where they once lived
- **archaic** (ahr **kay** ik) Old; Indians who lived in Wisconsin between 6500 and 800 BC
- **archives** A safe place for storing historical records and photographs
- **armistice** (**ahr** muh stis) An agreement to stop fighting
- **artifacts** (**ar** tih fax) Objects made by people
- **association** (uh soh see **ay** shuhn) A group of people joined together for a common reason
- **Axis** Countries who fought on the side of Germany in World War II, including Bulgaria, Hungary, Italy, Japan, and Romania
- **Aztalan** (**az** tuh lan) A Mississippian site in Jefferson County near the Crawfish River

B

- **bankrupt** Without enough money to pay what a company or person owes
- **barges** (**bahr** juhz) Long, flat boats
- **basins** Low areas
- **bat mitzvah** (bot **mits** vuh) In Hebrew, the words mean "Daughter of the Commandment." It's a Jewish ceremony in which a 13-year-old girl assumes responsibility as an adult by learning Hebrew and leading a religious service. The ceremony for boys is called a bar mitzvah.
- **blight** Disease
- **brass** A yellow metal made from copper and zinc
- **breeding** Mating and having young
- **brigade** (bri **gayd**) A large military unit, made up of several regiments
- **British** People from the island of Great Britain which includes the countries of England, Scotland, and Wales
- **brochure** (broh **shur**) A booklet, usually with pictures, with information about a product or service, such as a vacation brochure
- **buckers** People who saw logs into lengths
- **buckskins** Clothing made from the skin of a buck (deer)
- **butterfat** The fatty part of milk. Milk is usually sold according to the amount of butterfat it has.

C

- **Cahokia** (kuh **ho** kee uh) A large Mississippian site in southern Illinois near the Mississippi River
- **campaigns** (kam **paynz**) Organized series of actions and activities carried out in order to win something, like an election

•**capital** The city or town where the government of a country or state is located

•**capitalist** (**kap** uh tuh list) **economy** An economic system in which individuals own their property and their own businesses

•**capitol** The building in which lawmakers and other important government officials meet

•**cargo** Goods carried by ship or other kinds of transportation

•**cartographers** (car **tahg** ruh phurs) Mapmakers

•**cash crop** A crop grown to be sold off the farm rather than used on the farm

•**cast iron** Iron that has been shaped by pouring or casting into a mold

•**ceded** (**seed** ed) Given up

•**census** (**sen** suhs) An official count of all people living in a country or district

•**Central Powers** In World War I, Germany, Austria-Hungary, and Turkey fought together against the Allies

•**ceremonies** (**ser** uh moh neez) Important acts done at special times and places

•**child labor** Children working for wages in factories, mines, or on farms

•**churn** A machine in which cream is made into butter

•**citizens** (**sit** uh zuhns) Members of a particular country or state who have the right to live there

•**cities** (**sit** eez) Large, important centers of population and business

•**civil rights** The individual rights that all members of a society have to freedom and equal treatment under the law

•**Civil War** The war between the North and South of the United States, which took place between 1861 and 1865; **civil war** is a war between two groups of people in the same country

•**clan** A group of Native people with the same ancestor

•**clientele** (klI uhn **tel**) Customers

•**Cold War** The period between the late 1940s and the late 1980s when the United States actively tried to keep communism from spreading around the globe

•**colonel** (**kur** nuhl) An officer in the military, just below a general

•**colonial** (kuh **loh** nee uhl) Of or about a colony

•**colonists** (**kol** uh nists) People (or their ancestors) who left their country to live in newly settled areas called colonies

•**combine** (**kom** bIn) A machine on a farm, driven by a person, to harvest crops

•**communicate** (kuh **myoo** nuh kayt) To share ideas

•**communist** (**kom** yoo nist) **government** A system of government in which businesses and property are controlled by the state, and individuals have fewer rights than in capitalist societies

•**company** (**kuhm** puh nee) Group of soldiers

•**compass rose** A map feature that shows the basic or cardinal directions (North, South, East, West) and often, shows those in between, such as southwest and northeast

•**compromise** (**kom** pruh mIze) To agree to accept a solution to a disagreement that is not exactly what any side wanted

•**Compromise of 1850** The law passed by Congess that had several parts: First, California could enter the Union as a free state. Second, New Mexico, Arizona, Nevada, and Utah became territories—neither slave nor free. Third, slaves could no longer be bought and sold in Washington, D.C., the nation's capital. Finally, the Fugitive Slave Act was passed.

•**Confederacy** (kun **fed** ur uh see) The government of the 11 Southern states who fought the Northern states in the American Civil War

•**conservancy** (kuhn **sur** vuhn see) A group or organization that works to protect valuable things such as natural resources, forests, and wildlife

•**consolidated** (kuhn **sol** uh day tuhd) Joined together

•**constitution** (kon stuh **too** shuhn) In the United States, a written document that contains the rights and responsibilities that people have and describes how government works

•**continents** The seven large landmasses of the Earth. They are Africa, Antarctica, Asia, Australia, Europe, North America, and South America.

•**continuity** (kon tuh **noo** uh tee) Something that lasts or continues over a long period of time

•**co-ops** (**koh** ops) Stores or buildings in which members own shares of the business. Short for cooperative (koh **op** ur uh tiv)

•**copper** A reddish-brown metal that conducts heat and electricity well; a mineral

•**corporation** (kor puh **ray** shuhn) Large business company

•**coulees** (**koo** leez) Deep, narrow valleys, often with streams

•**country** (**kun** tree) An area of land that has boundaries and a government that are shared by all the people living there; a nation

•**county** (**kown** tee) One of the parts into which a state is divided

•**creameries** (**kreem** ur ees) Factories that turns cow milk into butter and cream

•**cultivate** (**cuhl** tuh vayt) To plant, grow, and harvest

•**curling** A sport where players push a large stone over the ice into the other team's goal to score points

D

•**dairy** (**dair** ee) **cow** Cow that makes milk

•**death camps** Places designed to kill many Jewish people at one time

•**decades** (**dek** aydz) Periods of 10 years

•**deed** Document that proves ownership of the land

•**democracy** (di **mok** ruh see) A system of government that allows people to choose their own leaders

- **demonstration** When people join together to protest something
- **depot** (**dee** poh) A railroad station building where people arrive and depart on trains
- **descendants** (dee **sen** dunts) Family members who are born after their ancestors
- **developers** People or businesses who build and sell houses and buildings
- **diversified** (di **vur** suh fId) **farming** Growing and raising a variety of crops and animals rather than focusing on one crop or one type of animal
- **document** (**dok** yoo muhnt) A written or printed paper that contains the original, official, or legal information that can be used as evidence or proof
- **dominated** (**dom** uh nay tuhd) Controlled something by using strength or power
- **Driftless Area** Southwestern Wisconsin and parts of the neighboring areas of Iowa, Illinois, and Minnesota that were never covered by glaciers
- **drill** To teach by having the learner practice something by doing it over and over again; to learn by doing something over and over again
- **drumlin** A long hill that looks something like an overturned canoe or teardrop

E

- **eaglet** Baby eagle
- **ecology** (ee **kol** uh jee) The study of the environment as a community of living things
- **economy** (ee **kon** uh mee) The goods, services, and money that are made and used by a group of people
- **efficiently** (i **fish** uhnt lee) Working without wasting time
- **effigy** (**ef** uh jee) **mounds** Human-made mounds created in shapes such as animals
- **elders** (**el** durz) Older people
- **elevation** (eh leh **vay** shun) The height of land above sea level
- **eliminated** (i **lim** uh nay tuhd) Removed
- **emancipated** (i man suh **pay** tuhd) Legally freed from slavery
- **Emancipation Proclamation** (i man suh **pay** shuhn prok luh **may** shuhn) An official announcement made by Abraham Lincoln on January 1, 1863, declaring that all slaves in Confederate states were emancipated or freed
- **emigrate** (**em** uh grayt) To leave one's country to settle in another
- **emigrated** (**em** uh gray tuhd) Left one's own country to settle in another
- **emigrating** (**em** uh gray ting) Leaving one's own country to settle in another
- **employed** Paid someone for working at the business, organization, farm, etc.

- **employment** A person's regular work or job
- **enameled** Made of a glasslike material melted and then cooled to make a smooth, hard surface
- **engineers** (en juh **nirz**) People trained to design and build bridges, railroads, roads, machines, and other equipment
- **enlisted** (en **lis** tuhd) Joined the military
- **entrepôt** (**awn** truh poh) Gathering spot
- **entrepreneurs** (ahn truh pruh **nurz**) People who start new businesses and are good at finding new ways to make money
- **environment** The natural world of lands, waters, and air
- **equal rights** Equality—the same rights for everyone
- **Equator** An imaginary line that goes around the middle of the globe like a belt from East to West.
- **equipment** (ee **kwip** muhnt) Tools and machines needed or used for a particular purpose
- **era** A period of time in history
- **eroded** Worn away by wind and water
- **escarpment** (ess **carp** munt) A steep, rocky cliff or long slope of land that is higher than the lands on either side of it
- **esker** A long, snake-shaped hill formed of rounded sand and gravel
- **established** (ess **tab** lish tuhd) Set up something, such as a school, church, club, or business
- **ethnic** Having to do with a group of people sharing the same home country or culture
- **Europeans** (yur up **pee** uhns) People from Europe
- **evaluate** (i **val** yoo ayt) To decide how good or valuable something is after thinking about it
- **evidence** (**ev** uh duhns) Information and facts that help prove something really happened
- **excavate** (**ek** skuh vayt) To dig carefully
- **exchange** (iks **chanj**) Act of giving one thing for another
- **execute** (**ek** suh kyoot) To put into action and enforce
- **executive** (eg **zek** yoo tiv) The head of state or governor
- **executive branch** The branch of government that enforces laws
- **exhaustion** (eg **zaws** chuhn) The state of being completely worn out
- **extinct** No longer existing
- **eyewitnesses** People who have seen something take place and can describe what happened

F

- **factors** Any one of the causes that helps bring about a result
- **factories** Buildings where products, such as lumber or paper, are made in large numbers, often using machines
- **features** (**fee** churz) Important parts or qualities of things

federal (fed ur uhl) Referring to a type of government where its smaller divisions—such as states—are united under and controlled by one government

fertile Good for growing lots of crops and plants

fixtures Things fixed firmly in place like a sink or a bathtub

formal Organized with a set of rules

formations (for **may** shuhnz) Shapes of something

forts Buildings built strong enough to survive attacks. Sometimes they were surrounded by walls or tall fences

foundry A factory where metal is melted and shaped

French and Indian War (1756–763) The seven-year-long battle between the French and the British for control of the trading forts and water-highways in Wisconsin, the Midwest, and Canada

frontier (fruhn **teer**) The far edge of a country where few people live

fugitive (fyoo juh tiv) **slave** Person escaping from slavery to gain freedom

Fugitive Slave Act A federal law passed in 1850 that required that all citizens help return fugitive slaves to their owners

fur trade The process of exchanging European trade goods for Indian goods, such as pelts or wild rice

fuse (fyooz) A long, slow-burning cord that is lit to set off a blast

G

galena (guh **lee** nuh) A shiny gray mineral used to make lead

geography (jee **og** ruh fee) The study of the earth, including its people, resources, climate, and physical features

geologists (jee **ol** uh jists) Scientists who study the earth's layers of soil and rocks

geology (jee **ol** uh jee) The study of the earth's layers of soil and rocks

ghetto A neighborhood in a European city where Jews were forced to live

glacial (glay shuhl) Having to do with glaciers

glaciated (glay shee ay tuhd) Once covered by glaciers

glaciers (glay shurz) Giant sheets of ice formed in mountain valleys or near the North or South poles

global Having to do with the earth and everything on the earth

globalization (gloh buhl uh **zay** shuhn) A connection among different countries through business and technology

Good Roads Movement People working together to have the state improve road conditions and build highways

gorges (gor juhz) Deep valleys with steep, rocky sides

governor The person elected as the head of the state to represent all the people in the state

granary (gran uh ree) A building for storing grain

Great Depression An event during the 1930s, when many people lost their jobs and homes, and people all over the United States and other countries suffered

Guernsey (gurn zee) A breed of cattle that is raised for milk

H

habitats (hab uh tats) Places and natural conditions where plants and animals live

harvesting Gathering in the crops that are ripe

headwaters The place where a stream starts before flowing into a river

hemisphere (heh mis pheer) Half a sphere

heritage (hair uh tij) Valuable, important traditions handed down from generation to generation

highlands (hy lundz) Hilly lands that are higher in elevation than the lands surrounding them

hijacked Took illegal control of a plane or other vehicle

hills Raised areas of land that are less than 2000 feet above the surrounding land

historians (hi **stor** ee uhnz) People who study and tell or write about the past

historic (his **tor** ik) Important in history

historic preservation (prez ur **vay** shuhn) The act of saving old places and spaces, taking care of what we have rather than tearing it down and building new places

history (his tuh ree) The study of the past

Hmong (mong) A language and group of people from Southeast Asia

hoboes (hoh bohz) People who are poor and homeless, and often ride freight trains looking for work

Ho-Chunk American Indian nation

hoisted Lifted up

Holocaust (hol uh kost) The planned murder of the Jews in Europe in the 1940s in which 6 million Jews, and others, were killed

Holstein (hohl steen) A breed of cattle that is raised for milk

homeland A country where someone was born or has lived

homestead A house with its buildings and grounds; farm with all its buildings

hydraulic (hI draw lik) Liquid-powered. Hydraulic machines work on power created by liquid being forced under pressure through pipes.

I

Ice Age A period of time, long ago, when glaciers covered much of the earth's surface. The last Ice Age was more than 10,000 years ago.

igneous (ig **nee** uhs) Created by great heat or by a volcano

immigrant (im uh gruhnt) A person from one country who moves to settle permanently in another

- **immigration** (im uh **gray** shuhn) Moving from one country to settle and live in another country
- **independent** Free of the control of other people or things
- **industrial** Having to do with factories
- **industrialization** (in dus tree luh **zay** shuhn) The development of large industries in an area
- **industries** Factories or plants that produce all kinds of goods
- **industry** A type of business
- **installed** Put in place
- **integrated** (in tuh **gray** tuhd) Included people of all races
- **interacted** Took action or engaged with something or someone
- **interpret** (in **tur** prit) To explain the meaning of something
- **interpreter** (in **tur** pruh tur) Someone who explains the meaning of something
- **interpreting** (in **tur** pruh ting) Translating
- **intersection** The point at which two things meet and cross each other
- **interstate highways** Large paved roads, designed to accommodate many cars and high speeds. Interstates have medians separating lanes going in the opposite directions. Interstate highways connect different states or cities within a state.
- **invaded** Entered by force
- **invention** (in **ven** shun) A new, important thing that someone makes or thinks of
- **investigate** (in **ves** tuh gayt) To find out as much as possible about something
- **iron** A strong, hard metal used to make things like gates and railings
- **islands** (**I** lundz) Areas of land completely surrounded by water
- **isthmus** (**iss** muhss) A narrow strip of land that lies between two bodies of water and connects two larger land masses

J

- **Jersey** (**jur** zee) A breed of cattle that is raised for milk
- **Jesuit missionaries** (**jezh** yoo wit **mish** shuh nair eez) Catholic priests who try to teach others to become Christians
- **judgments** Judges' solutions when people disagree on what a law means
- **judicial** (joo **dish** uhl) **branch** The branch of government that settles arguments about the way laws are carried out or applied

K

- **kame** A steep, rounded hill formed by streams of melting glacial ice pouring down a hole and depositing their load of dirt and rocks into a large pile
- **kettle** A scooped-out area that was filled with a large block of ice

L

- **labor** Work

- **labor unions** Organizations of wage workers formed to help them deal with issues such as the amount of wages paid for work and safer working conditions
- **land use** Decisions and actions regarding land and the environment
- **landforms** Features of the earth's surface, such as hills, valleys, and prairies
- **landscapes** (**land** skaypz) The shapes and forms of the land such as hills, plains, valleys
- **latitude** (**lat** uh tood) Lines, or parallels, that run from east to west around the globe
- **launching** (**lawn** ching) Putting a boat or other vessel into the water
- **league** (leeg) An organized group of sports clubs or teams
- **legislative** (**lej** uh slay tiv) **branch** The branch of state government that makes laws. The legislative branch has two parts. At the federal level, these are the Senate and the House of Representatives. At the state level, these branches are called the Senate and State Assembly.
- **legislators** (**lej** uh slay turz) Lawmakers who make up the legislature
- **legislature** (**lej** uh slay chur) An elected group of people who have the power to make laws for the state
- **livestock** Farm animals
- **locate** To find where something is
- **located** Found
- **location** The place or position where something is found
- **locomotive** (loh kuh **moh** tiv) An engine used to push or pull railroad cars
- **lodges** Cabins used for a short stay
- **logging** Harvesting trees to be made into wood for building
- **longhouse** A long, narrow wigwam built large enough to hold multiple families
- **longitude** (**lon** juh tood) Lines, or meridians, that run from the North Pole to the South Pole on the globe
- **lowlands** (**low** lundz) Fairly flat lands that are lower in elevation than the lands around them

M

- **machinist** (muh **shee** nist) A worker who shapes metal by using machines and tools
- **mansion** (**man** shun) A very large house
- **manufactured** (man yuh **fak** churd) Something made, often by machines, in a factory operated by many people doing different kinds of work
- **manufacturers** (man yuh **fak** chur urz) People who manufacture or make things, often with machines
- **manufacturing** (man yuh **fak** chur ing) Making something, often by machines, in a factory operated by many people doing different kinds of work
- **marches** Large groups of people walking together in order to protest or express their opinion about something

- **market** A demand for something, such as milk
- **Marquette, Jacques** (mahr **ket** zhok) A Jesuit missionary. He and **Louis Jolliet** (loo **wee** zho lee **et**) were the first Europeans to find and travel down the Mississippi River.
- **mascot** Something that is supposed to bring good luck, especially an animal kept by a military group or sports team
- **massacred** (**mass** uh curd) Fiercely attacked and killed
- **mastodons** (**mas** tuh dons) Large, hairy mammals, related to the elephant, that died out thousands of years ago
- **memoirs** (**mem** wahrz) Memories written by someone after the event or events occurred
- **Menominee** (muh **nah** muh nee) American Indian nation
- **merged** (murjd) Joined
- **Mesquakie** (mes **kwaw** kee) American Indian nation
- **metamorphic** (met uh **mor** fik) Changed by heat and pressure
- **Métis** (may **tee**) Of mixed blood or traditions
- **metropolitan** (met roh **pol** uh tuhn) Having to do with a large city
- **migrant** (**mI** gruhnt) A person who moves from one state or region of a country to another
- **migrant workers** People who move from place to place to help harvest crops
- **migrating** Moving from one region of the country to another
- **migration** (my **gray** shuhn) The process of moving from one region to another within the same country
- **militia** (muh **lish** uh) A volunteer army trained to fight only in an emergency
- **mineral** A substance found in nature than is not an animal or a plant. Lead, copper, gold, iron, and zinc are all minerals.
- **Mississippians** (mis uh **sip** ee uhns) Groups of Indians who lived in Wisconsin between 1000 and 1200 AD
- **monument** (**mon** yuh muhnt) Something set up to honor and keep alive the memory of a person or event. A monument can take many forms: a fountain, statue, building, or stone, for example.
- **moraines** (muh **rains**) Ridges or long hills that were once the side or edge of a glacier
- **movement** A group of people who have joined together to support a cause, as in the Civil Rights movement
- **mural** A painting created directly on a wall

N

- **navigate** (**nav** uh gayt) To travel in a boat, aircraft, or other vehicle using maps, compasses, the stars, and other devices to guide you
- **Nazi** (**not** zee) Describing the followers of Adolf Hitler who wanted to rid Europe of Jews and other peoples of Europe they considered "impure"
- **negotiate** (ni **goh** shee ayt) Discuss something in order to come to an agreement

- **neutral** (**noo** truhl) In a war, describing a person or country that does not support either side
- **New Deal** President Franklin D. Roosevelt's programs designed to help end the suffering of Americans during the Great Depression
- **newsboys** Boys from 8 to 17 who sold daily newspapers in the late 1800s and early 1900s
- **Nicolet, Jean** (nik oh **lay** zhon) The first European explorer generally believed to have landed in Wisconsin

O

- **obituary** (o **bit** chu air ee) A printed report of someone's death, often in the newspaper
- **Ojibwe** (o **jib** way) An American Indian nation
- **Oneota** (oh nee **oh** tuh) Native people living in Wisconsin between 1000 AD and 1630 AD
- **oral historian** A historian who talks to people to research their stories
- **oral tradition** The passing down of stories by telling them over and over without writing them down
- **ore** Rock that is mined because it contains valuable metal
- **orphans** (**or** fuhnz) Children whose parents are dead
- **outcrops** Groups of rocks above the surface of the ground
- **overalls** Loose pants with shoulder straps and a panel covering the chest

P

- **Paleo** (**pay** lee oh) Old
- **Paleo-Indians** The first people in Wisconsin, who lived here between 10,000 BC and 6500 BC
- **paper mills** Places where people use machines to turn wood into paper
- **pasture** (**pas** chur) Grazing land for animals
- **patented** Received a legal document that gives the inventor all the rights to manufacture or sell the invention
- **peat** Dark brown, partly decayed plant matter found in bogs and swamps
- **peaveys** (**pee** veez) Tools with long wooden handles and metal hooks on one end, used to move logs
- **pelts** Animal skins with the fur or hair still on them
- **peninsula** (peh **nin** suh luh) A piece of land that sticks out from a larger land mass and is nearly surrounded by water
- **Pentagon** A building with five sides that is the headquarters of the U.S. Department of Defense
- **perishable** (**pair** ish uh buhl) Likely to spoil or decay quickly
- **persistent** (pur **sis** tuhnt) Refusing to stop or give up
- **petition** (puh **tish** uhn) A letter that many people sign to express their feelings about an issue or to ask those in power to change something

- **pharmacy** (**far** muh see) A place where medicines and drugs are stored and sold
- **physical boundaries** (**fiz** uh kuhl **bown** da rees) Natural features like rivers, lakes, or mountains that separate counties, states, or countries
- **pioneer** (pI oh **neer**) One of the first people to work in a new and unknown area
- **plains** Level or nearly level land
- **plank roads** Roads typically built of wood planks two inches thick and eight feet long, which were nailed to four-inch squares of wood
- **political** (puh **lit** uh kuhl) Having to do with politics, or the way a city, county, state, or nation governs itself
- **political boundaries** (puh **lit** uh kuhl **bown** da rees) Boundaries that governments create to separate counties, states, or countries
- **political** (puh **lit** uh kuhl) **party** A group of people organized to win elections and gain political power
- **politician** (pol uh **tish** uhn) Someone who runs for or holds a government office
- **pollutants** (puh **loot** uhnts) Things that pollute or make dirty
- **polluting** (puh **loot** ing) Making dirty
- **portage** (**por** tidj) A location on a river or lake where things are carried from one shore to another
- **pottery** Pots and other containers made from clay
- **prairie** (**prair** ree) A large area of flat or rolling grassland with few or no trees
- **Prairie du Chien** (prair ee du **sheen**) An important city and trading center located where the Wisconsin River flows into the Mississippi River
- **preserve** To protect something so that it stays in its original state
- **primary sources** (**prI** mair ee **sor** suhz) The most important, original places, people or things from which information comes
- **Prime Meridian** An imaginary line that divides the globe into two equal halves, from North to South.
- **processed** (**prah** sest) Prepared or changed by a series of steps, such as wheat being processed into flour, or animal hides being processed into leather
- **processing** Preparing or changing something by following a series of steps
- **Progressives** People in the late 1800s and early 1900s who worked for positive change in government, education, and other areas
- **promote** To help with the growth and development of something
- **promoting** Helping with the growth or development of something and making the public aware
- **protested** Objected to something strongly and publicly

Q

- **quarried** (**kwor** eed) Dug out
- **quarries** (**kwor** eez) Places where stone is dug or cut

R

- **rationed** Allowed only limited amounts
- **ravines** (ruh **veenz**) Deep, narrow valleys with steep sides
- **reapers** Machines that people use to cut and gather grain when it is ripe
- **recreation** (rek ree **ay** shuhn) An activity meant to be enjoyed, like sports and games
- **recruiting** (ree **kroo** ting) Getting people to join the military
- **reformers** People who want to change things for the better
- **refugee camp** A safe place for people forced to leave their homes by war or disaster
- **refugees** (ref yoo **jeez**) People forced to leave home to escape harm after disaster or war
- **regiment** (**rej** uh muhnt) Part of the army (1000 soldiers) under the command of a colonel (**kur** nuhl)
- **region** (**ree** jun) A defined area of a place (state or country, for example) that has common features, such as a similar landscape
- **register** Official record
- **regulate** (**reg** yoo layt) To control or manage
- **Rendezvous** (**rahn** day voo) Place for meeting
- **replicas** (**rep** luh kuhz) Exact copies
- **representatives** (rep pri **zen** tuh tivz) In general, people chosen to speak or act for others. Some people elected to public offices are also known as representatives.
- **resented** (ri **zen** tuhd) Felt hurt or angry by actions done to them
- **resort** (ri **zort**) A place where people go to rest and relax
- **resources** (**ree** sors sez) Things that are useful or valuable
- **restore** Bring back to original condition
- **restricted** (ri **strik** tuhd) Kept within limits
- **ridges** Long and narrow chains of hills
- **rock shelter** Shallow cave
- **root cellar** A room underground for storing root vegetables
- **rural** (**rur** uhl) Having to do with the countryside or farming
- **rustic** To do with the country
- **rutabagas** (**roo** tah bay guhs) Large pale-yellow root vegetables sometimes called "Swedish turnips"

S

- **sacred** (**say** krid) Holy; deserving of respect
- **sampler** Hand-stitched cloth designed to show the skills of the person who stitched it
- **Sauk** (sawk) American Indian nation
- **sauna** (**saw** nuh) A Finnish bath that uses dry heat, or a bath where steam is made by throwing water on hot stones
- **sawmills** Places where people use machines to saw logs into lumber

- **Scandinavian** (skan dih **nay** vee uhn) Someone born in one of the following Northern European countries: Sweden, Norway, Denmark, or Finland
- **schooners** (**skoo** nurz) Sailing vessels with masts or tall poles that stick up through the boat's deck and sails that run lengthwise
- **secede** (si **seed**) To withdraw or leave one organization, often to form another
- **secession** (si **sesh** uhn) Withdrawing from or leaving from one organization, often to form another
- **secondary sources** (**sek** uhn dair ee **sor** suhz) Sources having less importance
- **sedition** (si **dish** uhn) Moving others to take action against a government
- **segregated** (**seg** ruh gay tuhd) Separated or kept apart from the main group
- **segregation** The act or practice of keeping people or groups apart
- **serve** To do your duty in some form of service
- **shanties** Small, simple, and temporary buildings
- **sharecroppers** Farmers who were so poor that they had no money to rent the land they farmed. To live on the land, they gave the landowner a "share" of what they produced.
- **shot** Small balls or pellets to be fired from a gun
- **silage** (**sI** ludj) Grain, grass, or corn that is cut, chopped, then packed into a silo
- **silo** (**sI** loh) A tower used to store food for farm animals
- **silt** Fine particles of soil washed along by flowing water to settle at the bottom of a river or lake
- **site** A place where people lived, worked, and worshipped; where archaeologists find artifacts and features
- **slash** The branches and parts of the tree too small to saw during logging
- **slave** Someone who is owned by another person
- **slavery** The practice of owning people and making them work
- **sloughs** (slooz) Marshy or swampy areas with slow-moving or standing water
- **slugger** A baseball player who hits lots of homeruns
- **smelted** Melted so that the metal can be removed from ore
- **smelting** Melting ore so that the mineral can be separated from elements that are not useful, such as sulfur
- **social** (**soh** shuhl) Having to do with the way people behave in groups and live together as communities
- **sod** The top layer of grass and soil
- **soil** The top layer of earth, dirt
- **Soo Locks** The part of the canal built at Sault Ste. Marie that can raise and lower the water level, so that boats can be raised or lowered to get to and from Lake Superior
- **sources** (**sor** suhz) The places, people, or things from which information comes
- **sphere** (sfeer) A round solid shape like a basketball where all sides are the same distance from the center
- **spiritual** (**spir** uh choo uhl) Having to do with the soul and the spirit
- **sponsor** A person, people, or organization that agrees to help refugees who enter the country
- **standard** The banner, symbol, or flag of a military group or nation
- **states** One of the parts into which the United States is divided. Wisconsin, Illinois, Michigan, Minnesota, and Iowa are all states
- **steamboats** Large wooden boats powered by steam created in a coal-fired engine. Because of this power, steamboats could easily carry people and goods upriver. Unlike schooners, steamboats could travel on windless days.
- **stereopticon** (stair ee **op** tuh kon) **card** A pair of photographs mounted side by side on either glass or cardboard, and also called stereo views. When people look at the card through a stereopticon viewer, the photo looks three dimensional.
- **stewardship** (**stoo** wurd ship) Personal responsibility for taking care of something that is not one's own
- **stonemason** Person skilled in building with stone
- **straits** A narrow channel connecting two bodies of water
- **subsistence** What is needed to survive
- **suburbs** Homes and shopping centers located beyond the main settled areas
- **suffrage** (**suf** rudj) The right to vote
- **supervised** (**soo** puhr vIzd) Watched over or directed
- **surrender** (suh **ren** dur) To give up
- **survey** (**sur** vay) To measure an area in order to make a map
- **survived** Continue to exist or live
- **suspected** (suhs **pek** tuhd) Believed to be bad without proof
- **swamps** Wet, soft lands
- **symbols** (**sim** buhls) Designs or objects that represent something else
- **synagogue** (**sin** uh gog) Place of Jewish worship
- **systematically** (sis tuh **mat** ik lee) In a systematic or planned way

T

- **Taliesin** (tal ee **es** uhn) Frank Lloyd Wright named his house Taliesin which means "shining brow" in the Welsh language
- **tanning** Making leather from animal hides
- **taxes** Money paid to the government
- **technician** (tek **nish** uhn) Someone trained to work with any specialized equipment
- **technology** (tek **nol** oh jee) The use of science and engineering to do practical things, such as make businesses and factories work better
- **territory** (**tair** ih toh ree) An area of land that belongs to the United States, but is not a state

- **terrorist** Someone who uses violence to threaten or attack others
- **Thailand** (**tI** land) A country in Southeast Asia
- **threshed** Separated the grain from the parts of the plant that can't be eaten
- **till** A combination of clay, silt, and, pebbles, and larger rocks
- **timber** Trees that were cut to be made into wood for building
- **tobacco** (tuh **bak** oh) A plant with large leaves. The leaves are chopped and dried to be used for smoking or chewing.
- **topographical** (top uh **graf** uh kuhl) Showing details of the physical features of an area, including hills, valleys, mountains, plains, and rivers
- **topography** (tuh **pog** ruh fee) The detailed description of the physical features of an area, including hills, valleys, mountains, plains, and rivers
- **tourism** (**tur** iz uhm) Traveling and visiting places for pleasure
- **tourists** (**tur** ists) People who travel and visit places for pleasure
- **townships** Square-shaped pieces of land, six miles on each side, divided into 36 sections
- **tragedies** (**traj** uh deez) Very sad events
- **translate** To turn one language into another
- **translation** (tranz **lay** shuhn) A change from one language to another
- **transport** Bring
- **transportation** A system for moving people and goods from one place to another
- **transported** Moved from one place to another
- **transporting** Moving
- **treaties** Official written documents between nations
- **tributary** (**trib** yuh tair ee) A stream that flows into a larger waterway
- **troops** Soldiers
- **trough** (trawf) A long narrow container from which animals can eat or drink
- **turbine** (**tur** buhn or **tur** bIn) An engine driven by water, steam, or gas passing through the blades of a wheel that makes it turn. Turbines are often used with other machinery to produce electrical power.
- **turning point** Major change

U

- **U.S. Congress** The part of government where laws are made. Congress is made up of the House of Representatives and the Senate.
- **Underground Railroad (UGRR)** Not a railroad at all but a network of abolitionists who helped fugitive slaves find their way to free states or to Canada before the Civil War
- **Union** The United States of America
- **unite** (yoo **nIt**) To make one
- **uplands** (**uh** plundz) Rocky cliffs and steep valleys
- **urban** (**ur** buhn) To do with or living in a city

V

- **valleys** Areas of low ground between two hills
- **veins** (vaynz) Cracks or layers in rock filled with a mineral
- **vessels** (**ves** uhlz) Ships or large boats
- **veteran** Someone who has served in the armed forces, especially during a war
- **Veterans of Foreign** (**for** uhn) **Wars** A group of veterans who help each other by serving their community
- **veterinarian** (**vet** ur uh nair ee uhn) A doctor who treats animals
- **veterinary** (**vet** ur uh nair ee) Having to do with animal medicine or surgery
- **volcanic** (vol **kan** ik) Having to do with volcanoes

W

- **wages** Money paid for work done, especially work done by the hour
- **War of 1812** (1812–1815) The war in which troops from the United States fought British troops for control of American land claims in North America. When the United States won, the British no longer had any real power over trade and other businesses.
- **waterfowl** Birds, like ducks and geese, that spend their lives on or near water
- **watershed** The area of land that drains into the same waterway
- **waterway** River, lake, or other body of water on which ships and boats travel
- **welders** People who join to pieces of metal or plastic by heating them until they are soft enough to bond or join together
- **wetlands** Areas covered with water for all or part of the year
- **wheat** A plant with a grain that can be made into flour to make bread and other foods
- **widow** A woman whose husband has died
- **widower** (**wid** oh ur) A man whose wife has died
- **windlasses** Tools with two handles and a long rope used to lift heavy things like a bucket of lead ore
- **Women's Relief Corps** (kor) A group of women acting together to honor all citizens who have served our country in any war
- **Woodland Indians** Groups of Indians who lived in Wisconsin between about 800 BC and 1630 AD
- **Works Progress Administration (WPA)** A Federal New Deal program, started in the Great Depression that gave people jobs building parks, roads, and bridges
- **World Trade Center Site** The site where the World Trade Center buildings stood before September 11, 2001

Z

- **zinc** (zingk) A blue-white metal that is used with other metals and for coating metals so that they will not rust

Index

Illustration Credits

Photographs identified with WHi are from the Society's collections; address inquiries about such photos to the Visual Materials Archivist at Wisconsin Historical Society, 816 State Street, Madison, WI 53706. Credits read counterclockwise, beginning at the upper left of each page.

CHAPTER 1 Page 5 WHi 1906, Fire at the Wisconsin state capitol; WHi 9566, Raising *Wisconsin* statue; WHi 10450, The Wisconsin state capitol under construction; WHi 23123, Surveying fire damage **Pages 8 and 9** Letter from John Cronk, courtesy of Wisconsin Historical Society Archives; Boaz spear point, courtesy of the University of Wisconsin Geology Museum; Mississippian spear point, courtesy of the Wisconsin Historical Museum; Jacques Marquette journal entry, courtesy of Wisconsin Historical Society Archives; Mai Ya Xiong sponsorship card, photo by Marcus Cohen; Announcement of escaped slave Joshua Glover, courtesy of Wisconsin Historical Society Archives; WHi 3553, St. Augustine's Church; WHi 5172, Map of Wisconsin, 1848 **Pages 10 and 11** Mississippian spear point, courtesy of the Wisconsin Historical Museum; Boaz spear point, courtesy of the University of Wisconsin Geology Museum; Letter from John Cronk, courtesy of Wisconsin Historical Society Archives; Mai Ya Xiong sponsorship card, photo by Marcus Cohen; Announcement for escaped slave Joshua Glover, courtesy of Wisconsin Historical Society Archives

CHAPTER 2 Pages 14 and 15 Photo of Ice Age Trail sign, courtesy of Ice Age Park and Trail Foundation; Photo of winter scene on Ice Age Trail, courtesy of Gail Piotrowski; Photo of Ray Zillmer, courtesy of Ice Age Park and Trail Foundation **Pages 22 and 23** Photo of Madison isthmus, courtesy of *Wisconsin State Journal* **Pages 26 and 27** Photo of University of Wisconsin–Stevens Point students overlooking Greenbush Kettle, courtesy of Karen A. Lemke; Photo of Green Lake Public School students on Parnell Esker, courtesy of Thomas Eddy; Photo of University of Wisconsin-Stevens Point students on Garrity Kame, courtesy of Karen A. Lemke; Photo of snow-covered drumlins, courtesy of Todd Fonstad **Pages 30 and 31** Aerial photo of Apostle Islands, courtesy of the Wisconsin Department of Natural Resources; Photo of Amnicon Falls, courtesy of the Wisconsin Department of Natural Resources **Pages 32 and 33** Photo of Rib Mountain, courtesy of the Wisconsin Department of Natural Resources; Photo of Roche-A-Cri State Park, courtesy of the Wisconsin Department of Natural Resources **Pages 34 and 35** Photo of confluence of Mississippi and Wisconsin rivers, courtesy of Wyalusing State Park; Photo of Kohler-Andrae State Park, courtesy of the Wisconsin Department of Natural Resources **Pages 36 and 37** Photos of state parks/forests, courtesy of the Wisconsin Department of Natural Resources

CHAPTER 3 Pages 40 and 41 Photo of James Frechette, courtesy of Museum of Natural History, University of Wisconsin–Stevens Point; Photo of James Frechette bear sculpture, courtesy of Museum of Natural History, University of Wisconsin–Stevens Point **Pages 42 and 43** Photo of layers of trash exhibit, courtesy of Wisconsin Historical Museum; Photo of shifting dirt at Apple Branch, courtesy of the Wisconsin Historical Society Archaeology Program; Photos of tools/artifacts, courtesy of the Wisconsin Historical Society Archaeology Program **Pages 44 and 45** Photo of Boaz mastodon, courtesy of the University of Wisconsin Geology Museum; Photo of Boaz spear point, courtesy of University of Wisconsin Geology Museum; Photo of Paleo spear point, courtesy of the Wisconsin Historical Society Archaeology Program **Page 47** Photos of Crow Hollow tools/artifacts, courtesy of the Wisconsin Historical Society Archaeology Program **Page 49** Photos of Woodland tools/artifacts, courtesy of the Wisconsin Historical Society Archaeology Program **Page 51** Photos of Mississippian tools/artifacts, courtesy of the Wisconsin Historical Society Archaeology Program; Photo of Aztalan Mound at sunset, courtesy of the Wisconsin Historical Society Archaeology Program; Photo of Ramsey incised pot, courtesy of the Milwaukee Public Museum; Photo of Aztalan house replica, courtesy of the Wisconsin Historical Museum **Page 53** Photo of turtle-shell-bowl fragment, courtesy Wisconsin Historical Society Archaeology Program; Photo of Dambroski longhouse excavation, courtesy of the Wisconsin Historical Society Archaeology Program **Pages 54 and 55** Drawing and photograph of Lizard Mound, courtesy of the Wisconsin Historical Society Archaeology Program; Photos of Ho-Chunk basket, beaded bag, Woodland pot, courtesy of the Wisconsin Historical Museum; Photo of rock art, courtesy of Wisconsin Historical Society Archaeology Program **Pages 56 and 57** Photo of projectile points, courtesy of the Wisconsin Historical Society Archaeology Program; Photo of Aztalan house replica, courtesy of the Wisconsin Historical Museum

CHAPTER 4 Pages 60 and 61 Photo of Old World Wisconsin Camp Day, courtesy of Old World Wisconsin Historic Site; Photo of hikers, courtesy of the Wisconsin Department of Natural Resources;

Photo of girl studying in library, courtesy of Hine Family; Photo of Wade House blacksmith, courtesy of the Wade House Historical Site **Pages 62 and 63** WHi 24509, Ojibwe woman harvesting wild rice; Photo of Marvin Defoe building canoe, courtesy of Marvin Defoe; Photo of buffalo herd, courtesy of the Wisconsin Department of Natural Resources **Pages 64 and 65** Detail of Jean Nicolet from Wisconsin Historical Society mural; Detail from *Landfall*, courtesy of Wisconsin Historical Society Archives **Pages 66 and 67** Jolliet's map of North America, courtesy of the Library of Congress; WHi 43575, Excerpt from Marquette's journal; WHi 1982.448.1, Detail from *Marquette and Jolliet* by Frank Zeitler **Page 68** WHi 35065, Drawing of beavers; Photo of beaver hat, courtesy of the Wisconsin Historical Museum; Photo of Montreal canoe, courtesy of the Canadian Museum of Civilization **Pages 70 and 71** WHi 5434, Sampler made by Elizabeth Baird; WHi 5210, Elizabeth Baird portrait; Photo of toy cradleboard, courtesy of the Wisconsin Historical Museum **Pages 72 and 73** Photos of Forts Folle Avoine exterior, Ojibwe interpreter, trading post interior, courtesy of Forts Folle Avoine **Page 75** WHi 4170, Augustin Grignon portrait; WHi 42230, Fort McKay **Pages 76 and 77** WHi 6125, *Fort Winnebago*; WHi 2398, Juliette Kinzie portrait; WHi 2733/1942.473, Solomon Juneau portrait; WHi 43571, Juneau House **Pages 78 and 79** Photos of beaded powder horn and silver earrings, courtesy of the Wisconsin Historical Museum; Detail of Jean Nicolet from Wisconsin Historical Society mural; Jolliet's map of North America, courtesy of the Library of Congress

CHAPTER 5 Page 83 WHi 3142, *View of the Great Treaty Held at Prairie du Chien* **Pages 84 and 85** WHi 26888, *The Pipe Dance and the Tomahawk Dance*; WHi 43574, Treaty of Prairie du Chien **Page 87** WHi 43572, Crawford County map; WHi 9026, Cross section of lead mine; Photo of mining bucket, courtesy Pendarvis House Historic Site **Pages 88 and 89** WHi 11706, Portrait of Black Hawk; Photo of powder horn, courtesy of the Wisconsin Historical Museum **Page 91** WHi 43573, Map of New Diggings; WHi 3553, Photo of St. Augustine's Church **Pages 92 and 93** Wisconsin territorial seal, courtesy of Legislative Reference Bureau; WHi 2617, Portrait of James Duane Doty; WHi 38589, Original Madison plat map; WHi 27177, Portrait of Henry Dodge **Pages 94 and 95** WHi 5172, Map of Wisconsin 1848; WHi 11632, Drawing of Madison from University Hill by Adolf Hoeffler **Pages 96 and 97** Photos of contemporary Wisconsin capitol and interior rooms, courtesy of Legislative Reference Bureau **Page 98** Photo of Doty peace pipe, courtesy of the Wisconsin Historical Museum

CHAPTER 6 Page 103 WHi 7196, Photo of Ethnic Pride Day Celebration **Page 105** WHi 44792, Irish emigrants embarking from Queenstown, Ireland; Photo of Hmong welcomers, courtesy of *The Capital Times*; Photo of the Harrell Family, courtesy of George Harrell; WHi 12356, Beloit Chicago & North Western Depot postcard **Pages 106 and 107** WHi (x3) 38996, Richard Thomas; WHi (G5) 1445, Pendarvis & Trelawny Houses; WHi 37576, Pendarvis & Trelawny Houses after restoration; WHS (x3) 385559, James Carbis **Pages 108 and 109** WHi (x3) 27857, John Greene; Photo of gravestones, courtesy of Old World Wisconsin Historic Site; WHi (x3) 28102, the Greene family **Pages 110 and 111** WHi 35844, Koepsell house before move to Old World Wisconsin Historic Site; Portrait of Sophia and Fredrich Koepsell, courtesy of Old World Wisconsin State Historic Site; Photo of interior of Koepsell house at Old World Wisconsin State Historic Site, courtesy of Loyd C. Heath; Exterior of Koepsell house, courtesy of Old World Wisconsin Historic Site; Close-up of half-timber building style, courtesy of John Motoviloff **Pages 112 and 113** WHS (x3) 26412, Family in front of house; WHi (X3) 26410, Maria Ketola knitting; WHi(x3) 26417, Heikki and Maria in wagon with one horse; WHi(x3) 26416, Farmyard with windmill; Contemporary photo of pannu kakkuu, courtesy of Kori Oberle **Page 115** Photo of Goldberg family, courtesy of Wisconsin Historical Society Archives; Photo of Katz family at Marilyn's Bat Mitzvah, courtesy of Wisconsin Historical Society Archives **Page 117** *Life is Hard* album cover, courtesy of Cris Plata; Photo of Cris Plata singing, courtesy of Cris Plata **Pages 118 and 119** Photo of Mai Ya in traditional dress, © Bob Rashid; Photo of Mai Ya and her family, courtesy of Xiong family; Photo of Mai Ya's child sponsorship card, courtesy Marcus Cohen; Photo of Mai Ya reading to her brother, ©Bob Rashid; Photo of Mai Ya at UW–Milwaukee campus, courtesy of Xiong family **Pages 120 and 121** Stoughton Norwegian Dancers, used with permission

CHAPTER 7 Page 125 Runaway slave wood cut, courtesy of Wisconsin Historical Society Archives; WHi 6270, Joshua Glover portrait; Newspaper ad for return of Joshua Glover, courtesy of Wisconsin Historical Society Archives **Page 127** WHi 39663, Schoolhouse detail; Abraham Lincoln letter, courtesy of the Library of Congress; WHi 39661, Little white schoolhouse, Ripon **Page 129** WHi 1838, *Camp Randall* by Louis Kurz; Letter from John Cronk to Charles Palmer, courtesy of Wisconsin Historical Society Archives **Pages 130 and 131** WHi 11474, Patriots of St. Croix recruiting poster; Part of roster from the 29th Wisconsin, courtesy of Wisconsin Historical Society Archives; WHi 1909, Swearing in Native American Civil War recruits; WHi 45509, Statue of Col. Hans C. Heg; WHi 3399, Peter Thomas **Pages 132 and 133** WHi 7536, Old Abe; WHi 48226, Rufus Andrews; Letter from Rufus Andrews, courtesy of Wisconsin Historical Society Archives **Pages 134 and 135** WHi 36009, Cordelia Harvey; WHi 10028,

Photo of Soldiers Orphans Home; Photo of peg leg, courtesy of the Wisconsin Veteran's Museum; WHi 34323, Lucius Fairchild; Photo of Lucius Fairchild's housewife kit, courtesy of the Wisconsin Veteran's Museum; Photo of Lucius Fairchild's vest, courtesy of the Wisconsin Veteran's Museum **Pages 136 and 137** WHi 36793, Grant County's Soldier Monument; WHi 39824, Milton House; WHi 1884, Painting of Lucius Fairchild by John Singer Sargent; Photo of Civil War re-enactment, courtesy of Wade House Historic Site

CHAPTER 8 **Page 141** WHi 25044, Cranberry pickers; WHi 1874, Harvesting cranberries in Wisconsin; WHi (Rashid) 15, Northland Cranberry, Inc. **Pages 142 and 143** WHi 9000, Lead mining blast furnace; WHi 39775, Detail of lead mining map; Photo of lead pig, courtesy of the Wisconsin Historical Museum; Photo of poll pick, courtesy of the Wisconsin Historical Museum; WHi 38321, Zinc Works; WHi 23372, Ashland ore docks; WHi 23380, Gogebic Range miners **Pages 144 and 145** Photo of Fossebrekke farm, courtesy of Old World Wisconsin Historic Site; WHi 4510, Sketch of Rodolf farm **Pages 146 and 147** WHi 1914, Farm laborers with reaper; WHi 28955, Men working tractor and threshing machine; WHi 41161, *Residence of Mr. Martin Luetscher II, Town Honey Creek, Wisconsin* by Paul Seifert **Pages 148 and 149** WHi 27790, Andreas Larsen Dahl; WHi 27545, Cutting grain; WHi 26427, View of farmyard with windmill; Agricultural census report, courtesy of the Wisconsin Historical Society Archives **Pages 150 and 151** WHi 37268, Silo under construction; WHi 33796, Jersey herd at the fair; WHi 26649, William Hoard; *Hoard's Dairyman* magazine cover, used with permission **Pages 152 and 153** WHi 23041, Wisconsin creamery; Photo of butter churn, courtesy of Stonefield Historic Site; WHi 40880, Dairy Progress map; WHi 3238, Barron Co-op Creamery; WHi 33283, Casper Jaggi; WHi 5585, Babcock with butterfat tester; Photo of Babcock butterfat tester, courtesy of the Wisconsin Historical Museum; Photo of curd rake, courtesy of the Wisconsin Historical Museum **Pages 154 and 155** WHi 3679, Buckers in Florence, WI; WHi 5826, Logging crew posed in camp; WHi 1963, Sunday in lumber camp bunkhouse; WHi 24425, Sunday washing; WHi 1960, Loggers dining at camp **Pages 156 and 157** WHi 1958, Loggers loading sled; WHi 1894, Lumber raft on the Chippewa River; WHi 6316, Hauling logs with oxen; WHi 37826, Chippewa Lumber & Boom Company log driving crew; Photo of log mark hammer, courtesy of the Wisconsin Historical Museum; WHi 5048, Log jam on Chippewa River; WHi 32611, Cook's tent in log drive **Pages 158 and 159** WHi 31707, Man amid logs at pulp mill; WHi 10565, Clearing stumps; Peshtigo River from *Haper's Weekly*, Nov. 25, 1871, courtesy of Wisconsin Historical Society Archives; WHi 2209, Birds-eye view of Peshtigo **Pages 160 and 161** WHi 1964, Loggers pose on railroad tracks; Regrowth of forest, courtesy of Wisconsin Master Loggers Association

CHAPTER 9 **Page 165** WHi 29997, Village of Cochrane; WHi 5780, Bird's-eye view of Ashland **Pages 166 and 167** WHi 28081, View of part of the city of Milwaukee; WHi 11428, Bird's eye view of LaCrosse; WHi 6081, Schooner *Moonlight* **Page 169** WHi 24906, Mineral Point Railway Depot; WHi 24660, Wisconsin and Michigan employees; WHi 31640, Green Bay Harbor; WHi 24904, Milwaukee railroad yards **Page 171** WHi 38179, Lehigh Coal and Iron Company; Photo of Horlick's box, courtesy of the Wisconsin Historical Museum; Kohler tub, courtesy of Kohler Archives; WHi 18460, Butchering hogs **Pages 172 and 173** WHi 6920, Pfister and Vogel Tannery; Photo of Pfister and Vogel Tannery workers, courtesy of Milwaukee County Historical Society; WHi 35694, Allis-Chalmers Manufacturing Company; WHi 2045, Allis-Chalmers interior **Pages 174 and 175** Photo of Edward P. Allis, courtesy of the Milwaukee County Historical Society; Photos of Harley-Davison backyard shop, early motorcycle, and Harley-Davidson factory 1919 all courtesy of Harley-Davidson, Inc. **Pages 176 and 177** Photo of Sholes typewriter, courtesy of the Wisconsin Historical Museum; WHi 1940, Hooping the curd; WHi 36512, Jeffery car; WHi 2081, Tire factory interior; WHi 23519, J.I. Case gas tractor **Pages 178 and 179** WHi 7612, Workers pouring molten metal at International Harvester's Milwaukee Works; WHI 39877, Parker Pen screw machine department; Photo of newsboys, courtesy of the Milwaukee County Historical Society; Cover of *The Newsboys World*, courtesy of the Wisconsin Historical Society Archives; Bicycle workers, courtesy of the Milwaukee County Historical Society **Pages 180 and 181** Photo of "I am for Bob for Governor" button, courtesy of the Wisconsin Historical Museum; WHI 2390, Photo of Fighting Bob La Follette speaking from a wagon; WHi 5586, Mr. La Follette's strongest card; WHi 30148, La Follette campaigning by train; WHi 2415, Belle Case La Follette addressing farmers **Pages 182 and 183** WHi 7439, Farmer's Market, 1875; WHi 6945, Downtown Milwaukee, 1930; WHi 38187, Superior Harbor; Photo of *S.S. Meteor*, courtesy of the Milwaukee Public Library

CHAPTER 10 **Pages 186 and 187** WHi 40516, Early automobile in Bonduel; WHi 16192, Connor Radio Store interior; Photo of Reed School exterior, courtesy of Wisconsin Historical Society; WHi 41021, Boarding the school bus; WHi 45011, Photo of Reed School interior **Page 188** Photo of Wade House, courtesy of Wade House Historic Site; WHi 49394, Early road conditions **Pages 190 and 191** WHi 37953, Ross' Teal Lake Lodge; Pamphlet cover for Lucky 13 highway, courtesy of Wisconsin Historical Society Archives; WHi 7568; H.H. Bennett and dark tent at Gate's Ravine; WHi 49133;

Camping at Devil's Lake; Brochure for Richards & Cox resort **Pages 192 and 193** WHi 33439, Four women and truck; WHi 10261, Rodney Williams; WHi 40882, Sedition map; Detail of gold star on Wegner Grotto, courtesy of Wegner family **Pages 194 and 195** Unemployed men in line for jobs, courtesy of the Milwaukee County Historical Society; Tent city in Lincoln Park, courtesy of the Milwaukee County Historical Society; WHi 49392, New Deal road work; WHi 5751, Rustic Bridge at Copper Falls; WHi 49393, WPA-built cabin **Page 197** WHi 12284, Girls bring in old bed for WWII scrap drive; Photo of women welders at Manitowoc Shipbuilding Co., courtesy of Wisconsin Maritime Museum; Photo of Major Richard I. Bong, courtesy of the Bong Heritage Center; Photo of launching of *Peto*, courtesy of the Manitowoc Public Library **Pages 198 and 199** WHi 6838, Washing dishes; WHi 40850, Woman rubber worker; WHi 35573, Presenting wreath on Armistice Day

CHAPTER 11 **Pages 202 and 203** WHi 40222, Half cloverleaf intersection; WHi 2027, Family in living room; "Give Earth a Chance" pin, courtesy of the Wisconsin Historical Museum; WHi 11519, North Central Plane; WHi 44185, Legislator using computer **Pages 204 and 205** WHi 1941, Family bomb shelter; WHi 47424, Joe McCarthy; Sgt. Risteen and Mr. Kim, courtesy of Landon Risteen; Letter from Risteen to his parents, courtesy of the Wisconsin Historical Society; Photo of old Korean man, courtesy of Landen Risteen **Pages 206 and 207** WHi 10845, Family fun at home, 1955; WHi 8655, World Series traffic jam; WHi 40966, Sun Prairie development model; WHi 40397, Building I-94 with earthmover **Pages 208 and 209** WHi 2290, Aldo Leopold; Photo of Leopold walking out of the Shack, courtesy of University of Wisconsin–Madison Archives; WHi 1888, Portrait of Chief Oshkosh; Photo of E.M. Griffith, courtesy of Wisconsin Department of Natural Resources; Photo of Walt Bresette, used with permission; WHi 48016, Photo of Gaylord Nelson speaking on Earth Day **Pages 210 and 211** Photo of Vince Lombardi, courtesy of the Neville Public Museum; Photo of Curly Lambeau, courtesy of the Neville Public Museum; Photo of Brett Farve jersey, courtesy of the Wisconsin Historical Museum; WHi 8937, Deering Works baseball team; WHi 26355, Henry Aaron, 1954; WHi 6224, Warren Spahn, 1953 **Pages 212 and 213** *Fishing by Torchlight* by Paul Kane, courtesy of the Canadian Museum of Civilization; WHi 10150, Hunting prairie chickens; Photo of three generations of deer hunters, courtesy of Wisconsin Department of Natural Resources; Photo of fish decoy, courtesy of the Wisconsin Historical Museum; Photo of duck decoy, courtesy of the Wisconsin Historical Museum; Photo of snowboarders, courtesy of the Wisconsin Department of Tourism; Photo of ice fishing on Black River, courtesy of the Wisconsin Department of Tourism; Photo of Casey FitzRandolph, courtesy of Casey FitzRandolph **Pages 214 and 215** Photo of ERA button, courtesy of the Wisconsin Historical Museum; Photo of "Stop Treaty Abuse" pin, courtesy of the Wisconsin Historical Museum; Photo of "Honor America, Honor Treaty Rights" pin, courtesy of the Wisconsin Historical Museum; WHi 4993, School desegregation pickets; WHi 28114, Vel Phillips **Pages 216 and 217** Photo of Lance Sijan, courtesy of U.S. Air Force; WHi 1903, Anti-Vietnam war demonstration; WHi9333, pro-Vietnam war demonstration **Pages 218 and 219** Photos of Blackhawk helicopter and Jalowitz's pharmacy unit in Kuwait, courtesy of Stacy Jalowitz; Photo of Ground Zero quilt, courtesy of Lois Jarvis; Photo of Seagrave Fire Truck sent to NYC, courtesy of Seagrave Industries **Pages 220 and 221** Photo of Dousman House at Villa Louis Historic Site, courtesy of Wisconsin Historical Society; Photo of Apostle Island kayakers, courtesy of the Wisconsin Department of Tourism; Photo of circus wagon, courtesy of the Wisconsin Historical Society

CHAPTER 12 **Pages 224 and 225** WHi 44050, Cocoon around *Wisconsin* statue; Photo of Harold Thomas cutting hay, courtesy of Driftless Area Land Conservancy **Pages 226 and 227** WHi 1921, Frank Lloyd Wright, 1930; Photo of Taliesin, courtesy of Pedro E. Guerroro (Used by permission of the Frank Lloyd Wright Foundation ©2007); WHi 6375, Tree Planting In Chequamegon National Forest; Photo of deciduous forest in Pattison State Park, courtesy of Dr. Scott Nielsen; Students at Madison School Forest, courtesy of Kerry M. Motoviloff **Pages 228 and 229** Photo of family at Gibraltar Rock, © Zane Williams; WHi 11711, Rock of Gibraltar in the Richmond Memorial Park; Photo of Wisconsin capitol, courtesy of Legislative Reference Bureau